AQUIFER

Other books by Jonathan Friesen:

The Last Martin
Aldo's Fantastical Movie Palace

AQUIFER

A NOVEL

JONATHAN FRIESEN

BLINK

BLINK

Aquifer
Copyright © 2013 by Jonathan Friesen

This title is also available as a Blink ebook.
Visit www.zondervan.com/ebooks.

Requests for information should be addressed to:
Blink, 3900 *Sparks Dr. SE, Grand Rapids, Michigan 49546*

This edition: ISBN 978-0-310-73183-2 (softcover)

Library of Congress Cataloging-in-Publication Data

Friesen, Jonathan.
         Aquifer : a novel / Jonathan Friesen.
              pages   cm
         Summary: In 2250, water is scarce and controlled by tyrants, but when
    sixteen-year-old Luca descends to the domain of the Water Rats, he meets
    one who captures his heart and leads him to secrets about a vast conspiracy,
    and about himself.
         ISBN 978-0-310-73182-5 (hard cover : alk. paper)
         [1. Science fiction. 2. Water supply — Fiction. 3. Despotism — Fiction. 4.
    Secrets — Fiction.] I. Title.
    PZ7.F91661Aqu 2013
    [Fic] — dc23   2013023874

Cover design: *Cindy Davis*
Interior design: *David Conn*

Printed in the United States of America

14 15 16 17 18 19 20 /DCI/ 19 18 17 16 15 14 13 12 11 10 9 8 7 6 5 4 3 2 1

To Isaac

PROLOGUE

S top the winch!"

Mape pounded the hull of the boat and dropped his hook-end pole with a clank. He squinted through the netting. Thousands of flopping shrimp dripped and glistened, reflecting the last rays of sunlight.

But the grotesque creature, the white beast bound in weed — it didn't move at all.

"I think you oughta come up here, Jasper."

"I'm in no mood for whinin' tonight." Jasper sloshed across the deck toward his ship mate. "I hired you to haul, not to feel sorry for the poor little fishes, or to complain about the by-catch. You wanted to shrimp off Scott Reef, and that means scoopin' a dolphin or two." He pointed at the net. "Now swing that haul over the floor and dump ..."

Jasper's eyes widened then narrowed as the catch flowed onto the boards. He had seen everything the sea owned.

Almost everything.

"That's no dolphin." Jasper angled himself closer. "That beastie has a claw."

"What d'ya think it is? Sea turtle? Mermaid?" Mape let out a short, sharp laugh and then fell silent.

Swells from the Indian Ocean slapped the side of the boat, and a salty breeze blew cool and stiff across their leathery faces. Jasper shivered. An inside-out shiver. But he wouldn't let Mape see it.

Mape was an impressive specimen — muscles rippled across his worked body. He didn't possess the average hauler's portly, barrel-chested physique. But a captain like Jasper, who worked the prohibited northern waters, couldn't be choosy, and Mape had approached him in a Derby tavern. How Mape knew Jasper needed a new mate was still a mystery.

"We ain't bottom trawling ever again," Mape whispered, scanning the horizon in all directions. "You know what they do to bottom trawlers. You know what our net does to the coral — "

"Shut up. When I want your warnings, I'll ask for 'm. Net's drained. Pull'er in." Jasper turned. "Beastie was in the wrong place at the wrong time, that's all."

Mape grabbed his pole and stretched it out, clamped the hook into the metal arm, and grunted the hanging net in and over the deck.

"That's bone stickin' out!" Again, Mape dropped his pole. "Human bone inside a shackle. I ain't cutting it free."

Jasper cursed and removed his machete from behind the water barrel. The blade was standard equipment for a shrimper. Water rationing codes were difficult to enforce this far from the mainland, and on extended trips Jasper routinely hauled more than his allotment. Extra fresh water in a slug of a boat made him an appealing target for all who lived on the fringe, and the sea alone remained wild, worked by wild men and water pirates.

It's why Jasper loved it. The sea wasn't safe, but it was still free — free of the codes and of the accursed Amongus, the peacemaker's

Watchers and secret informants. For all Jasper knew, his own wife had been one of them. On land, the Amongus were everywhere.

He struck the metal arm, sparks flew, and the net fell. Jasper mumbled as he stepped forward and cleared the wriggling shrimp with his boot.

"I'll be. 'Twas a woman. Four weighted shackles, hands and feet. Not much left to her." He poked at the strips of flesh with his machete. "Been down there a long time."

"How long?" Mape blurted, then cleared his throat. "How long, do you think?"

"It don't matter. Five years, maybe ten judging by the decay."

"So, what do we do? We bring her in, right?"

Jasper was silent. He slipped the tip of his machete beneath one of the iron rings and carefully raised it to eye level. "It's heavy. Lass didn't have a chance. Bring a light."

"Right away." Mape tripped over the hook box and disappeared below. He returned with a small sphere in his hand. He handed it to Jasper, who rubbed it, setting off a reddish glow. "What do you see, boss?"

Jasper held the light up to the shackle and turned the ring over in his hand.

The light sphere thudded to the deck.

"The peacemaker's mark is etched on here," Jasper hissed. "Out! Everything out!" He flung the shackle over the edge. "The net. The catch. The body—"

"But she was—she is—human, right? Shouldn't we tell someone?"

Jasper grasped Mape by the neckline and yanked him near. "We never pulled this lady out of the sea. We weren't here. This day never happened." He shoved Mape backward and grabbed the net. "Help me, fool!"

Mape stumbled to his feet, fisted the netting, and together the two men slid the catch to the rail.

"Up and over," Jasper said.

"I told you, I ain't touching that thing."

Jasper paused. "I can't do this alone." He forced his hands through his dreads. "We'll make a deal. You help me get her out and there'll be ... there'll be no more bottom trawling."

Mape swallowed hard. "Okay, then." He winced and slid his palms beneath the bones. "One. Two. Thr — Hold on! Look on her leg, below the iron."

"I don't care what's on her leg. Even if it's solid — "

Mape released the net and reached his fingers through the mesh, snapping the ankle bracelet free. He slipped it through the netting and squinted. "Look at it. Gold's what it is, I say. There's some marks on it. Letters. Maybe a word."

Jasper snatched it from Mape. "A word? Must be old. Back from the Scratchin' Time."

"Gonna throw it over with the rest?" Mape licked his lips.

Jasper thought. "No. It's worth four months labor. When we reach the dock late tonight, it'll be dark. We'll melt it and sell it. We split the credits seventy-thirty."

"But I saw it — "

"Sixty-forty, and that's all on that." He tossed the anklet so it landed next to the light. "Now grab on, and let's take care of her."

Mape grinned. "Right."

They grunted and rolled the net over the edge. Jasper listened as one thousand credits worth of gear splashed into the dark waters below. He slid down into the bottom of the boat, panting. Mape slipped down beside him.

"We could have turned her in, Jasper. They may have

bumped up our water rations for finding an undone. She had to be an undone."

"Reward us? Bah. The PM wanted her down there where she'd never be found. I don't suspect he'd hand out gifts if I brought her back up."

"You're right." Mape stood, and slipped out of his jacket. "When I dumped her below, that was the peacemaker's directive: she was not to be found."

Jasper looked up, mouth agape. *Could he be . . . ?*

"But this one causes wrinkles from the grave," Mape continued, "and I needed confirmation her punishment was done correctly." He took a deep breath, walked over to Jasper's auxiliary fresh water tank, and pitched it into the sea.

"All these months with an Amongus," Jasper whispered.

"It only took you twelve weeks to see to it. Did you really believe you were beyond our reach, that staying out at sea would protect you?" Mape sighed. "It's been no pleasure fishing with you, so gladly I'll take my leave. Maybe now I'll get some rest." Mape grabbed his bag and strapped it to his back. "I'll be waiting for you on the dock in Derby. You'll need to be" — he paused — "debriefed on the situation you've experienced. We wouldn't want you spreading inaccurate information."

Jasper inched back toward the machete. Once debriefed by an Amongus, the mind was never the same. Jasper had seen it too many times.

Mape watched him for a moment and shook his head. "Such a brutal instrument, and not one a citizen should possess. I'll be waiting, Jasper. Please hurry. The quicker we're done . . ." He looked around the shrimp boat. "The quicker we can return you to the sea."

Mape turned and dived over the edge.

"No!" Jasper lunged at the blade and jumped to his feet. He watched his once-trusted crewman swim toward the coast with alarming speed.

"Jasper, you fool," he muttered to the wind, then limped to the wheel and turned the boat mainland. "You'll return me to the sea, all right. In irons!" He kicked the empty water barrel. "Of course Mape was one of them. For months, he wants to shrimp the same stretch of reef?"

Think, old man.

Without fresh water, south to Derby was his only option. He could try to reach Broome, but that would take two more days, and if he didn't report in to Mape tonight, they would certainly assume he had headed that direction.

But he had to head south, toward shore, if he wanted to live …

"I won't be debriefed," Jasper whispered, and spun the wheel sharply. The boat creaked and groaned, its nose swinging to the north.

Jasper sank back on the bench as the boat chugged toward the deep sea. He sighed, his head thudding against the hull.

It's been a good run. Forty years, the sea dog. A man couldn't ask for more.

He glanced to the left, at the red light and the anklet that glinted on the boat's deck. He stretched and gently picked it up. "What good does gold do me now?" He stared at the scratches.

Jasper glanced at the tip of his machete, then out over the ocean. "Lady of the Sea, since I soon will share your fate, I christen this boat in honor of you …" He lowered his blade and carefully etched the letters from the band into the damp wood of the deck.

LUCA

Jasper doused the light and closed his eyes.

Lady, I hope what you did was worth it.

CHAPTER
1

Two Years Later

L eft, slight jog right, sharp right, left, left ..."
        I stand in front of the Australyan Sea and whisper the
mantra that is mine alone to remember. Twice a day, I repeat
the order, as I have for the last ten years, as I will until the day
I die.

"Veer left, lower your head, left again ..."

My mind holds a mystery: directions to a land I've never
seen. A land five miles beneath my feet. I kick at the sand.

My journey there is inevitable, but I'm in no hurry to
descend that far, to a world of blackness and shadow, where a
race known as Water Rats scurry about. Father says that I cannot imagine what lies below, what manner of creatures extract
the fresh water our parched planet needs, and pump it, with
unseeing eyes, to the surface. This is good. My imagination

provides many sleepless nights as it is, and if my nightmares are accurate, when it comes my turn to descend, I will die of fright.

"Nine hundred forty seven paces straight away …"

The yearly transfer will one day fall to me, the Deliverer's son, as it falls to Father now and fell on his fathers before him. Every seventh day of the seventh month, Father gathers rods of light, descends toward the heart of the earth, and exchanges them with the Rats for a promise — one more year of free-flowing fresh water. For both Toppers and the creatures below, it's a life-giving trade. The Deliverer returns, and the Toppers rejoice.

Father does not.

A successful exchange should please him most of all because it means my father's work is done for the year. Instead, he slumps through the streets of New Pert, his gaze downcast. Citizens avert their eyes. A superstitious lot, they know he is Other and assume that the pained look on his face reveals the enlightened nature of his thoughts.

They don't know he wanders our shoreline in the moon-light searching, waiting — for whom, I do not know. They don't share his burden or hear the forbidden sobs that shake him.

That is mine alone to see. The slow death of a savior.

One day, the territory of New Pert will treat me with the same grim reverence, once my schooling is complete and my child-hood no longer extracts from them a greeting. I will then become Other. All because of the directions floating around my mind.

I hope Father lives to one hundred and twenty.

Tonight, Father and I are left to our thoughts and ourselves. A quiet shanty on the sea is our payment for shouldering the weight we bear, the peacemaker's way of rewarding us with just enough privacy to make living bearable.

A gentle breeze crosses my face and heads toward Father's

dock, where his boat gently sways. The dock stretches out into the Shallows, a natural gift created by the waves that crash over the reef. Without the sea's fury, water stills and pools in the rocks and coral. This evening it glistens pink beneath a reddening sky.

Father sits on the edge, still as stone, his feet dangling off the dock into the water and his hands stroking his prized possession: hundreds of papers bound in leather. We don't speak of things illegal, but I wonder why he carries it and risks the Amongus's wrath. There are many things I don't understand about Father.

His back is hunched and scarred; his memory is broken. But if I were to go to him, to drop down and place my head on his shoulder, I know what I would hear.

"Left, slight jog right . . ."

Ten years ago, Father's debriefing stole his thoughts and muted his feelings, if the rumors be true. Father will not speak of his crime. "She was worth it." It's all he will say, and my questions float away unanswered. I do know the Amongus did not dare touch the order, the precious directions to the Water Rats' world.

I stare out past the thin white reef line. Afrika. Beyond the sea lies Afrika. And beyond it Sowt Amerika. We're taught that people still inhabit those lands, and that remnants of past nations gather around the pipes sent out from our diverters. But a life thousands of miles from the only consistent source of water? Rains are so scarce; that distance so great. How would they tell us if their pipes failed? It's all hard to believe, and I wonder if my best friend Lendi is right: Australya, perched upon the Aquifer, the buried rock bed source of all fresh water, is home to the only Toppers that remain.

I sigh and stare out toward the distant lands, wondering if there is another fifteen-year-old boy staring back at me. I doubt I will ever know. So much water between us.

So much salt water.

"Right ... right ..."

I lose my way in the sequence. Five hundred twelve random turns are difficult for a wandering mind to hold. Yet forgetting is not an option.

"Last march of the undone!"

The cry comes from outside our walls, from down the street. It is loud but emotionless, tearing me from my thoughts.

Father glances toward me, shakes his head, and crawls back inside himself.

Not today. They can't hold a march today, so close to the water exchange!

I run toward the gate and pull. And pull. The heavy wooden doors swing open at last.

People line the street before me. Silent people. Friends and family come to see the guilty one last time. It is one thing to be debriefed, to have one's memory robbed and the past reset. That is for small offenses.

It is quite another to be undone.

From this, there is no return.

Today, the crowd is larger than usual. Though bans on strong emotion are mandated by the PM, and enforced by his Amongus, we are allowed our curious fascination with death. Marches of the undone become little spectacles. Even the young show interest. And where they gather, so also do the carts. Merchants selling treats and drinks — though this near an exchange, the drinks set parents back quite a few credits.

In the distance, a particularly loathsome Watcher approaches. All refer to him as Reaper; all except Father, who has named him Barker. This Amongus is shrill and proud and I hate him. Every ten steps, his voice raises.

"Last march of the undone!"

He strides toward my open gate, face forward, his gaze fixed on me. I cannot bear to stare back. Barker halts, turns, and hollers the lie that haunts my dreams.

"I will now seek the Deliverer's judgment to affirm each sentence. The condemned will wait outside."

The Watchers' plan is brilliant and insidious. Citizens of New Pert dare not argue with the savior of the world, and from appearances, Father and the Amongus work together. After all, the Deliverer who risks his life for all would not condone a sentence imposed without just cause.

If only Barker would actually speak to my father.

I can't help thinking the peacemaker doesn't know. If he and his Council of Nine are as unerring as we're taught, the PM can't possibly know this deceit of his Amongus, his Watchers.

Barker pushes by me, and I stare at the faces standing single file outside the gate. Four men, two women, one child.

One child?

It is rare that a child is undone. Not an Eleven. Not one from my school.

Not Walery.

I've spoken to him twice. There is nothing abrasive about his manner. I can't imagine him causing a wrinkle.

Barker vanishes within our walls, presumably to speak to my father. Only I can see both the Amongus and the accused. Barker stretches and strolls to our water cask. He lifts it and drinks long and deep before setting it down and wiping his brow.

Undoing people must be hard work.

"They're all innocent." Father speaks, his voice barely reaching my ears. "I pronounce them all innocent."

He is, as always, ignored. In this one act, this one

compassionate act, the most important man in the world is ignored. Why doesn't he toss his papers into the sea and stand? Why doesn't he break from his darkness and show himself at the gate, where the accused and the onlookers could see his opposition? Barker would have nothing to say.

I don't understand my father.

I glance down the street. Walery's mother stares at me, her chin quavering. Her husband is stoic. I can't stomach their gaze. I back through my gate and duck behind our canoe, because some horrors should not be experienced from out in the open.

"Come in, each of you," Barker calls to the doomed. His voice is calming, hypnotic. Why does he soothe before the kill? Filing in, only Walery looks afraid, not yet resigned to his fate. The gate swings shut, and Barker points at Father. It is a good thing that from a distance the papers are indistinguishable. I don't know how many debriefings my father could stand.

"Your Deliverer, Massa, has sealed your sentences. Helia, you incorrectly coded ten children. Into the boat. You are undone. Jordane, you failed to surrender your child to the Developers. Into the boat. You are undone ..."

Liar! The sentences are a sham. I should have destroyed the Amongus boat anchored in the shallows.

"Walery, for speaking information that could incite rebellion against the PM. Into the boat. You are undone."

Incite rebellion?

I peek over the canoe. All the adults are aboard. Barker turns and marches back toward the gate. Walery stands, frozen in the sand.

"It's time now, Walery." Barker speaks so gently. "Get in with the others. Helia will steer you out to sea."

Walery nods and shuffles toward the Shallows. Barker

quickly slips out the gate — his job here is finished. I stand. Furious. Throughout New Pert, it will be believed that my father was responsible for this. He not only gives life, he also takes it away.

But today, I am filled with more; a sense that if I do nothing and watch them go, as I have hundreds of times before, something in me will be undone too. I leap forward and race to Walery.

"Don't get in."

He doesn't look up. "Where should I go?"

It's a fair question. Out of fear, his family will not receive him back.

I pause and stare at Father. He sits on the dock, yet he has never been farther away. The next moments are mine to direct.

"All of you. You don't need to go. My father did not condemn you. You can go right back out the gate."

Helia smiles. "It's all right, Luca. This is our fate. Come, Walery." She holds out her hand.

"Stop! Think. This is not how it has to be. There is nobody watching you."

Jordane's gaze shifts from me to the boat, and he bites his lip. "Maybe — "

"No," Helia says calmly. She grabs Walery's hand.

"Wait!" I say. "I'll take him." I point to Father's boat. "I'll take Walery myself. I want to speak to him before he is undone."

Helia pauses. "Very well." She hands me four shackles. "You are the next Deliverer."

Jordane pulls up anchor, and another boatload of people sail themselves to their end. They will swing around Rottnest Isle, help each other into irons and chains, and jump.

After all, we are a peaceful society.

CHAPTER 2

I stand by Walery and watch the boat fade from sight.

"What do you want to talk about?" Walery asks.

I have not thought ahead that far, and I stare at the sandy-haired Eleven. He is thin, very thin. The shackles I hold would likely slip off his wrists. He looks me in the eye, and I am uncomfortable. Lowers avert their gazes around Uppers. Especially me. But Walery's eyes hold no fear now, though he stands minutes past a certain death.

"I guess we should discuss where you want to sleep." Outside the walls, voices murmur. The remnants of a crowd. "I can't let you leave, at least for a while."

"You aren't going to use those?" He nods toward the chains. "Massa really didn't ..."

I shrug and shake my head.

Walery looks to the sky. "How many others have you and the Deliverer saved like this?"

Inside, I ache. The knot that formed inside me while I hid behind the canoe twists and tightens.

Deliverer. Right. During marches, neither Father nor I are worthy of the name.

"Nobody. I've watched and watched and stopped no one."

Walery's face turns grim. "But you did stop me."

"I did. Now go into the shanty, turn left, and you'll see a small door leading into a storage room. Father never goes in there, and he will be preoccupied tonight. Grab some food and water from the kitchen on your way. I'll come get you when Father is gone."

He stares at me, unsure. "If I'm caught, I'll be undone for certain."

I guide him toward the house. "You already were."

"Luca!"

"Go now!" I hiss, and shove him toward the door. I wait until he disappears inside and then turn. "Yes, Father Massa?"

He massages his forehead and continues his vacant stare out to sea. "Who am I?"

I approach him slowly and call from the beach, "You're my father."

"Why are so few memories with me? What did I do?"

I've heard the story from Lendi's father. Of the day the Amongus sealed off the entire wharf district of New Pert, so monumental was the occasion, so terrible the task. The day the Deliverer was debriefed. What Father had done, of course, Lendi's father did not know. Surely nothing so forbidden as hiding an undone.

"You've never shared your crime, but you're my hero, and a great man. And tomorrow, you'll be great again." It is the reply I've learned to give, the one that quiets him.

Not tonight.

"Yes, but son, have I loved you well?"

My father stands and faces me. Nowhere else in the territory will I hear the word *love*. It was Father who taught it to me, taught me to guard it, taught me not to fear it.

This word is our word. Mine for you. Yours for me, should you choose it.

I was only five, and newly returned to him after being raised by the Developers for my first years of life. My memory doesn't reach those earliest years; I don't even remember the people who cared for me. But all that matters now is one recollection: Father said he loved me, and at five, I knew the word's meaning, I felt its warmth.

I pad toward the dock, and my father joins me on the shore. He is forty, but already his strength is spent, and the hand he places on my shoulder keeps him aright. Though his face is dark and weathered, his eyes are soft. Gentle eyes peering from beneath dreadlocks, thick and unruly, the distinctive hairstyle of all New Pertians. Yet his face holds no apprehension. There is still a wildness and a freedom his debriefing could not tame. It sets him apart from all others in the territory, including me.

Could the Developers have made an error? Their record keeping is impeccable; it has to be in order to return one hundred thousand babies to the proper parental set five years after those children are born. But there is little of Father in my face.

I am short and weak. The shortest of all my agemates. Father is tall and courageous, even now.

Yes. Short and weak and pale and thin, nothing like him. Perhaps my blond hair and gray eyes came from Mother Alaya, although I will never know. Her name is the only piece of her I will ever own, and she is the one topic Father does not allow me to broach.

I peek at the wall that separates us from our neighbors. Eight feet tall and topped with broken bottles and shards of glass. I strain into the breeze, listening for footsteps outside the gate. No Amongus sensed the emotion in Father's question. We were fortunate. Displays of feeling cause wrinkles, and wrinkles rarely go undetected.

"Yes, Father Massa, you have done very well." I lower my voice and gesture toward the shanty. "But now you need to eat. What would you like?"

He reaches his arm around my shoulder and draws me close, my body a whisper compared to his frame. His eyes are focused and clear. "What is your first memory?"

I pause to think. The question feels safe and neutral. "Darkness."

"Mine too."

"I dream of darkness, Father Massa. But I'm never afraid. I ... I ..."

"Finish, son."

"It feels like safety. I wake peaceful. Is that normal?"

He draws a deep breath. "No, it is not normal. But it is good."

We walk toward the shanty and reach the back porch.

"Turtle soup." Father nods, his voice clear and strong. "I want turtle soup tonight."

I step back. "That will take some time to catch and boil. There are other options."

Father furrows his brow. "Yes, Luca, but is it the sixth of the seventh? It feels like the sixth. I will be reciting all night. Bring it to my cot."

I watch my father disappear through the door. Inside, no orbs are lit—a comfort with darkness is the one trait both Father and I share. Walery will be safe, but Father's request means I will not see Walery for hours. He will certainly be afraid when I do, though he likely will not know how to show it.

I slump toward the boat.

Why did he have to ask for turtles?

~

Only one turtle remains in the Shallows: Old Rub. I paddle out to the area I have come to call the Graveyard, where eight giant rocks poke above the waterline. In the moonlight and from a distance, they resemble a cemetery.

I drop anchor near the largest stone. I have spent entire days watching Old Rub paddle happily around the markers. She alone knows my secrets. Wrinkles are harder for the Amongus's dials to detect offshore, and surrounded by the Shallows, Old Rub has received my angriest tears. We've sat together and bathed in the sun on this rock.

Tonight, I will chop her head off on it.

I unfurl the hoop net and set to work on the poles, driving them into the sandy bottom, but there is no need. Old Rub knows I'm here and surfaces to greet me. Does she forgive me for slaughtering her children? How could I explain?

I need meat for Father. He has few pleasures left. When I make him turtle stew, he relaxes, and it warms me. I feel I have my father back. Sometimes he speaks of shimmering stone and laughter, of places I don't know. He speaks my name, and for a while we are father and son. All from a taste that resurrects a faded memory.

Old Rub seems to understand how I need my father, a feeling none of my agemates could comprehend. She seems willing to give up her own for me, though she dives before the knife falls. But between her and me, the relationship is different. There is trust.

Strange. Love I learned from my tormented father; trust I learned from a turtle.

"Hello, Rub," I whisper, the words catching in my throat. "It is the sixth of the seventh, and Father asked for turtle soup. Do you know what this means?"

Old Rub treads water. The great boney shell of the Guinea turtle spikes above the waterline, like a small, mountainous island.

"It's late. I can't buy meat from the wharf." I gaze from the stone to the washing cask. I will plunge Old Rub's head and body beneath the waterline until the bleeding stops. I will scrub her shell and flesh with the catch brush, then paddle her to shore, where I'll boil her until her feet and head turn white.

I will kill my friend for my father.

Old Rub floats motionless, near enough to grab, and I lean over the edge and pause. "No. How can I save a stranger and undo a friend in the same day?" One tear falls into the Shallows. "I'll say I couldn't catch you. That there are no more turtles. Father doesn't know. He'll understand, and I'll make him lobster. Under the weight of tomorrow's importance, he'll forget." I peek over my shoulder. "Now swim. Far from here."

Old Rub doesn't move, and I push at her side with my oar. "You can't live here. There will be more requests for stew, you stupid turtle!"

I strike her shell and she submerges.

And I weep. I weep for my loss. I weep from relief and joy. I weep because I'm not allowed to weep, and of all my agemates, I alone seem to feel the need.

I weep because I'm all alone.

Old Rub resurfaces and slowly climbs onto the rock. She

lays down in the indentation on the rock's surface and slowly stretches out her neck.

Old Rub is a turtle with a pea-sized brain, yet she knows more about sacrifice than I do. She is willing to give my father what I was not, and I feel shame.

I sniff and draw the boat close to my friend. I remove the knife from its sheath.

"You will not feel it. I promise. Thanks for being my friend." I raise the knife — and then hear a shout from the shanty.

Father!

The blade splashes into the water, and I look toward the wall. Ten men crouch on the top, their feet unaffected by the shattered glass that would deter the most persistent thief.

The Amongus are here.

"Father Massa!" I paddle furiously toward the dock.

"Luca!" Dad's voice pushes strong through the darkness. "Fill my five casks with water. Prepare the boat for my descent. I'll return tomorrow. Remember that I love you. And your package ... it's safe. I removed it from the storage room. I'm very proud of you."

Why do you share your feelings in front of them? Why make it so easy for them to condemn you?

"Father!"

The Amongus jump backward off the wall, leaving a dreadful silence. Was it my tears? My words to Old Rub? Did I cause the wrinkle that drew them? Or was it Walery? Did they come for him? I leap to the deck and run inside. There is no sign of resistance, but Walery sits shaking at the table and Father is gone.

CHAPTER
3

It is the seventh of the seventh, and my agemates are jittery. Each home has prepared for the Feast of Exchange; every parent has given final instructions: Avoid Luca in school today. He must remain calm. His father descends this afternoon.

And they obey. Even Lendi and Javo, Fifteens like myself.

School is about to begin, and students move silently through the streets. Though we shuffle side by side, nobody will speak and risk a wrinkle.

My mind wanders to the colors of New Pert. So much gray. I'm told there once were plazas of green, when the rains fell often and grass grew lush. Freshwater trees sprung toward the skies that nurtured them. Father tells me the world was beautiful.

But sprinkles are now so rare, they do little more than extract squeals from the young. The plazas have browned and cracked, yielding shrubs both brittle and yellow. It is not so on the outer islands, where saline-tolerant plants and trees give the illusion of a healthy world. Yet all know the truth: the earth itself cries out to drink, and won't bring forth life until satisfied.

Together, we all file into the building of concrete and stone. Our school, Pert #3, is a circular tower, as are all the other schools. Identical on the outside, and I assume on the inside, and all built in the same year, the year of the New Education. Our teachers tell us that was the beginning of our golden age. Father once said it was the year freedom died.

Freedom is a word I don't truly understand.

School will dismiss early; when Father returns tomorrow morning and crosses his arms over his chest in the symbol of agreement with the Rats, the annual Holiday of Jool — Water Day — will begin. It will last three days. Father will be cheered throughout the festival. The water rations will be temporarily removed.

And then Father returns to his private hell.

That is the pattern, the expected. But there is no certainty this year. Not with Father taken and Walery in his place.

It turns out they had quite a long talk while I spoke to Old Rub. I wanted to ask Walery to tell me everything Father said, but my anger wouldn't allow it. How could Father share words with an Eleven and silence with me?

I long to tell someone about last night, about the visit from the Amongus, but my position does not allow many close friendships. At least that's what I tell myself.

I could tell Lendi about Old Rub, how she seemed to understand. Lendi loves animals, and would appreciate that part of the story. It's unfortunate his father makes coats. Lendi doesn't have the heart to be a tanner.

But there will be no chance to share with him this day.

A wide space opens before me. Students, uniformed in

red and gray, part as I climb the spiral ramp that leads to my classroom. Fives quickly disappear through their doors. I walk behind Lendi, circling upward until I reach the second-highest floor. I glance up. It is not long until schooling is complete.

Lendi and I turn into room 1510 and sit as all students do, in a wide circle that faces outward. My chair is comfortable, as is my view: a screen, changing images every ten minutes. Presently, an eagle soars through a blue sky. And in the center of the scene — the eye of the eagle — is a dial, the same one carried by the Amongus to monitor the emotional climate of New Pert, placed to sense my wrinkles.

We are often reminded how peaceful our world has become, a world without a police force or prison, where crimes and uprisings have nearly disappeared. But we've paid a price. The emotional root of all conflict — fear, anger, love, especially love — is prohibited. The goal of our schooling is to master a life of total self-control. A life without wrinkles, without feeling, without soul. The exercises in school are endless.

But in truth, for most, they're no longer needed. Generations of life in an emotion-neutral world have bred these dangerous urges right out of people.

Why do I still feel them so strongly?

Anger. Loneliness. Hope. They burn in me. Only me.

I stare at my eagle eye, and my dial stares back. Each of us faces one tuned to our individual frequency, the one given to us at birth. My arrow hangs and quivers. This is not good. A quiver is acceptable; a swing is dangerous.

Here again, I am Other. I was not given a frequency implant. These mistakes do not happen, and surely my attending Birther was undone for the error. But I am now too old for my heart to accept the personalized signal implant, and I stare at my unsynced dial, a first-generation model able only to note changes in body temperature. Such instruments are much more prone to error.

Behind me, in the center of the circle, Teacher Two drones on. I miss Teacher One. He had become too passionate in his defense of the New Sydney uprising and was replaced. Rumor has it he now works an outpost oil field. Let his passion burn to pump oil, or something like that.

Teacher One had sounded like Father did yesterday.

Father. My hands sweat. The dial jumps, spins, and quivers again. *Calm, Luca. Calm.*

Behind me, the door creaks, and boots strike the floor slow and heavy. I stare at my screen, and a man in a crisp, red uniform steps between my eagle and me.

"Luca. We need to talk."

I stare at the bulge in his shirt pocket. A dial. An Amongus.

"My dial isn't synced. I don't know what emotion it registered. We were in the welcome. There's little passion in that."

The Amongus turns, his dreadlocks swishing down across his back. He approaches my dial, and I start to recite in my mind.

Left, slight jog right . . .

The monitor falls quiet.

"Would you please replace my dial?" I ask. "I'm getting tired of these faulty readings."

He removes the monitor, turns it over in his hand, and glances at the teacher. "Keep your welcome calm. You may continue."

When the door shuts, I smile. More than once my Birther's error has saved me. I can't understand my agemates. I've schooled with them for ten years, and never once has any dial twitched but mine.

Today's lessons, as they always do on the day of descent, focus on history, the History of the Exchange. The class hears the annual retelling of Rabal and the gold mine.

It was he who first discovered it, the bed of fresh water rock deep below the ocean floor. The thirsty world had no choice but to give to him allegiance, and all countries became one.

"But how fortunate to swear fealty to such a wise man, the first PM. Soon the once-necessary evils of this world were gone, and surrounded by the Council of Nine, Rabal and his wise sons established the security we now take for granted."

Blah. Blah.

"Such fortune was not had below ..."

The tone of the story darkens, and my stomach flips.

"The nine miners who had worked alongside Rabal made a fateful choice: to stay below, to live near the mantle of the earth. While they took on the important task of providing life-giving water to the people above, I don't suppose they realized they would devolve. From human in form to little more than rats, crawling on all fours in the darkness. And there they would breed, and multiply. It's to them that Massa will descend today to make the trade on which our lives depend."

Lendi glances my way with eyebrows raised. He knows the task will one day fall to me.

Teacher Two pauses. "Please stand for your recreative minutes."

"Happy Birth Hour," whispers Lendi, leaning over.

"I forgot."

"You always forget. The curse of a seventh of the seventh birth hour. I consider it my job to remind you."

At quarter of noon, I will turn sixteen, and be escorted up the stairs to the next room for the last months of my formal schooling. I'll miss Lendi. He's already a Sixteen, but was detained. Hopefully, he'll join me soon.

"How does your father look?" Lendi asks.

"He's strong," I lie.

Lendi exhales slowly. He is an anxious sort, always concerned about Father's wellbeing. I suppose it makes sense. His life depends on the man.

"Back to your positions." Teacher Two points to the clock. 11:45.

"Class, Luca will be moving up today. Wish Luca well."

Nobody speaks. They can't. Their parents have given them orders, and on this day alone, Teacher accepts their disobedience.

"On behalf of the entire class, I wish you well."

I nod and stare at my eagle.

"Save me a good seat." Lendi speaks, and I hear the smile in his voice. I shift in time to see the wiggle on his dial. The door opens and the Amongus returns. He whispers to Lendi, who rises.

"And while I'm here," says the Amongus, "I will escort Luca to the Sixteens."

I rise and join Lendi. He'll only be chastised, but that's still quite a sacrifice for a mate.

The three of us exit the door and circle higher.

"You shouldn't have said anything," I say.

"You do."

"My position is somewhat more protected than yours."

The Amongus opens the door to the circle of Sixteens. Nobody but the teacher turns to look.

"I have a new student for you." The Amongus pushes me through the doorway, and then grabs my shirt. I glance over my shoulder. "Wish Massa good luck." He smirks.

Amongus never smirk.

I whip around. "What do you know about last night?"

The door slams, and from behind me the teacher speaks gently. "Your presence, though honoring, cannot be accompanied by these outbursts."

"It won't."

The room clock clicks twelve and all rise. "When we return from Holiday, we will be visiting the Hall of the Old. Prepare to be disturbed. Good day." The teacher strides out into the hall. My peers rise and part and exit, each one cupping their hands as they walk by. It's the universal gesture given to my father, who fills each hand with water, with life. Now as a Sixteen, it is given to me.

I stand alone in the empty room. It's time to go home. I'm afraid of the man I will see.

CHAPTER
4

"Father Massa, I'm home! What do you need me to do?" I bang through the screen door, and slow. Father's hammock sways gently in the main room. There is no breeze.

I feel cold, though the day is warm.

Of course. Today he will recite the path of descent in the sitting area, repeating it backward and forward. He says the route must be known both ways, for there is always the return journey to the surface.

I pull the sheet that shields Father's sitting chair from the rest of the shanty.

He slowly lifts his head.

"Father Massa, I was worried." I glance around. "Is everything well? Have you checked the boat —"

He raises his finger to his lips and stands. His eyes are fiery and clear, and I warm in that terrible, wonderful gaze.

"Come, son." He tousles my hair and takes hold of both shoulders. "Let me look at you. There is so much of your mother in your face. The child of hope, that's what she called you, and you turned out well."

"Uh, thank you, Father Massa." Words falter. He is changed. "What happened to you? Where's Wal—" Father slaps his hand over my mouth.

"What happened to me? Well, the brain is not meant to be tinkered with. As we've known for far too long, debriefings can steal memories, but"—he smiles broadly—"occasionally after too much tinkering, those memories find their way home." He sighs. "There's so much I need to tell you, but not now." I feel the strength in his arms, the certainty in his voice. It is Father, but not one I've known. He slowly releases me.

I rub my mouth. "You're so—"

"Late. Massa is late to depart."

I swing around. The sheet rips from its clasp and an Amongus approaches, while two more block the doorway.

"Ignore them, Luca. I'm not late," Father says, his voice soft and tender. "I can't stop looking at you. How long have I been gone?"

"Get up, Massa," the Amongus hisses.

"My mind, how long has it been absent?"

"Years," I whisper, and peek toward the door. And in the corner of my eye, there is a tickle I can't explain.

"Up, Man!"

The Watchers push my small frame aside, and I land with a thud. They stride toward Father.

He stands and points at each of them in turn. "Leave my home. You will not touch my son again."

They stare at each other, and Father steps forward. "Out. Get out." He bends and gently lifts me to my feet. "I wish to speak with Luca."

Father shoves the lead Amongus, who raises his fist.

"Hold it, Mape." His companion leaps from the door and grabs Mape's arm. "Only he knows. He can't be hurt. Not today."

Mape slowly lowers his hand. "Not today." He turns, and along with the others steps out of the shanty.

Father kneels. I kneel as well. "Luca, I have a job to do, and then we will talk. In the meantime, you have taken on quite a task. Your bravery yesterday means you must now care for the package you rescued. You will need to find a place for it."

"Not here?"

Father slowly shakes his head. "Here is safe and good, but only for you, son."

Inside, I warm. He said Walery couldn't stay, but I warm. Because I can. I matter. I'm his son.

Father looks at me, deep and full. The stare reaches places the dials never find. Does he see my fear? My sadness, and the emotions that have no names?

He rises and hoists his backpack over his shoulders. A beam pierces from inside the pack. Even though the light rods are in their inactive state, there is no way to fully contain the glow. "How was school today?"

"It was … uh, fine. I moved into the Sixteens."

"Sixteen! Three more months of school, and you are done. Finally a young man. No more a boy."

"Ow!" Lendi stumbles into the shanty and crashes into Father, who doesn't flinch.

"Why is this boy prowling about?" Mape follows him through doorway.

Father raises his eyebrows. "A good question."

I step forward. "When you're gone, he sometimes comes over to keep me company."

Lendi turns a slow circle. "I swear that's all. I didn't know there were any Among — I mean Watchers here."

"Seems I should leave so you can enjoy each other's company." Father kisses my forehead. I turn toward Mape. From his pocket, I hear the whirring of his dial. "I'll see you early in the morning, my son, after the celebration begins."

Dad leaves, and Lendi and I walk to the door. Outside, Father is escorted to the end of the dock, where he climbs into his boat.

"There's far too much water in this vessel for one man." The gentle swells carry Mape's words to the shanty.

Father pays him little mind, and unties the rope. "You've never descended. You don't know what's needed."

"Hmm. Go now," Mape says. "The world waits."

"Not until you leave my gates. I would not abandon Luca and Lendi to you."

"He's right. They'll come back," Lendi whispers. "They'll go and come right back and we'll be debriefed and I won't remember my parents and — "

"Shh!"

The Amongus back away from the dock. Father starts the engine and calls, "Your dials. Toss them to me."

The dials. During the New Sydney uprising, several Amongus had been attacked, their dials removed, and with them, their authority. They had quickly been undone. An Amongus without a dial was nothing, and even unfeeling citizens found relief in their embarrassment.

Mape shakes his head.

"Fine." Father reclines in the boat. "You came to see me off. Let's wait until others come, and you can explain to the waiting world why I'm still at the dock."

"We have to do it, Mape," his companion says. "There is no option."

Mape reaches into his vest pocket and removes the dial. "You feel you have control. Because of your position, I will do this. But ..." He glances toward us. "A penalty will be paid."

"No, it won't." Father reaches out his hands and catches three dials. "Accursed things. You'll get them back when I return. Now it's your time to go. You're late."

The Amongus quickly disappear. Father waves to us. "Luca, the path in your mind—give it to no one else. If you are asked, you'll know what to do." He speeds out toward the reef. "Oh!" he yells back. "Please clean my closet."

"He took their dials." Lendi backhands my chest. "Luca, did you see that? How can he do that?"

I breathe deep. I don't know the answer. But I've never been so proud.

CHAPTER
5

Clean the closet?

C   I run to the back of the house and throw open the door. Walery steps out, wide-eyed. "Are they gone?"

"Luca?" Lendi calls. "Where are you?"

My mind races, and I shove Walery back inside, slamming the door. "In Father's area, Lendi. Come on in." He appears, and I lean back against the closet. "So, where do your parents think you are this time?"

"Caesar's, as always. His place in Scarboro makes for a long trek, and the idea of staying overnight makes sense to my parents." Lendi grabs my arm — another rare physical touch. "I need to show you something."

I wait, and my friend chews his lip. Fortunately for him, the Amongus don't patrol New Pert when Father drops below the surface; his anxiety will go unnoticed. Even the Watcher's lives are on the line.

I peek at Lendi's fingers tightening around my forearm.

"We can't talk here, but I found something. You'll want to see it, Luca. This is the only day we could go unnoticed."

"Where —"

"No questions, all right? Just follow. I'm already a walking wrinkle, and thinking about it only makes it worse."

It's a day for secrets, and my body tingles. Lendi's mouth is a risk, but that increases my urge to confide about the boy in my closet. "I've got something to show you too."

Lendi puffs out air. "You know I blab. You know ... Oh, fine, what is it?" I step away from the door, and Lendi slowly pulls it open.

"Why is Walery in your father's closet?"

"It's somewhat of a story."

Lendi lowers his voice. "Wait. I saw him in the march. Wasn't he undone?"

"Does he look it?"

Lendi peeks. "No. But he's supposed to be undone, isn't he?"

I say nothing.

"He came through your gate, and somehow you hid him."

More silence.

"And nobody knows about it but you, and now me. Blime! I can't keep this kind of confidence. You know that." Lendi drops to the floor and squeezes his dreadlocks.

I sit beside him. "It's okay, mate. Now, what was your news?"

"My news?" His breathing quickens. "Yeah, my news! Maybe my news will help me forget your news."

I gesture to Walery, and he steps out while flattening his shirt. "You're not going to slam me back inside again ..."

"Wasn't planning on it." I grab a fish from the cold box and drop it into Walery's hands. "The place is yours tonight." I offer him a quick slap on the back. "Lendi and I are going on a little trip."

Walery presses his toe into the wooden floor. "I could ... I could come with you. It's, uh, really dark here, and really ..."

Lonely. The word you're looking for is lonely. You haven't been allowed to talk of it, but there it is. I know it well.

"I think it's far too soon for you to be outside this house. Even Lendi knew about your scheduled undoing." I wince. "Sorry, Lendi. Anyway, I need to find a place where you can stay. Forever. Perhaps the Northern Territories. A different district. Father knows people. Stay here until he gets back, okay?"

Walery raises his palms and lets them flop back down. "Yeah, you're right. This is just a strange place." He glances around. "So quiet. So full of something."

It's called emotion. That takes some getting used to as well.

I touch Lendi on the shoulder, and then together we push out the door and into the heat of afternoon. The streets of New Pert are nearly deserted. We wander along the Swan River and toward its lagoon, around which citizens' homes huddle. Dotted among the dwellings, remnants of massive buildings stand in decay. The Swan is the heart of New Pert, both a magnet for those who remain and an image of what's been undone.

Millions used to fill the city, but no longer. Thirst has seen to that.

Today, the shoreline is deserted — no bikes, no scooters. Not on the eve of Water Day.

Lendi leads me across the river and then veers toward Freemanl Wharf, close to the sea, where only a few tardy fishermen are frantic at work tying down their boats and hauling in their catch. In another hour, even the most secret alleys of the wharf will be uninhabited.

Only the water mission will remain open. All day, every day, it collects extra from donors and gives water to the destitute for free. Father sends me daily to contribute.

Lendi's face is tense and his gait quick; odd for my friend. There are no jokes. There are no words.

There have always been words between us.

Lendi first approached me when we were Sixes. He grabbed my swing at the play yard and twisted it, and I swirled and fell on my back while he laughed. His reprimand had been severe, but I felt an immediate kinship with the wild, jittery boy.

"You know, Lendi, Tamari's home rests near the wharf."

At the sound of her name, his legs slow, and he flashes me his most-controlled look. "Yes. Why do you mention — "

"Because you never do." I raise my palms. "You just stare and stare. She could be your match. You could ask your father to make the request."

Lendi freezes. "And just when have you ever heard of any request being granted? No, I have a better chance saying nothing."

I glance down. "She's pretty." I sweep my hand before my eyes. "I can see it now. The Joiners are pleased to announce the selection of Lendi, son of Beldi the Tanner, and Tamari, daughter of Jokthan the ... What does her father do?"

"Veterinarian." Lendi covers his face with his hands and peeks at me between the cracks. "Have you ever heard of a tanner joining a vet? It will never be! She would save critters and I would skin them!"

I frown. "That does seem to be an inherent contradiction ..."

Lendi circles me. "I will likely be joined to Lorna, the plump future baker."

"You will eat well — "

"But who can eat when the girl they ... When another man

42

joins the girl, they …" Lendi cannot finish his sentence. He can't name what he feels. He only knows the heart whisper is real, and that it makes him miserable.

"Perhaps we should pay Tamari a visit," I say quietly.

"Oy, mate. Would you have me undone? Come!" He mutters and grabs my arm, and we hurry past Tamari's home.

A breeze, stiff and swirling, flutters flags and carries a few muffled voices. Seadogs, grunting on the wharf.

"Luca?"

I turn toward Freemanl Pier. Seward bends over empty nets. He's the biggest scammer in New Pert, yet I always hope to see him. Seward never seems anxious, which always puts me at ease.

"Why out today?" He squints from Lendi to me. "Is Massa all right?"

"He's fine. In fact, he just left. Good fishing?"

Seward straightens and hints his crooked smile. "Always on the seventh of the seventh. I own the seas. I have the Freemanl to meself. Think I be wasting that chance?" He pauses. "You two be heading the wrong way."

"We are," I say. "Happy Water Day."

"Why do you speak to him?" Lendi hisses as we leave. "My father says he's a pirate."

"Mine says the same thing. Which is precisely why he's a good man to know. Father says to keep close eyes on your ene-mies — especially ones with large stashes of water on hand." I pause and lean into his shoulder. "Had we stopped at Tamari's, we wouldn't be having this conversation right now."

We turn inland from the shore and head through Kwinza sector and toward the old mine pits. We are far enough from home that we will walk back in darkness. Lendi hates darkness.

He turns down the wide road that leads to Glaugood.

"Why are we heading toward the mine?" I ask, and slow my pace.

Shadows dart on my left from inside old miners' quarters.

"Wishers," I whisper.

Lendi freezes. "Where?"

I gesture for him to follow and light-foot it toward the building. The window in the door is cracked, but what remains is smeared with mud. I carefully swipe the grime from it, peer in, and point.

Thirty, maybe more, kneel in a circle. Wishers often do that. Some say they practice an old magic, others claim that they fall into a trance. Father says they pray, though he doesn't know much beyond that.

It is rare to see so many in one place, given their status as enemies of the PM. They are a constant target of the Amongus; Barker has marched hundreds through our gate. Their crime? The frequency each was given at birth has somehow been silenced, overwritten. Amongus dials can't detect Wishers.

They wander the streets as free men and women.

I squint through the dark glass. The sight of them always thrills me, quickens me.

"What do you think they say?" I whisper.

"Leave them to their mumbling." Lendi tugs at my sleeve. "Come on, Luca!"

I pull free and press my ear against the crack.

"Has anyone heard the Voice today? Has anyone heard from God?"

They've lost their minds.

"I . . . I think the Voice spoke," a young girl pipes up. "I know I'm only an Eight, and the Voice has no business speaking to me, but—"

44

"Tell us, what did you hear?"

The girl's tone strengthens. "'The prophecy's fulfillment is in motion, even now.' That's what it said."

"Come on, Luca! Time is against us," hollers Lendi.

I raise my finger to my lips and peek back through the window. I see no one. I peer to the right and left, but the room is empty.

I sigh. Prophecies and voices. What's possessed them?

Lendi starts to jog, and I break free from the door with questions about a prophecy dancing through my mind. We climb over three fences and squeeze through rusted blockades. Lendi sprints ahead, stopping at the lip of the mine. I catch up, catch my breath, and stare down into the largest open-pit gold mine ever dug in Australya. Now it's a hole, a saltwater-filled hole three times wider and deeper than the Boddington excavation and stripped of all metals. Immense and abandoned, there's a heaviness about this place.

Lendi's eyes widen. "When Teacher One offered me the special assignment, the Dangerous Animal Pursuit, I thought, where could I go to look for an undiscovered species?"

"Dangerous Animal? He asked you to gather insects."

"Yes, but there was a bit of mystery in the request." Lendi nods large and slow. "Couldn't you feel the tension? My dial wiggled."

"Didn't see it. Go on."

"So I wondered where I might find even a strange insect, and it hit. Glaugood, a pit vacant for a hundred years. In all this time, there must be a new beetle or something crawling around near the bottom."

"It's filled with seawater."

"That's what I thought too. And it's a long way from home.

45

Still, I figured it would be worth a look, and the seventh of the seventh provides the only opportunity to safely take a peek. So last year, after Massa left and I left you, well, I did." Lendi jogs onto the dirt road that rings the perimeter, spiraling endlessly down into the basin. "Follow me!" He takes off in a sprint.

I test the firmness of the road with my foot. "You failed that assignment. You reported that you found no new insect species. And your dial didn't wiggle, so I know you weren't lying!"

Lendi doesn't slow. "That's right. I didn't find bugs. I found something else!" He waves to me. "Oh, Luca, I've been waiting a *whole year* to show this to you. Do you know how hard it is for me to keep a secret for a *day*?"

I do, and I stare down into the pit. Even half filled with water, Glaugood is massive and deep. Whatever gives my fidgety mate courage to descend must be worth the effort.

CHAPTER
6

An hour later, we're still stumbling downward. The road that once carried dump trucks of gold ore to the surface has, in many places, washed away. One misstep and we would tumble onto the next stretch of spiraling road, one hundred feet below us. The Amongus would not care that Lendi died. The world would mourn my passing.

I think about this. Left, slight jog right ... what lies in my mind makes my life more valuable than my mate's. It isn't right. The route should be given to all children — all should be forced to memorize it, right along with the pledge to Rabal and the present-day PM.

I'm not worth more.

"Thirty-one, thirty-two, thirty-three," Lendi counts as we pass each cave. "We need to hurry. It will soon be too dark for me to keep track." He mutters, "Large number thirty-four on the other side, with thirty-five ..."

His anxious recitation fills me with joy. He too knows a route. His life is certainly valuable.

I'll have to tell him.

But now, I have questions for my mate — questions about the caves, which were blasted, I know, into the sides of the mine. Why are some small? Why does the air chill me when I pass?

How deep do they go?

We quicken our pace. Lendi no longer glances at the path; he is driven, and his desire excites me. A tingle runs my spine, first up and then down. Excitement, the ultimate wrinkle. I descend, like my father descends. Right now, we both wind into the heart of the earth, toward the promise of water.

I am every bit his son, and the tingle strengthens.

"We are close. Cave fifty-four. I found it in fifty-four. The water is higher this year. We're lucky. Next year it may be too late."

Lendi stops. This is good, as water from the flooded mine now laps my shoes. My mate turns triumphant, his arms spread at his side. "Welcome to fifty-four!"

The cave is unremarkable, its mouth neither large nor small. But the damp air that floats from it smells of something Other, a scent I've never smelled.

"Yep. That smell is what stopped me last year. That and the water — I couldn't go down much farther. Come on." Lendi digs into his pocket and pulls out his red orb, which offers a pale glow. "I thought we'd need light, I just didn't think we'd need it so soon. Follow me."

He climbs over rubble and vanishes into the tunnel. I crawl after him, following the shadows and pinkish glimmer dancing on the walls.

The cave is broad and spacious, and Lendi is soon well ahead of me.

"Don't get lost!" he calls back.

"Don't go so fast!"

Minutes later, we still descend, and my ears pop. The walk is easy; the breathing is not. Foul air hangs like turtle soup — and I force it in, force it out.

"Lendi!" I turn a gentle corner. "Slow —"

I bump into my friend. Sweat pours from his face, and his eyes are large and bloodshot in the orb's light. "We're here." He points. "Through that pinch, in that offshoot. You won't find bugs. I'll let you go first."

I step back and bend, hands on knees, searching for air. "I'm a little winded. Maybe you should go first."

Lendi shakes his head. "You, friend."

Friend. Though I've never doubted it, he's never called me by the term. His voice — its cadence and strength — is different. His breathing, light and free. This is not the Lendi I know, and on the heels of that thought worms in another.

No! I shake my head. *Lendi couldn't be an Amongus.*

Yet it would be so like them. Planted in our lives, sleepers waiting to reveal themselves after information is gathered.

Lendi saw Walery! He saw the Wishers. My heart both rejects and aches with the betrayal.

"Remind me." I straighten and peek back up the tunnel. "Where do your parents think you are?"

"Caesar's. Or was it Kern's? I forget, but it doesn't matter. Once you're inside, you'll forget all about what was said to reach here."

I step back. "Why will I forget?"

"Trust me." Lendi advances and hands me his orb. "Go in."

I reach out and take the light. I can't outrun him; I never could. He's always been quick, strong. A little too strong. Why didn't I see?

"I'll go." I march by him and drop to my knees. "No matter what, you've been the best friend I've had."

Lendi frowns and gestures toward the pinch. "It's getting late, we have a long walk back, and I'm not going to wait another year to show you!"

I creep forward through the tube, the rock rubbing my shoulders. For once, it's good to be small. What torment to be here forever! To be trapped. I think of Father, descending into the hideous lair of the Rats. Strange, I never asked if there were any tight passages.

I never asked him about Lendi either, and now my mate knows my greatest act of rebellion. Walery's rescue is an undoable offense. Would Lendi do the punishing deed in this cave? Nobody would find me.

The squeeze loosens, and I stand and hold up the light. And drop the light.

Lendi is not an Amongus.

He grunts in behind me and places the orb back into my hand. "Well? Not bugs, eh?"

Stacks and stacks of bound papers, large and small, lean against every stone wall. The musty smell is overpowering, the same smell hinted at near the mouth of the cave.

"I found them. Hundreds of years old, I'd say. From the Scratching Time." Lendi walks toward an open one, then bends over and hands it to me. "Books, right?"

"Books," I whisper. "Filled with words, words that nobody can read. And there are so many."

Father cherishes the one he has. I bet he'd love more.

"You've heard Teacher Two say it, and it's a quote from the PM himself: 'There's nothing so dangerous as a man poisoned by words.' Lendi picks up another book and shakes it. "But seeing them now, I don't understand the danger, why people fought and killed for them. Why did Rabal want a bunch of paper stacks destroyed?" Lendi scratches his head. "But here's the rub. If it's discovered I found a stash and didn't turn them in, I'll be undone. And if I do turn them in, it'll at least warrant a debriefing. It is the ultimate wrinkle." He sweats more profusely, and he wipes his forehead with each sleeve. "But I had to tell somebody. Before I destroyed them, I had to show you. Nobody else would believe me."

"Destroy them?"

"Do you know why I had to stay a Fifteen twice? Why I failed? All day, every day, I sit in school circle and stare at my dial. I don't listen to Teacher. I can't. I must will my dial still, because pounding inside are thoughts of this room, this cave. I can't hide it anymore, Luca."

He gnaws a fingernail and continues. "My father says what's scratched inside these can steal you, control you. I tell you he's right. I can't read scratches, but just finding them has controlled me. Books are not supposed to exist anymore."

I wander among the stacks. "Hard to see how a bunch of marks could hurt anybody."

I stare at the weapon in my hand; the one we're told brought ruin on the world. I flip the page, squint, and rub my fingers over the crinkled paper.

"This is called the Table of Contents," I whisper.

Lendi steps beside me. "What do you mean? How do you know?"

I can't answer. I'm not certain. But it's there, deep in the dark part of my mind. "It's divided into sectors, called chapters. Each chapter into para … paragraphs, sentences, words, letters, and sounds. That's how you use one. Make the sounds your best mate."

"Stop it, Luca!" Lendi grabs the book from my hands and throws it to the ground. "This was a mistake. We need to leave." He takes a matchbook from his pocket. "We'll start the fire and leave."

"Fire? We can't burn these. They're … they're history."

"They're evil, Luca. And it's the only way. The water will rise, some will float out, someone will find them, we will all hear, and I won't be able to keep my emotions in check. I'm cursed, Luca, until they're destroyed."

Lendi is right; if a book is discovered, he will not be able to control himself.

For the third time in two days, I lie. "Let me do it, mate. It's the best way. Go, and leave me the matches." I lower my voice. "I'll take care of them."

"You'd do that for me?" His anxious tone returns.

My feet splash into a puddle. "The cave mouth is above the waterline. How did water — " I raise the orb. "There's a crawl space in the corner. Did you follow that tube? Where does that go?"

"Who cares?" The Lendi I know has returned. There is no more determination, only concern. "We need to go now."

"Go." I ease him toward the entrance. "I want to follow that cave. I'll be fine — I know the way home."

"And you'll burn these."

"I will."

Lendi presses the matches into my hand and ducks into the pinch. "Don't say too long. It's almost dark." He pauses.

"And beware. There's something about those stacks. The very thought infests the mind."

He's gone, and I lower myself to the floor, my mind thoroughly infested. I inch forward beneath the rocky outcrop into the offshoot. Water licks my chin, laps against my ear.

I press my face into the small pocket of air, and thankfully the ceiling soon rises. The orb illumines the rocks above and I stand, dripping in a small chamber. And soon jerk back.

A skeleton reclines in the corner, submerged to the waist. Rags float off its bones and its arm reaches up to a hollow in the stone. Stark white fingers grasp a book resting in the crevice.

I swallow hard. No shackles ring the wrists or ankles; this one's life wasn't taken. This person chose his end. "Who were you?" I raise the light to the book. "You must've wanted to keep this one safe." My fleshy fingers join boney ones on the book's cover. "Problem is, water's seeping in from somewhere. It's going to reach your prize soon, then it will flow up the rise into the bigger chamber as well." I give thought to Lendi, and then my father. Finally, I think of this ancient one, whose last act was to guard this stack of pages.

"Honestly, how important can it be, lying hidden for centuries? And I did make a promise to my mate."

I dig for the matches; wet and useless. *So much for that.*

Father must be nearing his exchange. Father. He would know what to do.

Take the book, Luca.

The command is so distinct, it strikes me as audible. A gentle voice, both familiar and safe. I scoff at the thought. *That's what I get from letting Wishers inside my head.*

"I'm losing it, but, hey, I tell you what," I address the skeleton.

"I can keep this book safe for you." I grasp it, and a boney hand splashes near my knees.

I stumble backward. "Sorry, I really need to go."

Back through the cut, into the bookroom, and through the pinch. I stand and start back up the tunnel, emerging onto the broad path. Lendi runs on the other side, nearing the top.

There's nobody waiting for me, and I slowly plod with my ancient book. To hold this thing, this banned thing. To find a stash the Amongus missed, and bones protecting it. It frees me. Tonight, I too feel like a Wisher, living outside the Amongus's domain. To be unobserved on this day of descent. To feel the thrill of the find, knowing I will not be questioned or worse.

To be my own person, making my own choices ...

I clutch the book, the book that destroyed Lendi's year and empowers my night.

"You will not be burned," I whisper, and wrap the contraband in burlap.

What a gift for Father. And there are hundreds more ...

But there will be no other night, not for another year. I need to get them all while the streets are clear, and the Amongus are in their homes.

I clutch the book to my chest. I know a way, and break into a run.

"I'll be back."

CHAPTER
7

I sit on Freemanl Pier, the moon low and red in the sky, its light dancing on the waters deep.

There is nobody out tonight, not a soul in a city of ten thousands. It is the collective hold-your-breath. My father is at the center of an event that brings the entire world together. For once a year, the world feels, and what it feels — though it does not know it — is dread.

I never want to be the center of that event.

What if I fail?

My secret rests on my lap. I stroke the book's cover like Father strokes his. I will not open it until I'm home.

Not ten feet in front of me, a great light suddenly blinds me.

Seward.

His boat eases to shore, and he quickly douses his floodlight and ties the prow to the pier.

"What manner of fool is out tonight?" he hisses. "I carry a load that — "

"It's not best for a respectable businessman like yourself to be found carrying?"

"Aye. That's a way of puttin' it. But I struck well tonight. I'm finished. Move off, I need to unload on the winched dolly." He glances both right and left, lowering his voice. "Best you not see."

I slowly stand. "I need your help. I need it tonight."

"At two in the mornin'? There's a craziness about you."

I grimace, thinking what to share, what to hold. "I've found a treasure. I need you to help me get it to my home."

Seward's face turns sly, and inside he's thinking, calculating, I'm sure of it. He wonders how he can remove the treasure from my possession.

"This deal be from one pirate to another ... Why didn't ye just come out with it, lad? For this, I'm always here." He lowers his face so it is equal with mine, and the smell of fish and ale overpowers. "What manner of treasure?"

I glance at the burlap in my hand. "To possess it is to be debriefed. Perhaps undone. Do you still want to know?"

Seward whitens and straightens. "I'm already in a pickle with them. I need no more reason for their ... special attention." He takes a step past me, and I grab his shirt.

"I know the gruesome task you do. The retrieval of the undones from their watery dropping point. Father told me." I kick at the dock. "You perform this service for the Watchers, the Amongus, and they wink at the water casks you steal."

Seward exhales slowly. "So Massa tells you all my good traits—"

"If your mates knew just who your employers were, it wouldn't sit well. Would it?"

"What do you want, little blackmailer?" His eyes twinkle.

"No." I step back. "No questions. Can you sit with that?"

Seward stares out over the sea, waiting, it seems, for the sea to answer. Then it does.

"Can I get more than your word for the silence you'll keep?"

"My word is all I have." I nod. "As the future Deliverer."

Seward rubs his face. "Luca, you are a pain. Help me unload." He pauses. "Can you stand the sight of an undone?"

I think back to the guard of the cave. "Oh, I imagine so."

I am wrong.

The skeleton was unreal, distant. An unknown collection of rotting bones. As I drag the recently undone across the deck, I can't help but wonder about their families, their children and parents. Seward and I hoist his retrievals into bags. Zipping the clasp over their fixed gazes, I know one thing: They are human. No different than me.

We finish Seward's work and he flashes me a glance. Does he almost look ashamed? I try to soften my gaze, to let him know it's okay, he's okay, but beneath the light of moon he turns from me and unties from the dock.

Seward's boat moves silently through the water. Though engine powered, there is not a sound but the lap of waves on the hull. It's a boat made for stealth, not for speed.

"Glaugood. What is here to you?" He pulls into the old mine's port.

I shake my head. "I'll need the dolly and whatever wraps and straps you have."

"Body bags are the best I can do."

"Very good." I hop out and gesture for the dolly.

"Luca, wait. I can only give you four hours." Seward peeks at the sky. "If you be needin' to be emptyin' a cave, you'll not reach it and back. But —"

"But?"

"You forget, the mine is filled to sea level."

"So ..."

"So, we're in a boat, and I be the great Seward of the Seas. The mine has crumbled. We float in."

"Brilliant!" I leap back into his craft. "Lead on, noble pirate."

Minutes later, we leave the open sea and silently glide beneath an arch of stone.

"Glaugood." Seward glances around. "To be sure, much gold was found, but they dug too near the sea, and the sea always reclaims her own. Many times I have hidden in this basin. I've found it a very private port." He clears his throat. "I'm none too pleased to share it."

"This is the last time I'll come. Promise."

We float into the water-filled mine. "We need to find cave fifty-four. I'm turned around. Can you take me around the perimeter?" I stand and squint. "I can't see to the top to count, but I'll know it by the smell."

It's easier than I think to locate the cave. The scent is more pronounced than it was two hours ago. Seward tosses his anchor into the cave's mouth, and I slosh my way into it.

"Twelve bags is what I got." Seward pitches them forward, where they land at my feet. I stack and drag them down the tunnel. Once inside the bookroom, I place my orb on the floor and stuff books. Sweat pours down the small of my back, mats my hair and stings my eyes, but soon every bag is filled, and I back through the pinch, hauling each load into the larger tunnel.

Father, I wish I had your strength ...

Hours pass, and finally I lug the last bag of books through the squeeze and onto Seward's weighted boat.

"Done." I collapse beside him and we float back out to sea. The feat I performed would have been nothing to Lendi, but my arms scream.

"Get me to the Shallows."

"What are they, Luca?"

"I don't think you should know. I don't think that's safe."

Seward shrugs. "Books never are."

I fire him a glance.

"Oh, wipe that look from ya. What'dya think I be doing while you loaded me down with your illegal cargo?"

Of all the people to know. A pirate ... who works for them.

"Fine." I fold my arms. "The tables are turned. What can I pay *you* for silence?"

Seward leans back. "Getting to it now. That's good, that's good. Yes, I do imagine some type of hushing valuable is in order. But credits do me little good — they are obtained easy enough." He glances at the sky. "But no amount of money destroys the enemy I can't fight. This accursed darkness. It is hard to work at night. Always at night, beneath the pale moon and the feeble light of the orbs. My flood light alerts too many of my presence. After all, there be pirates on the waters." He winks. "Often I've thought how quickly my job be done if I had a light rod to see. Small, focused, piercing ..."

"Father gets those from the PM, and only once a year."

"He does not!" Seward snaps, and just as quickly calms. "Apologies." He wipes his brow. "Some folktales are hard for me to endure. Massa gets nothing from the PM. He gets rods from the Nine, the Council." Seward pauses. "Can you handle a truth?" He glances down, his hands forming the shape of a make-believe bag. Seward slides open an invisible zipper and reaches inside. He pulls out a fistful of air, lifts it in front of my face, and opens his hand. "There is no PM."

I stare at Seward, who offers his nearly toothless grin. "Are you surprised that we live in a leaderless world, young Deliverer?"

"But we learn about him in school and recite the pledge ..."

"And they told you every book was destroyed. I want a light rod for my silence."

"But Father receives just enough. No extras, just enough to pacify the Water Rats."

Seward sighs, and slows the boat. "Would you like me to start dumpin' the discovered?"

"No!" I grab his wrist. "No. I'll find a way. Give me some time."

"A little." Seward glances up. "We're here." He rubs his arms and gently guides us toward the mainland. "Tell Massa I said hello."

I frown as the boat skims the reef and eases into the Shallows.

Dawn breaks, and we glide past the Cemetery. Old Rub swims at our side. I lean over and stroke her shell.

"Old Girl, you'll never believe it."

CHAPTER
8

I wake from a deep sleep, my nerves on fire.

I'm always nervous on this day, the day Father returns from the exchange. Not because I doubt him or his memory — the route is permanently fixed deep inside — but because of the Rats.

From the docks of Freemanl to the boroughs of Scarboro to banks of Garden Isle, rumors of the Rats spread in hushed tones. Speculation about their cruelty mixes with the knowledge that miles beneath our feet the hideous crawl around, and we rely on the hideous for every sip of water we drink.

Yes, the PM devised the system of diverters, the labyrinth that carries water to the four corners of the world, but those pipes are buried ten feet down, as low as most Toppers dare descend. Below that — below our feet — is the Rats' domain. Mindless, soulless, and meeting with my father.

What if they eat him?

"What's in the bags?" Walery asks, rolling over in Father's cot. "They stink."

The books remain stacked in the cellar. Their stench does not.

"It was supposed to be you," I snap, and remember the bloated bodies from Seward's boat. "I'm sorry. Just tense, I guess."

Seward is long gone, and I shake my head, clearing it of worry about my father's arrival, and the Ceremony of Rebirth where he will announce his success to the world. Four words from Seward take residence, alter the shape of my thoughts.

There is no PM.

Seward is a liar, a thief, and a pirate. But his words didn't seem to hold deceit. I'll ask Father; during a break in the proceedings, I'll ask him. He'll know.

"What are you thinking about?"

"The PM," I say.

"Does he impress you?"

"I don't know. I've never seen him."

"It's good to question things like that. It's good to question the leaders and the rules and the punishments."

Toppers don't say things like that, and I scratch my head. "You're an unusual kid."

Walery breaks into a big grin. "That's what they said on the Bottom Floor."

The Bottom Floor. We first heard about it as Sixes. Though the higher we schooled, the more the story slipped into myth. A floor beneath the ground? Beneath the Fives? Where the schooled kids never rose? The rumor was that those sent there stayed, year after year, their attitudes ill fit for the climb.

"So all those times I saw you on the way to school, you were heading ... down? What did you do to end up there?"

Walery swings his legs over the edge of Father's hammock and stares. "Two small crimes, really. I looked around, and I thought. That's it." He scoots forward. "Luca, don't the controls feel wrong to you? The prohibitions, those wicked dials. I see your discontent. You feel it too — that we were made for more than a tame life. We were made to *feel*."

I lean back and instinctively peek at the door, waiting for Amongus to burst in.

"Everyone on the Bottom feels this way?" I whisper.

"They have the potential to, so we're watched, even encouraged."

It makes no sense. "Encouraged to think like this? But why?"

"From what group do you think the PM's Council of Nine is selected?"

I'd never given it any thought.

"There always must be nine, and even those on the Council eventually succumb to age undoing. When that happens, the PM must choose a replacement. Below, we are referred to as Feelers; we are the pool from which the Nine are chosen."

I stand and pace. "But they were about to destroy you."

"Yes. During the last Replacement, my agemate was chosen. It was no longer in their best interests to keep me. They had taught me too much."

"Such as ..."

He takes a deep breath. "Luca. L-U-C-A. Massa. M-A-S-S-A. They teach us to read, to scratch. If chosen for the Council, it is a necessary gift. If not, it is a sentence which leads to undoing."

The smell of the books wafts up from the cellar. "So you can read. You can read any scratch, no matter how old?"

He cocks his head. "What do you know of reading?"

"Little. Listen, I need to go take my place at the ceremony. You need to stay here. I'm sorry for that, but when I return, we'll talk, yes?"

Walery lowers himself down. "Yeah, let's talk. You saved me, and I've been thinking of ways to repay."

"You don't need to —"

"I have an idea. I know your burden, Luca. I know what you will one day face. I likely know more than you do, as we are taught everything below. For instance, I know what you fear."

"The Rats."

"No," he says. "Forgetting. Letting your father down. He's entrusted you with the world. What if you dropped it? You would be heartbroken, yes, but more than that, you would look at your father and feel … ashamed."

I scramble toward my dressing area and open my closet. With my back to Walery, I release one tear. He sees what he can't see, what nobody can see.

"How do you know this?" I ask, but do not turn.

The floorboards creak, and I feel his hand on my shoulder. "The how doesn't matter. This is where I can help. I can scratch the route down for you. Think of the relief. You would never forget. No more worries of shaming Massa."

"But I can't read." I spin and face him.

"I'll help you. I can teach you."

I wipe my face. "I need to prepare."

Walery steps back, and I pull the sheet between the two of us. There must be a PM to teach him all these things. How else could an Eleven understand?

I dress for the event that defines my life. My finest clothes, my most colorful shirt. For the next three days, emotions are

64

allowed. Wrinkles are allowed. We will rejoice for yet another year of life made possible by my father.

I open the door and glance back over my shoulder, first toward cellar steps, and then at Walery, resting again in Father's hammock. He swings back and forth without a care in the world, his leg hanging lazily over the edge. He is far too comfortable in the Deliverer's quarters.

So many questions for Father.

～

I join the masses moving toward the Swan River. On its banks rises the amphitheater, and we will funnel through its creaking turnstiles. Once inside, nobody speaks. A quickly hushed cry, a nervous cough — these are the sounds of this moment, when wails of children are considered bad omens. A young wail from behind sets the somber on edge, and faces darken.

The amphitheater is old. Though patched and repatched with concrete, it still appears ready to crumble. It once housed the dark arts of this world, though that's all the information I've received. Walery may know more. Once a year, fifty thousand cram through its gates. All those who do not fit will line the river, gathered at one of the many watching stations. Many purposely choose to view the ceremony on the screen; the tension inside is too much for them.

I don't have that luxury.

I reach the theater and breathe deep. The Ceremony of Rebirth is the only event that brings together every citizen of New Pert. Only the young, those under five, remain far from the proceedings and under the Developers' care.

I push through the gate, and whispers gather.

Sixteen.

The next Deliverer is of age.
The next Deliverer has come.

My presence brings relief to the people, and I stride in practiced confidence to my chair directly in front of the Birthing tunnel. It stretches down to the Swan, and from it Father will soon emerge.

Father's boat is certainly already anchored at the tunnel's far end. One glimpse of his face, the folding of his arms, and Holiday will begin. I've come to hate the event, the attention, my place in front of the crowd, but this year I can't wait. I have so many questions. Prophecy questions. PM questions. Walery questions.

Most of all, there is the big stash of books I long to give him.

I assume my seat and the whispers vanish. Above the tunnel, a large clock marches off the time, each tick amplified in the vacuum of this occasion. It's five of eleven, too soon for a return, but already the crowd bristles. They should know that even if Father returns early from the exchange, he will pause at the tunnel's entrance; he must emerge between eleven o'clock and eleven fifteen.

The clock is all there is ... that and the fountain. I peek to my right. Standing atop the granite block, a cloaked man stretches out marble hands, and from his palms water spews. The symbol of every Topper's hope, this is the only fountain allowed in the city, and it never runs dry.

Thanks to Father.

The clock clicks eleven. Tension fills the theater, and I fix my eyes on the timepiece. Only once did Father emerge at eleven. What would be the fun in that? When the task falls to me, I won't be so predictable. Perhaps I'll race out at ten o'clock, or linger until noon. Maybe I'll tweak the signal of success. Cross my fingers or cross my eyes.

I stare down at my hands. With each click of the minute hand, whispers grow. After twelve minutes, I shift, and a grown woman cries.

I squint into the tunnel. In the distance, a shape appears. I stand and approach, and the tension breaks. Behind me, the crowd sighs and cheers, their voices connected to my steps. The floor shakes and rumbles as all rise to join me in welcoming Father.

The clock clicks 11:16. The figure appears, and silence falls. A chilly, confused silence.

It's not Father.

But it must be my father. I glance over my shoulder and force a smile, to let them know it's all right. But the truth forces the smile away and I stumble back to my chair.

It's an Amongus. One without a dial.

It's Mape.

Sobs and screams fill the theater. The Amongus raises his hands for silence, and quickly receives it.

"New Pert, World, I bear good tidings from Massa." He folds his arms over his chest. He nods toward the camera, as my father would, and proclaims, "The world is again reborn!"

Something is wrong. No cheers accompany this moment.

It's not my father.

"It was an excruciating exchange for our Deliverer. Wrong turns were made. An exhausted Massa authorized me to deliver the comforting word. He will be available to speak after his recovery."

He doesn't make wrong turns.

"Where is Massa now?" a lone man calls from a back row, giving voice to my heart.

"He is resting comfortable on the PM's isle. However, the PM has made a decision. The PM, the one whose wisdom has created the comforts we enjoy, the upholder of peace in this world . . ."

He continues, reciting the words we recite each morning in school, and my mind wanders.

Wrong turn? There are many things I hold against Father — his unwillingness to talk of my mother, his unwillingness to tell me why I feel so Other. He alone could understand the pangs of loneliness that strike.

But a wrong turn? His dedication to the route makes this impossible.

". . . this great man has determined that Massa's time as our Deliverer has come to an end. Massa's errors have shown that the burden has become too great to bear. Yet the Fates have smiled on us and our children, because as one Deliverer rests, another has emerged. The new Deliverer is of age!"

From out of the tunnel march three more men. They approach my chair. "Come, Luca."

I glance beyond them into the tunnel. "Where is Father? None of you have the right to use the Birthing tunnel. Only a Deliverer may walk it."

One lifts me by the shoulders and spins me around. "World, behold your new Deliverer!"

I look over the confused crowd, their faces a reflection of my own. One by one, they reach out cupped hands.

And it sinks in. A different, more terrifying exchange has just been made.

"No," I yell. "My father is your Deliverer, he'll be fine following his rest." More hands stretch toward me. "When has he ever failed you?" I turn to the nearest Amongus. "Where is he? Where have you taken him?"

"Smile for the world," he whispers. "Your father is undone."

I shake — a tremble that weakens my legs and speeds my heartbeat. The world starts to spin, and I break free from his grasp and run into the tunnel.

"Father Massa! Father, where are you? Please ... please ..." I'm quickly surrounded.

A face blurs through my tears, an Amongus, but I don't care that he watches me weep. "Luca, we need you now. After your schooling is completed, we will take you to the PM for the official transference of all that belonged to Massa, but for now, your face must hold steady. The world looks to you now. You, Luca. You may mourn later without consequence. Do you understand?"

No, I don't! My head swims, while I slowly nod.

There is no PM. I'm hiding books. Father is undone.

Outside, the crowd chants my name.

I am the Deliverer.

CHAPTER
9

I spend the day of rejoicing resting in the Graveyard with Old Rub.

"Father's gone. Walery is nowhere to be found. I'm sure they extracted him during the ceremony." I splash the water with my fist. "Look at me. I can't even rescue one boy. How can I provide for the world?" I exhale hard, and lie back on my thinking rock. High above, one small cloud moves in front of the sun, and I'm bathed in shadow. "I think this shanty falls to me."

Old Rub is still, wondering it seems, her feet treading gently in the water.

"You know how I told you to leave? Forget that, okay? I don't know what I'd do here alone."

Where is the ache, the one that should fill me? Yes, there was shock, and maybe it still numbs my mind. But shouldn't I miss Father more? Instead, I feel for me.

I glance at my home, slip off the rock, and swim to shore. I clamber up onto the dock, and run my hands across the boards where Father used to sit. Such a lonely life. It is one thing to feel Other. It is far more painful to feel it completely alone. I scoot forward on the decking and swing my feet as he had, letting the hot afternoon sun bake me dry. Outside the gate, on the street, beat the unique sounds of Water Day — shouts and squeals, buoyed by water and ale that flow in equal measure. There is no line before the water mission, not during Holiday. Water is free, abundant. Firecrackers whistle, children laugh — the one time all year they are allowed to do so.

Your father is undone.

For me, there can be no rejoicing.

"Cheer up."

Lendi stands on the beach. "You look awful. Or is this the new expression of the highly exalted Luca?" He jogs out to me and cups his hands. I slap them down.

"Come on, then." He gestures with his head. "Fireboomers at the wharf tonight. Maybe your father would enjoy them. People long to wish him well. So many want to offer him their thanks."

"Lendi, I …"

What would happen if Lendi knew? Questions would flow and my answers would spread.

How was Massa undone? I don't know.

Did he even finish the exchange? I don't know.

"I don't think Father would enjoy them." I blink hard. "I'm not feeling well myself."

Lendi nods and shrugs. "A strange ceremony today. My father says it's for the good. He says Massa was close to breaking and that it's your time. And to think, I am the Deliverer's best friend. I should receive something for that." He backhands my shoulder. "Let's go inside. Nobody should spend Holiday alone."

71

I follow my mate off the dock and through the front door. Lendi whips around, his shaking hand raising to his lips.

"That smell. I'll never forget that smell." He grabs my shoulders. "Tell me you destroyed them."

My mouth opens, flops shut, and opens again. "Okay, I destroyed them. There, in the corner, are the balled-up clothes I wore. I'm sure their odor still fills the shanty."

Lendi walks over and bends down. He breathes in and his face relaxes. "Yeah, they stink. Thank you. You don't know how tormented I would've been."

He glances around the room.

"Where's your father? I should think he's back from the isle by now, and I'd like to thank him for his years of facing the Rats."

Clearly, he's not recovering upstairs, and my mind races. "On hot days, he rests in the cellar, where it's cool."

Oh no, Luca, you fool.

"Now that you mention it ..." I round Lendi's shoulder with my arm and pull him toward the door. "Let's go see those boomers and let Father rest."

"Yeah, but I bring gratitudes from my family." Lendi steps outside and returns with a long coat. New Pertian red, inlayed with a gold sunrise on the pocket — the PM's mark. "Father can't remember a time when Massa wasn't his Deliverer. He's been hard at work on this garment for months. He received special permission to use the mark." Lendi admires the symbol. "Father says it's his finest work ever." Lendi holds it up to himself. "Maybe someday I'll make one for you."

My mate is so proud; I can't take that away.

"It's handsome, and Father will be pleased to wear it."

Lendi gently folds the leather. "I promised my father I'd pass this on, and report the look on Massa's face when he sees it. I'll be quick."

"Wait, Lendi." I reach for his arm. "Do you trust me? That there are times when my father should not be disturbed? This is one of them."

Lendi thinks for a moment, grins, and pulls free. "Good to know. I will only disturb him a little." He bounds down the stairs.

Five minutes pass, then ten. Finally, Lendi climbs the stairs, his face blank.

"Do I trust you, Luca? You can ask me this? You lied to me. You brought the cave to your home." His chin quavers. "When they are found, and they will be found, what am I to do?"

"You were never to know, mate. They, like that coat, were to be a gift for Father. I never meant you harm."

Lendi whips his gift onto the heap of musty clothes. "Don't call me mate."

In a moment, I am again alone, but this alone feels deeper. There is no father and there is no friend and neither will return.

There is only me.

And a turtle.

In time the revelry ends, and New Pert slips back into itself. Tight-lipped greetings and hushed talk blanket the streets. Occasionally a child, still loopy from Holiday, runs or hollers. Time will train this out of them.

I enter school the next day, and it feels different, as I feel different. I will climb to the top floor, but that isn't it. It's the weight, the sliver in my mind, the task I will perform not some-time, but next year. If I fail, every face I now see will perish of thirst.

Why did this curse fall to me?

I start the spiral, all the while thinking of Walery. There is no doubt I will see him soon — during the next march of the undone. This time, Barker will remain until Walery pushes off. I glance down, but see no doorway to the Below, no hidden entrance missed all these years, and I bump into a group of Twelves.

"I'm sorry. My fault," I say. They cup their hands and back away.

Right. The separation between the world and me is now complete. I belong nowhere.

I peek up and see a familiar figure. Lendi!

I push through the ascending crowd and reach his side. He clears his throat and cups his hands.

"Knock it off, mate. It's me, Luca. To you, always just Luca."

"Yes, Deliverer, as you say."

He turns into the Fifteens' room. I stand statued in the doorway and watch him take his seat. His gaze fixes on his dial. It wiggles, and he flashes a desperate glance my way. I have no words of comfort.

Emile does. "Calm now, Lendi."

A pleasant Fifteen, she reaches over and strokes Lendi's shoulder. He recoils at her touch.

I slump and traipse higher.

I have ruined his life.

CHAPTER 10

"You have attained the level of adulthood, memorized the codes and conduct needed for a waveless life in a great society." Teacher speaks calmly. She has clearly mastered her own lessons. "Your parents have trained you, and your occupation awaits. Indeed, the next great moment in your life will be a Joining. As Sixteens, find assurance in the fact that your parents have relayed your personality information to the Joiners. These last three months are therefore a formality, a chance to fill in cracks that were missed in your formation. The exception is today."

Teacher stands on the crumbling stone steps of New Pert's only museum. The building, set back from the Swan's inlet and surrounded by rubble, is unique in every way, from its creamy white columns to its marble exterior.

Children walk around it, wondering aloud. Adults are quick to respond, silencing all questions before they are fully formed.

The museum is to be experienced only once, and then never discussed again.

In this way, it's like my mother.

"We will knock and wait. Once we are permitted entry, follow me quickly inside. I will take my leave of you and return here. The Curator will guide you through the Hall." Teacher pauses at the door but does not turn. "Should you feel ill or faint, you may return to me. Feel no disgrace if you must leave early. It is a most ... disquieting place."

I glance at my twenty agemates. One boy and one girl already look green. They will not last long.

Teacher opens the door and we file in, the thick, wooden door closing silently behind us. I gasp.

It is beautiful. Statues, marble and perfect, stand in all stages of undress. The ceiling lofts high above, and is covered with an image, striking and vibrant and lifelike. It's a man, his arm outstretched and powerful, attempting to touch the finger of a smaller, desperate figure. Who has the skill to create such a thing? Who knew such a thing existed?

I break my gaze from the ceiling and my brow furrows. My agemates and my teacher shield their eyes and stare down at the marble floor, their faces visibly shaken. Many clasp their hands and slowly raise their pointer. Right finger, then left finger. Relaxation exercise number three.

"It is called a painting, and it will remain on the ceiling," Teacher says. "You may be experiencing a ... concern. That is normal. It will pass when we are through the entry room."

"I don't want to stay here," Kyrie whispers. Normally a pretty, self-assured Sixteen, her body trembles. She backs slowly toward the door.

"Then you should go."

The voice is strong and comes from behind me. I spin.

This woman's skin is unlike that of New Pertians. It is creamy and smooth, like the marble around us. Her hair is dark, as are her eyes. For an Older, she is beautiful.

"I am the Curator of the Hall. Fear is what you are feeling now, though you will not be told this in school. I assure you that there is nothing to fear above ... or below. I would like to give you a tour, but if you cannot endure beauty, you certainly cannot endure the exhibits."

She pauses and stares at me. "Hello, Luca. I'm especially glad you've come."

"Uh ... me too."

"Class," says the Curator, "unclench your hands and gaze upward."

Ten. Ten do. "Teacher, you may take the fearful out onto the steps. No doubt I will be sending you more shortly."

Teacher seems happy to leave, and when the door closes behind us, the Curator places her hands behind her back, staring at each remaining student in turn. "What you just were is brave. It is another feeling. It often holds hands with confusion, that sense of not knowing what course of action to take."

"How can you speak so freely of feelings?" I ask. "Aren't you afraid of the ..." I glance about the room. "The Amongus?"

At the mention of them, six more agemates leave. Four remain.

"Their dials do not work within this stone, but I do not think I would alter my welcome if they did."

One more student out the door.

"So I have three. Three ready to experience the Hall of the Old. Prepare to feel."

The other two retreat, and the Curator gestures me forward

through a marble arch. I peek at her, and she smiles. Not the cold smile of outside, but the warm one. The one I saw on Father before …

I step into a room filled with pedestals. It's different, but not disturbing. "This is it? This is the Hall of the Old?"

The Curator nods. "In this room, you will find history's greatest threats to humanity. That is, if you believe what I am going to tell you." She winks.

"Should I believe you?"

The Curator gently bites her lip. "What a marvelous question! Sometimes yes, sometimes no."

I cock my head. "But how will I know?"

"You won't. But trust your feelings. Trust that sense inside, the sense that will, if allowed, become a Voice. It no longer speaks to your agemates, but it still calls to you."

"But I don't know you and you don't know me —"

"Call me Wren. Now we are introduced. If you will allow me to finish the tour …"

I take a heavy breath, and she beckons me to follow.

"I was speaking of threats. For example …" She guides me to a marble stand, which supports a tiny black box. "Behold, the smart phone. If in possession of one, you, Luca, could speak to anyone else in the world … from your dwelling. Anywhere. Anytime. And they could say anything without fear of punishment."

"But how?" I reach out and touch the case.

"Each person was assigned their own numeric code. They entered the code into the phone and then spoke to each other, saw each other." She sighs. "But imagine — ten billion people thinking their own thoughts. Expressing themselves. When your ancestor discovered the Aquifer and the power it gave him, he feared these devices would inevitably lead to rebellion." She touches the phone. "It wasn't difficult to move the masses from a personal external code of freedom to an implanted internal one of bondage, which is where you now stand."

"Wait, slow down." I hold up my palm. "I want to know more about the Aquifer ... And you know things about my *ancestors*? I don't even know basic details about my mother."

Wren pauses and breathes deeply. "Your mother. Yes, I move too quickly, and with far too much liberty. I must stick to the tour."

She leads me to another display. "Over here, the expandable tablet, or ET for short. Same thing: Too much interaction. Too much sharing of ideas. Dangerous to the PM and the status quo."

"You mean Rabal."

"And his sons. They realized that a citizenry that cannot share ideas cannot rise up in protest. But enough of this technology. Let me show you my personal favorite."

She leads me to a glass case, and I wince. "What is that?"

"The de-evolution of man. Behold the Water Rat."

Rumors I've heard of their appearance claim they are gruesome. The truth is the stuff of nightmares.

Bent over, crouched on all fours, the stuffed rat snarls. It is hairless, and stares at me with eyes twice human size. It has no fingernails, and the bones of its spine rise and fall, some protruding from its skin, its posture no doubt due to a lifetime of crouching. Its hands and feet are abnormally flat and large, likely for padding over uneven layers of rock.

Wren continues. "Nine miners accompanied Rabal when he discovered the Aquifer. But unlike the first PM, these nine called for their families to join them, and together they discovered a life below. Unlike Rabal, they never surfaced. Hundreds of years later, their ancestors still extract fresh water from the Aquifer and demand light rods in exchange."

Water Rats. *There's no way I'll be able to descend to them.*

"Is that a him or her?" I ask.

"Our museum houses one female specimen." She clears her throat. "And that statement you can believe."

"This is what the Rats have become? And my father ... well, me ... I go down and make an exchange with those things?"

Wren hints a smile. "They control the freshwater rock bed we call the Aquifer. The last known source of water on this earth. You best make friends with the idea."

She gestures for me to come nearer. "But, of course, Rabal was most concerned with something he considered much more dangerous ..."

She points to a thick tome. I walk toward it. "A book." My heart races. "Is this one dangerous?"

"Only insofar as it leads you to another, and another, and perchance finally to the one book Rabal feared above all things." The curator cocks her head. "Do you remember books, Luca?"

Does she know? Has Lendi broken so soon?

"How would *I* remember? This must be the last one in existence."

"Look here, my poor liar," she whispers. "Can you read it?"

I shake my head. "No, I can't." I blink, and stare at the strange cover. "T ..."

The curator nods. "Yes. The letter *T*. Keep going."

I rub my fingers over the scratchings. "T-O- ... T-O-M ... Tom S ... S ..."

"Tom Sawyer. A book scratched, or written, by Mark Twain."

My mind swarms. "How do I know some of the letters? How can I sound out the scratches? Why am I so Other?" I breathe deep. "Why did they undo my fa — "

I stare at Wren, whose eyes widen.

"Undo?" She bites her lip and glances toward the arch. "I have more words to say, but I will show you instead."

She walks toward a small door, opens it, and disappears downstairs. I slowly follow her into the darkness, my hands grazing smooth marble on either side. At the bottom, the hall turns, turns again, and in the distance a light appears.

I follow the glow and emerge in a room filled with a dozen easels.

"Paintings." I reach out my hand, and draw it back. "You painted that ceiling?"

"No," she says. "I only paint what I've seen."

She strides to an easel and whisks off the fabric covering.

I step forward and gaze at a most beautiful image. I have watched the sun dance on the sea, and observed the sea offer back reflections of the sky's splendor. I've seen the Northern Mountains, the high country where rare snows still dust the land in magnificent white. My position as Massa's son has allowed me to leave the district from which most never venture.

But I have never seen a sight like the painting.

Created in cool blues and grays, with streaks of yellow criss-crossing the canvas, I am struck and settled at the same time. The subject of the painting is unclear, but it draws me, as did Father's voice. I want to see it, whatever it is.

"Tell me," I say. "Where can I see this beautiful thing?"

She removes the canvas from the clips that hold it taut, rolls it, and slips it into a metal tube. "As you like it, you may keep it. It is my gift to the Deliverer. But Luca, hear this. Everything,

everything that happens — all your losses and your pains — all is because of this. Everything desires this."

She reaches the tube to me and I grasp the other end. We stand in silence, connected by this beautiful, mysterious object, staring at each other. Her eyes speak, and though I don't know what they say, I can't help but gaze.

"I, uh, really should return to my agemates. They're waiting for me on the steps, I'm sure."

"No. School was over an hour ago." She releases the painting. "You are dismissed home."

I back toward the hallway and stop. "Could I quickly see the others?"

"Yes. You can see them all." Wren raises her eyebrows. "But not today."

"But this is my day. My one day at the museum. I come — "

"Anytime you like. Deliverer's privilege."

My spine tingles, and I clutch the painting to my chest. "When are you open?"

"Whenever you knock."

"You better not say that." I shift my weight from foot to foot. "I might come at midnight."

"Whenever you knock."

I stroke the tube. "Well, okay then. I'll ... uh ... I'll see you soon."

I dash up the stairs, bash my head on the marble overhang, and stumble into the Hall of the Old. I rub what will certainly become a mighty lump, but I hardly feel it. I feel something else, a warm else. An else I haven't felt since Father left.

I don't feel so alone.

I skip outside and down the stairs. It's a distance to my house, but I don't mind. My thoughts travel from the book to my painting and back again. I'm not sure what I would tell an Amongus — I'm wrinkling something fierce — but I feel light like I haven't before.

Tom Sawyer. He didn't look like a dangerous boy.

~

Yes, I decide, I should hurt more for Father.

No, I decide, I should not spend so much time dwelling on myself.

During the nights, the guilt of my selfishness overpowers. Noises were more familiar with him here. Moon shadow was comfortable and safe with him in his cot.

But we hardly spoke. I hardly knew the man.

I push his memory out when it forms, and focus on the Curator. Her words fill my days.

Weeks pass, and soon Wren's paintings line the walls of my cellar. My nighttime excursions to the museum fill my mind; whatever is taught in the circle of Sixteens is lost on me. I walk empty streets in shadow, her canvases hidden beneath my coat, feeling very much the pirate. Maybe this is how Seward feels.

But I must take them. It's a shame to conceal such beauty in Wren's basement, where light can't dance off the color and shade. Possession of a painting must warrant a debriefing. I've not heard of a prohibition, but there must be one. Living with Father has taught me the Amongus are never far away.

I spend hours staring at Wren's work, and during sleep her paintings invade my dreams, along with new sounds of her laughter and singing.

Perhaps it's some strange fume from the paint, but I'm okay with those intrusions. The sounds are so welcome to hear.

"Luca?"

I sit across from Wren on the top floor of the museum, where sunlight streams through the sky roof. "Would you like to learn how to read? All the words."

All the words of all my books. Of Dad's special book.

"Of course I would. But if the Amongus found out ... I mean, that's worthy of undoing, for most people."

She says nothing.

"Aren't you going to guide me or encourage me one way or — "

"I'm going to let you choose. Your thoughts are precious. You don't need mine on the matter."

Would I like to learn how to read?

I remember Walery. He, too, offered to show me. He is likely undone. How could I place my new friend in the same danger? "It's not allowed."

She pours herself some tea. "Outside these walls, true." She stares up into the blue sky and then back down. "I may have a solution. I give you permission to forget how to read outside the museum. I will simply teach you to read inside."

I glance at her sideways. "Is that how it works?"

"Absolutely not." Wren sips from her cup and removes a book from inside a table.

"Is that it?" I lower my voice. "You know, the really danger-ous one?"

She pauses, and then sets down her tea and the book and folds her hands.

"Years ago, before our Great Thirst, before the countries had boundaries, and before the Great Wars ... thousands of years before, rain fell. It fell with fury, and soon the rain from above joined with the waters beneath our feet, and this earth was covered, above the highest mountain. One family alone prepared, was alone tossed by the waves, and alone survived the deluge."

"Who were they?" I ask, eyes wide. I can't imagine that much water.

"I don't know." Wren sighs. "But since I do not have the dangerous book, I thought I would at least tell you a dangerous story."

"So it's filled with stories?"

"Stories and prophecies. I only know a few, those remembered and those that come to me in the stillness. But enough on that for now ..."

Stories and prophecies.

Wren reaches for her thin volume. Yellowed pages crackle as she pulls back the cover. "Even the safest of books are useless without the reading. Let's meet the sounds."

I offer a slow nod. Wren writes the letters in her book. It's amazing how quickly the shapes and curls form on my lips over the next hours. Scratches take on weight, purpose. One scratch plus another scratch equals not two, but one — one word.

"Luca can lear ... lear ..."

She underlines the words with her finger. "Just keep sound flowing through each scratch."

"Luca can learn to rea ... read."

Wren smiles. "I will give you a reading test tomorrow. Unfortunately, it would not be safe to send this book home with you, so you'll just need to repeat the sounds in your mind. I trust your memory."

I think about the books smelling up my shanty.

"No problem. I look forward to the test."

CHAPTER
11

L *earning to read is tougher than I thought.*
    That, or the books I rescued put up a tougher fight than Wren's. There are few one-syllable scratches, and every page is a challenge.

I dig for the thinnest book — a pamphlet, really — plunk down on a pickle barrel, and stroke the wrinkled pages.

"The Consti ... Constitution Act. Whereas the peop ... people of New South Wales, Victoria, South Australia, Queensland, and Tasmania, hum ... humbly relying on the blessing of Almighty God, have agreed to unite ..."

I blink and swipe sweat from my eyes. "Relying on the blessing of Almighty God. Whatever that means." It's tough reading, but I'm doing it. I pump my fists, and read the line again.

People form the union. Not the PM or the Council of Nine? The people?

I whisper, "If the idea spread, it would change everything."

Outside, the familiar sound of wash and motor.

"Luca! Are you there?"

Metal thumps gently against the dock, and my heart pounds. "Father?" I jump up. "Father Massa!"

I race up the stairs, through the house, and burst out the door. "Father Mass —"

"I'm sorry to disappoint, mate." Seward holds up his arms and lets them flop. "Believe me, I'd give my arm to know his fate. But I do bring strange tidings of the man. Come aboard —"

I already am.

"Please speak!" I grab his long coat and yank. "Father's not here. What happened to him? They told me nothing."

Seward loosens my fingers and leans back. "They know only what they be told. Lots to blame the Amongus for." His jaw tightens. "Lots. But not knowin' the truth can't be held against 'em."

"They publicly announced that he was fine, that he just needed rest." I crumple down on the bench.

"He's not fine?" he asks. "There be more to their story?"

I peer up at Seward, his lip bulging with baccy. *Should I tell a pirate?*

"They told me something else in the tunnel."

Seward turns and spits. "They told you he was undone."

I jump up. "How do you know this?"

"Because Mape just told me. Mape, the most unpleasant one of the lot. Sit down, I be speaking hushed as we go."

We float with engines off over the reef, and my muscles calm. Distance from mainland relaxes the heart, and thoughts flow more freely.

"So listen to Seward through and through, and then you can add your piece."

I make a motion to zip my lips and glance over the sea, still and calm as glass.

"Quite a sight, isn't it," he begins. "Not a breeze. Not a wave. Dead as recent business, and without restating the obvious, it's a nasty one I'm in."

"I know. I helped you retrieve a group of un —"

He grabs my fingers and lifts them up in front of his face. "This be one ineffective zipper."

"Sorry." I motion for him to continue.

"In the past months, I've only been asked to make two retrievals. One, you rudely interrupted. The second set was dunked the day before that … the day before Water Day, if you can believe it. The morning of their undoing, Mape told me the count. 'They'll be three men and two women.' A few days ago, that's who I bagged."

"He didn't mention a child? I remember that march. I remember seeing a boy …"

"You remember wrong." He tongues his cheek and gently puffs out air. "An unfortunate trait for a Deliverer, I might be addin'. Only five there were. No child."

I pause and think about Walery. The events around his rescue and his stay in the shanty were so crazy; he could have danced through my imagination. I could have dreamed him up.

"So fine, you found five," I say. "Go on."

"I be paid by the head, or the body as it is. Mind you, the job is grim, and I pull no satisfaction from seein' them that were undone, but it does keep me alive. But two retrievals in as many months? There's no livin' in that. And I have to wait the allotted thirty days. A month or more they must rest on the sea floor before I can winch them up and extract my fee from Mape."

I rub my shoulders. I could not do Seward's job.

"Then last night, after a day of honest thievery" — he points to three water casks — "I return to the wharf and he be waiting.

Mape, that rat of a man. He tells me he has a special retrieval. Just one. 'Not worth my time,' I says. But Mape said he could change that. He offers thirty times the price for the extraction, and a year's worth of credits for my silence. Luca, please understand, it's hard to turn down that much — "

"Father," I whisper.

"When he told me Massa's name, it was all I could do to hold me supper in place. He asked if he should search out a retriever from Derby, but I pulled it together. 'No, I be your man,' I says. 'I need the credits.' But in my mind, I think, I don't believe the body is Massa's." His voice cracks. "And I need to know."

"Not my father's? Not undone?"

"Luca, think it through. Would your father make an error?"

"No, I always said he couldn't — "

"Even if he did, if he be punished, destroyed, the Watcher's actions would leave this world in your hands. They don't know how well you know the way, or even if you truly know it. Massa's undoing is too big a risk. Unless . . . unless they pulled from his mind the path." He grabs my arm. "Do you think they could do that?"

"I . . . I don't — No, he would give them the alternate," I whisper. "He made me memorize it. It's an alternate set of directions. 'For use when pressed,' he always said. It never made sense until now."

"Ah, Massa, they could not pull the path from you. An alternate." Seward laughs aloud. "Arrogant, stubborn trickster of a man. They could not break you. Now I be sure of it."

My mind whirs. "How do you know my father?"

"A different story for a different time." Seward places his fingers nearly atop my eyes. "For now, I need these. I go to retrieve Massa, and a body I will surely find, but will it be his? You know it best. It will have been a month below. Bodies change, bloat. Sharks gnaw. I need to know if the man I retrieve is him. It may be a horrible sight, Luca." Seward's leg bounces. "But what if it's not him? Would the risk of horror not turn to sudden joy?"

Father Massa, alive! The possibility buoys me. "Take me."

One half hour later, Seward kills the engines three miles north of Rottnest Isle and drops two anchors. The mainland is no longer visible in the darkness, and I wonder how this pirate can locate a floating spot with precision.

"Don't have the promised light rods, do ya?" He rolls his eyes. "We may need some renegotiating. Grab the winch arm with that pole." He points toward the rear of the craft. "I like havin' a mate. Should savin' the world ever get boring, consider yourself hired."

"No chance." My hands shake as my pole hook clanks against the magnetic claw.

"Push it out." Seward squints. "Left a little ... a little more, there."

I unhook the pole from the arm, and Seward releases the winch, watches the claw splash into the water. Down, down it sinks, while Seward holds an orb over the surface. He stares at the sea, watching the ripples calm while the line slips between his fingers.

"'Tis right below us."

Slack doubles the rope, and it coils on the surface of the water. Seward holds up his hand. "Got it." He slowly cranks the winch.

Either way, what comes up will change my world.

The surface churns and Seward pauses. "Not the way these

things should be done. If it be him, this will heap pain upon pain." He rubs his face. "You don't need to be party to this."

I cock my head. For a pirate, Seward has a side I don't often see; it's something I don't ever see, except in Wren, and in those last precious minutes with Father.

Father.

I swallow hard, nod, and step back.

Seward slowly lifts the claw. The body lifts limp from the water, a small waterfall spilling down from the catch back into the ocean. Shackles of iron — a wrist ring, ankle rings, and chains — stick fast to the metallic pinchers, and Seward pulls the mechanical arm over the boat.

My heart sinks.

The face is already bloated beyond recognition, but the clothes and the backpack, they are Father's.

"It's him," I say quietly. And I weep. I've wondered when the dam would break. Each time it got close, the waters held back, but not now. Now they flow salty and loud, and I crumble into the bottom of the boat.

"Luca, lad, I don't have words ..."

I peek up. Seward faces the last glow of the orb, and in that light I see a tear.

Seward cries.

We float silent and motionless with our sadness. The night falls, and my sobs choke back to whimpers and finally sniffs.

"Please," I say. "Can we get him off that hook?"

Seward gentles my father into the boat. He removes a blowtorch from beneath his seat and carefully burns off the shackles.

"Cursed things," he says, and kneels down beside Father.

"He looks so different." I scoot up on the opposite side. "His face — "

"Water does strange things to a man. Strange things. It twists the flesh, distorts the mouth, bends the nose —"

"Removes scars?"

Seward glances up, his eyes large. "No, lad, it leaves the evil acts done above intact." He slowly rolls the body onto its front, lifts the light orb, and we both lean over the back to peer between the shoulder blades.

I fall to my haunches. "It's not there. He had a scar, jagged and ugly. That's not something that can be wiped away, is it?"

Seward rubs his stubble. "That one would be there. It was too large, too deep."

"How do you know it?"

He climbs to his feet, and his words come slow. "I gave it."

I scurry backward. "You stabbed my father?"

"No," he says quietly. "I knifed my brother."

I blink. Brother? Seward?

Uncle?

Seward shakes his head, and his gaze clears. "The reasons will not be discussed now, as we have bigger problems." Seward hauls the body into a bag, zips it tightly inside. "This is not Massa. So why go to great lengths to hide the fact? To produce a body? To convince everyone he's gone?"

A deceit like this makes no sense. "It would be a day of wrinkles, for sure. The entire world would mourn. If everyone knew I alone held the route, they couldn't endure it." *Especially not Lendi.*

"No, they couldn't." Seward paces and mumbles. "What does the Council gain? What do they want? What does everyone want?"

I think of Wren. "The Aquifer?"

Seward turns to me and smiles. "Yes, Luca. I see it now." He slaps his thigh. "They thought they'd extract the route to reach it from weak Massa. Instead, they received the alternate, and you can be sure they tried that path many a time. By now, they know they be fooled. But there is one other who holds the key that lived in his mind."

I face his gaze. "But I could be brave. If they ever ask me, I could give the alternate, like Father."

"You be brave, lad. No doubting it. But for them, there be a far easier, and quicker, way to get what they're after. Especially since your alternate matches Massa's."

He points to me and then over the edge of the boat.

"What would happen if you too be undone?" Seward scratches his stubble.

"Me?"

"With no Deliverer, the people would demand action from the Council. They would rise up until the Aquifer was taken by force."

"But," I say, "they don't know the way down."

"No, not yet." Seward squeezes his forehead between thumb and forefinger. "But if Massa believed you had met your end, that you could not make the exchange, he would be forced to reveal the true route to his captors. His heart be too big to watch millions thirst. The Age of Deliverers would be over. The Council's Amongus would follow the route, take control of the Aquifer. The Nine would finally control the earth."

My head swims.

"So why fake Father's undoing?"

"People fear change, unless there is no other way. My guess be the Council will show this body, and your body, as proof that a new course must be charted, and once the Aquifer is taken, the Nine will emerge as saviors of the world."

I should be following Seward's reasoning, but my mind is stuck on one question. "So Father's alive?"

"Are you listening to nothing, boy? I guarantee, he'll stay alive as long as you do. If you be gone, and he shares this route, he's no longer needed." Seward starts the motor. "I fear they mean to undo you, Luca. You can't go back home."

"What's wrong with home? I have to go home. To Old Rub and my books and paintings —"

"Even now, Mape waits for me at Freemanl." Seward rubs his hand over his face and stares off. "If I turn this body in, I give you my word, you're next to be taken."

I jump to his side and clutch his sleeve. "Then don't turn it in!"

He glances at me. "We make another deal, eh, pirate?" Seward exhales. "Of course I will not be turnin' this body in, though I forfeit a fortune. I'll report the body washed, lost in the current to parts unknown — that is, if you swear *not* to stay on the Shallows."

"But Seward . . . where should I go?"

He reaches out and squeezes my shoulder. A touch, strong and sure. "We pick up what you need tonight. Then we leave the same hour. All sign of you must be gone by morning. We take only what fits in the boat."

"But we can't float around our whole lives."

"*We*." He laughs. "You speak as if we be in this together."

"You said if I ever needed a new job, I had one. Well, I need one now."

Seward falls silent and shakes his head. "A mate. My blood and my mate." He breathes deeply. "Ah, so it comes to me. It won't be comfortable, but I know your new home. It will be safe." He pauses. "My nephew once showed it to me."

I slump down to the deck. I know he means Glaugood. I know that's his plan, but my mind fills with another.

I need to reach Wren.

CHAPTER
12

Seward quiets the engine and rounds the wharf. Soon I'll see the Shallows and the shanty, maybe for the last time.

Right now, I see the spire.

It rises black on black into the night — a star-eating billowing plume — and with it Seward plunks down to the deck.

"Lad, I think we're late. The shanty burns." He pauses. "Their plan be underway."

"Then move faster! I need to get things out!"

Seward shakes his head. "You talk foolishness, boy. Only this trip kept you from fuelin' that fire."

I jump up and jam forward the throttle.

We power ahead. Seward tumbles onto his back and curses, and we round the bend. Flames leap into the sky.

The paintings. The books!

Seward scrambles to his feet, clutches my waist, and throws me to the deck. He lunges for the wheel, but it's too late and we crash into the dock. I tumble, my ribs smashing against the winch. I groan, push to my feet, and roll over the bow. I'm off and staggering into the blaze.

"Luca!" Seward's words fight through the hunger of the fire that bites and gnaws the dry timbers of the shanty. "You must stay alive. For Massa!"

I pause, then crash through the door. Smoke overpowers my eyes and thoughts, and I drop to my knees and crawl to the corner where I can see the laundry pile's silhouette topped by Father's new coat. I throw it aside, grab a balled-up shirt, and breathe through the fabric. My lungs still burn, but I breathe deep and throw myself down the stairs, landing with a thud on a stack of books.

Where are you? Where are you? I rifle through the piles. *There!* I find my two prized volumes — Father's and the skeleton-guarded book from the cave. Above me I hear a sharp crack, and the ceiling gives way. Sparks and timbers crash all around me.

Get out now, Luca.

The voice from the cave is faint, but clear.

Father? Who are you?

I cannot wait for an answer. I jump up, books tightly pressed to my chest, and stumble upward. Heat overpowers, and I close my eyes, picture the floor plan of the home I know so well, and hurtle in the direction of the door. I strike mesh, and burst through the screen and onto the porch, followed by a billowing belch of smoke. Gasping, lumbering, I limp toward the boat.

Seward curses and grabs me.

"That be all you're taking. The fire spreads fast. I will allow no other run." He stares at the sky. "They will produce Massa's body — real or substitute, it won't matter. The world will believe you undone in this horrific 'accident.' If Massa believes the tales, the Council will get the route they crave. To that end, they will be looking for your remains to convince him. Let's see to it they find none."

I push against Seward but cannot pry free from his arms. So much beauty, burning. So much in those books I'll never learn.

Two books were all I could save.

Seward throws the boat in reverse, and we churn backward. "Here."

He slaps a paper against my chest. "Nailed to the dock, it was. Scratching, if you ask me."

I grab the light orb and hold it close.

Not safe. Time to go down. Meet you there. Wren

"Must have fallen out of one of them books," he says.

"'Not safe. Time to go down.'" I squint at the message. "Not safe. That's what it says. I know it's not safe — I get that part. It's the down part."

Seward winces and groans. "Nephew. Who's it from?"

"A lady I know at the museum. She works there."

"Only one lady works at the museum."

"Are you familiar with her?"

He grins. "More than you know. We be making a change, of course." The prow of his ship swings violently.

I rest beneath the moonlight, Wren's letter clutched in my hand. Behind me, my house — my world — burns. In front of me, a pirate who happens to be my uncle. And between us, a corpse I don't know and the hope of a father alive.

How peaceful it had been today at the museum. Tea. We sipped tea, and Wren spoke musical words. Soothing words.

Her words on the page do not soothe.

The boat swings again, this time toward the north and west,

away from the mainland. Away, out to sea, farther out than I've ever been.

My life's in a pirate's hands, one who stabbed my father but who is also my uncle. He now looks at me, his eyes soft.

"You wonder about the knifin'."

"And many other things." Salt water sprays over the rails, and I feel a chill. I pull my arms inside my shirt sleeves and shiver.

"Do you wonder enough to ask?" Seward says.

"I'm scared."

Seward looks off. "Fool raised you right. But in this matter, anxious thoughts play no purpose. Massa turned out fine. As always."

I frown.

"A short story, for a long trip. Nestle down." He reaches into a basket and pulls out an apple. I extract one of my arms, and he tosses it to me. "Hear of your uncle's misfortune."

CHAPTER
13

A pirate I am, and no denyin' the claim. But it be truth that Massa and I came from the same womb. Has he told you about your second father?"

"Not even a name. He didn't ... well, doesn't ... like to speak of family."

"Good reason for that." Seward suddenly stands and cocks his head, listening. "Others have been out here this night." He lowers himself back down. "Let's float in the black." He switches off his floodlight. "Where was I?"

"My second father."

"Aye. His name was Janus — my father, Massa's father, and the Deliverer for sixty years. Fennel, that's your second mother, and Janus's wife."

"Janus and Fennel," I repeat. "Somewhere I've heard the names."

"Surely it be true, and you'll feel much more truth as I relay the tale. Two children they had, taken, as is custom, developed well, and returned. Seward, yours truly" — he bows — "came first. A year later, Massa was born. Your shanty was our home. My childhood home."

I prop myself up on an elbow. "You just watched your old house burn to the ground."

"I did."

"I had ... I had no idea."

Seward stretches. "You're a good lad. So, custom is, as you know, for the first child to be named Job Successor, and in our family, a mighty big job it be. The Deliverer. It was assumed that the privilege, the honored life, the freedom, would be mine." In the light of the orb, Seward's eyes glaze. "It should have been mine.

"But even at five, it was clear. Massa would grow to a giant of a man. He was strong and fast, sharp of mind. I ... I was slow of foot, of thought. And then came the dream."

I lean forward.

"Do you believe in the Fates?" he asks. "In dreams? Do you believe they hold the future, seeping glimpses into the mind in sleep?"

"Like a prophecy?" I shrug. "Father always said the Wishers believed in dreams and prayers and voices. Now I've seen it for myself. I know it's lunacy, but I think ... I think I'd like to believe. That there's more than life in the shadow of the Amongus. That there's hope from somewhere else." I drop my gaze and my apple core into the hold.

"Hmm." Seward smirks and falls silent. When next he speaks, his voice is soft. "Janus believed that we were guided from beyond. And so when Fennel dreamt of Massa holding rods in his hands, when she dreamt of Massa emerging from the Birthing tunnel, when she dreamt of ... Massa leadin' his son to a chair in a marble hall filled with light, well, Janus felt it a sign, and passed the future of the world to the younger, to your father. And to me, to me ..."

"You received nothing."

"Ah, the life of a pirate isn't nothing." Seward forces a grin, but it can't stay. "Days before Massa became a Sixteen, a rage consumed me. I waited on the rocks, waited for my brother to paddle near, and when he turned, I flung the knife. True it is that I wished him dead. And that was the last day I saw my father or mother. I left, and when the story rounded, there was a simple choice. A debriefing or a hideous job —"

"For the Amongus."

Seward raises his eyebrows. "My brother and I tried to mend it, but always my hot head or his stubborn pride snapped us short. I don't blame Massa. He wasn't the one with the dreams, and the violence be on my head — no fault lies with him. But Mother and Father, they should have come after me ..." Seward quiets, and then speaks with words meant, I think, as much for his own ears as for mine. "It is a hard thing to play the second, seeing that I arrived first."

I think of Walery, and the talk he had with Father while I almost sacrificed Old Rub. I think of all the nights I lay ten feet from Father wishing only that he would call my name and say ... anything. I know exactly what Seward means.

"But!" Seward speaks so loud I jump. "Watching him from afar, I wonder if perhaps I was the lucky one loosed from his burdened life."

"Piracy ever since," I say.

"Ever since." He slaps his leg. "But sleep now. The hours will soon tell if my gut spoke wisdom or doom. And if doom, we'll need all of our strength."

Strength. Oh, to be as strong as Lendi. I sigh at the thought. *He'll live a normal life. Even the tedium of tanning seems pretty great about now.*

I lie back in a pile of netting, and miss my mate. And the drift and the stars soon steal my thoughts.

~

"Luca."

I wake to a hand on my shoulder. "Speak softly, listen now. We be near your dropping point."

I feel my heart quicken as I raise myself from the makeshift bed. "What? Huh? How could you do this to me?"

Seward slaps his hand over my mouth. "I'll try again." He slowly releases my lips. "Not an undoing dropping point. Your and Massa's dropping point, the beginning of the route to the Rats. Massa starts his descent from a point on this isle. Surely he briefed you on the precise location."

My eyes widen, and I shake my head.

"Right. Then this be a futile attempt." Seward douses his orb. "But an attempt nonetheless. Peek over the edge, starboard side."

An island, cloaked with trees swaying dark on dark, stretches like a ribbon across the sea. Between the shore and us, hulking shapes dot the water.

"Amongus boats," Seward whispers. "Massa's isle be well known, but without the dropping point, I don't know what they're here for . . . Perhaps they be searching for the way down."

He places a hand on my shaking head. "Ease, mate. They're surely not here for you, who should be crisping well right now, so this fact works in our favor."

"Explain how bringing me here can be described as a favor!"

I hiss, and press into the bottom of the boat. "Why did you do this?"

"There's no place on this earth you can hide from them. They will scour the shanty, and when you aren't found they will search for you without end. Only with both you and Massa undone can they prove the Deliverer line is ended, dash all hope, and wrest control. But there is a place only you know how to find. One place, I think, that they cannot yet follow."

It becomes clear. Wren's message is clear; she wants me to descend. I think of the grotesque museum display: the teeth and claws and hunched-over form. I can't descend to that! I turn and vomit onto the deck.

"No bloke I've hauled in this boat has ever done that — of course, you are my first breathing passenger." He rests his hands on my shoulders and forces my eyes to meet his. "Do you trust me, Luca?"

"It depends." I wipe off my mouth. "Are you the man who helped me, or are you the man who knifed Father?"

"I be both."

I think on this. I have no choice. "What do we do?"

"Stay low, crawl to the back, and bring me three body bags."

I do the deed, and a light, strong and penetrating, lights up Seward's hull. I drop to my stomach.

"Identify!"

Seward pops up, hands outstretched. "It's your Seward! I wish an audience with Mr. Mape, if he be here." He lowers his voice. "Lay two bags open in the bottom of the boat and crawl inside the third."

"You do want me undone," I whisper.

"If that's what it takes to keep you alive. Crawl in!"

"Seward." Mape's deep voice chills me. "What brings you here? Was I not clear about your responsibility?"

"Yes, yes, as always, clear." Seward shields his eyes. "And as always, I let no detail fall. But unlike always, when I went to meet you at the wharf, you were not there. We had a deal, Mr. Mape. A thirty-spot and year's bonus for an important haul. I have him here."

Seward bends down and muscles the stranger's body into a waiting bag. He zips it shut, and then crawls to the magnetic claw, grabs the blowtorch, and quickly burns through an iron finger.

"What are you doing?" I start to sit up from inside my bag. "Now's not the time to destroy your equipment. I'm in a bit of a situation—"

"Silence. Your mouth be undone!"

I lay back down.

"Very well," Mape calls. "So how did you find me?"

Seward winces, and with his torch, burns a second magnetic pincher off the claw. A five-foot finger of iron rattles against the decking. "Ah, Mr. Mape." He peeks above railing. "You know the history between this undone and me. I went to Massa's home. Perhaps, I think, finally something might fall to me, something that should always have been mine. But the shanty be burned, torched, and Luca be crumpled on the dock."

"Still alive?"

"I did not stop to ask."

Mape hollers. "You told me Luca sleeps soundly, on his cot. That tonight of all nights, he would be there." The sound of hand slapping face snaps the air, and a boy cries out.

"I told you his pattern. I cannot account for anomalies!"

"Walery," I whisper.

"Hush." Seward grunts the metal pinchers into the third bag and seals it. He crawls over the undone and zips me up to the waist. "With fortune, I will see you soon. Without it, the pleasure to meet you has been mine ... Nephew."

"Wait." I grab my two books and pull them into the bag.

"You are insane, lad." Then, with one final zip, the world goes black.

"Bring the body to me." Mape's voice sounds muffled, and I reach up, find the underside of the zipper, and scratch it down a centimeter. Through the tiny opening, I see one bright star.

I see you, Luca.

The strange thought comforts, and my body relaxes. Our boat inches forward, and I rearrange the books, squeezing them against my gut. Moments later, strong fingers tap my head.

Be still. I get it, Seward.

"Why are there three bodies?" Mape stands directly above me, blocking out my star, and I hear his dial whizzing. My heart pounds. *Great, he got a new dial.* "Your emotions are causing quite a wrinkle, Seward. Unusual for you. What do you have to fear?"

"You. This is not the usual exchange. Not the usual place." Seward clears his throat. "The middle one is Massa. Would you take him?"

"With pleasure." Mape snaps, "I warned him that punishment would fall." Feet shuffle beside me. A stray boot catches my gut, and I suck in the gasp.

"And what of the other two?" The voice of Mape's companion.

"Ancient undones, no means to identify. Their bones came up attached to my claw. I call'm collateral bycatch, those done in before Mape and his efficiency took over. I'll carry this heavy one, if you would like to carry the other."

"Hardly worth the effort," an Amongus scoffs. "Tiny little bag-o-bones."

Hands slip beneath my back and lift. For a moment I'm weightless, then I land with a crack, my gut draped over an Amongus shoulder. I've been undone.

Seward knifed Father, now he's destroyed me.

Minutes later, I thud facedown onto the sand.

"Yes, Massa is the prize, but you'll all want to see the one I carried." Seward's voice nears and my bag rolls over, the zipper lowering halfway. I look up into the face of my sweating uncle. He calls back to the group. "Yeah, that one. The heavy beastie. You'll want a close look. Shackles of solid gold, it has." He winks and places my books firmly into my hands, then whispers, "Get ready to run. No stopping for books that fall."

I nod.

A distant zipper.

Thunk! The Amongus yell and groan.

"Hold on to your dials!" Mape's voice sounds pained.

Seward throws open my bag, I jump to my feet, and together we dash for the jungle. Ten steps, fifteen steps. I hear nothing but grunting, and glance over my shoulder. Ten Amongus are on their knees around the bag, the metal dials in their chest pockets stuck fast to the powerful magnetic fingers of Seward's claws. A rip of fabric. Mape breaks free.

"Leave the dials! Slide them out of your pockets! Luca is here!"

We reach the first row of palms. "From here, I have no plan." Seward huffs. "But if one of those books be scratched by Massa, best ditch them all."

I fall to my knees, brush sand over the covers, and pull palm branches over the stash. Seward hauls me upright the second my books are concealed, and we race forward, the shouts of men trailing in the distance, our feet stumbling over branch and root.

There are no sounds but the puff of my breath, the pound of my heart. Seward grabs my shoulder and we veer left. Down, down a slope. We run blind, the saline-tree canopy swallowing the stars above. At last he pulls me close and we collapse in a heap behind a fallen trunk.

"We hide here," he whispers. "They can't track us without the dials. But they'll soon catch up if we run."

I press my body into the bark and think. Were there any clues? Any words dropped by Father that would guide me to the entrance point? Seward must be thinking the same.

"He said nothing? Why would my brother keep it from you?" He grabs my arm. "You do remember the directions."

A moment of panic, and I close my eyes. *Left, slight jog right …*

"It's still there. I remem — "

"They ran this way." Mape's voice cuts thick through the night. "They're close. Very close. Spread out."

"They'll find us, mate," Seward whispers. "When I tap your back, we run. I toward the beach and you deeper in." He sighs. "I won't be seeing you again. Keep yourself alive — for you, for my brother. You're family."

He peeks over the log, gathers his breath, and taps.

"Mape! Amongus, follow me, you pack of vermin!" He's gone, and I hear steps pounding after.

No, Seward!

He's lost everything for me; I will not let him go. The thought of his pirate's smirk drowning in shackles is too much to endure. I leap up and give chase. I silently slip through the trees, the shouts of Amongus all around me.

"Oof." I collide with a chest.

Seward.

"Luca, you fooo — "

Up we sail, bound in a coarse net. We swing helpless thirty feet above the forest floor.

"This is not an Amongus weave," Seward hisses. "No, it is quality work. Someone else be on the island."

I raise my finger to my lips and point down.

Beneath us, a cluster of searchers circle. "Mape, we need the dials. Their fear wrinkles will flush them."

"We have no time. If Luca disappears below, we'll have to stand before the Nine. Do you feel like enduring that?" Mape kicks at the ground. "I do not want to struggle with Massa's mind again!"

I squeal, and Seward slaps his hand over my mouth.

"But Mape, Luca may not know where it is. He's never descended." An Amongus throws his arms into the air. "We need the dials to find them. There is no choice."

Mape paces, his fists tightening into balls. "No!" he screams. "This is *my* life! Always there is no choice." He exhales hard. "Fine! Fine. To the beach." He lets his head fall back. It cocks to the side as he peers up at us. "What would you say that is?"

"Looks to be a net," says another, raising an orb above his head. "A very full net."

"Hello, Luca." Mape waves, his voice calming. "What brings you here at night? And how do you come to know my employ?"

I should feel afraid, but I don't. I stare down at their ripped pockets, think of my father, and I feel I can do anything.

"Leave me be," I say. "I'm on private, Deliverer business."

The group sneers, and one bends over and grasps a chunk of wood. "Oh, of course, of course you are." He flings it upward.

"Uh." It strikes Seward hard in the back.

Mape holds up his hand. "While it would be entertaining to watch the two of you pummeled into pulp, Luca, we need some … information from you, so first let's bring you down."

"Seward! Luca! Close your eyes!"

I obey, and the world flashes light around me. Lightning, but there's no storm. A sunrise, but it's night.

Below us, shouts and screams and one calm voice.

"Two years of hiding from you, Mape, and now here you are, and ya can't lay eyes on me."

"Jasper!" Mape claws at the air.

"Oh, you do remember me. Well now, that's a nice thing." He clears his throat. "Sad to say, most of you will be blind — an unblinking stare at a light rod does that. But some of you may see in a day or two. I suggest you stay together. There be beasties on this isle, big and small, and none too friendly."

He sighs and stares upward. "Now for my birdies."

We lower in jerks and finally strike ground, but I don't move and I cover closed eyelids with my hands.

"You two can open up — light's doused."

I crack an eyelid and watch the Amongus stumbling, calling, gathering in a clump. I help Seward to his feet and turn toward Jasper. He is half bear; a wild, hairy, hulk of a man.

"Are you friend?" I ask.

"I hate them. They hate you. That's mates to me. But I was sent here, and instead of chatter I'd like to finish my job."

"Your job," I repeat.

"There's an opening I hear you need to find." He tousles my hair. "Massa's son. My pleasure. I've heard much of you."

"You have?"

Seward sets his hand on my back. "Not to interrupt, lad, but in case one of them shut their eyes in time, I'm thinkin' we best not be here when vision returns."

I nod. "Yeah. Um, Jasper? This is Seward. Massa's brother."

Jasper tongues his cheek. "Oh, we're quite well acquainted. More than once I've lost casks of water to this pirate."

"Entrepreneur." Seward chuckles. "We all scratch to make a livin'."

"Scratch! My books!" I break toward the beach.

"Curse those things." Seward follows, with Jasper not far behind. I dig up my buried treasure, and the three of us snake back deep into the forest.

"You know my father," I say.

"Aye." Jasper says. "I reckon better than most."

"How, bloke?" Seward barks. He follows the two of us, and the mistrust oozes from his words.

"He keeps me alive. There is no fresh water on the isle. Each year he brings me a supply, sneaks here every few months to replenish. It's a good thing. A man gets lonely by himself with only the beasties to keep him company."

"Why … do … you stay?" I huff.

"No choice after what I found." He whacks through the undergrowth with his machete. "Well, who I found. Mape was a mate, or so I thought, but the whole time we scooped, he was looking for an undone. A particular undone."

Seward sets his hand on my shoulder. "He lies. I would know about any retrieval that needed doing. I would have been sent, not a shrimper."

"Go on, Jasper." I pull free from Seward. Jasper looks into my face; the eyes that glisten beneath his shaggy brows hold concern.

110

"It was on Scott's Reef. I don't figure many undones get dropped there." He glances at Seward, whose eyes narrow. "The short version? We hauled her up in the PM's shackles, Mape jumped ship, and a debriefing was my lot."

Jasper takes a deep breath. "She'd been down there a long time." He runs thick fingers over his face. "This isn't mine to say, but I fear it falls to me. Luca, your father told me, and you should know." He stops, bends over, and whispers. "That night I was trawling for shrimp. Instead, I pulled up your mother, Alaya. I'm sorry, Luca."

Seward grabs Jasper. "This be the truth?"

"I have no reason to lie."

"My mother." I collapse onto my knees. "But what did she do?"

"Fantastic timing, shrimper." Seward shoves Jasper. "And when we need to move the fastest!" He pulls me to my feet. "Luca, there will be a time for your sadness, but now the sun rises."

Jasper nods and we quicken our pace. Mother, undone. Father, disappeared. Seward and me, pursued.

What is it about our family? What don't I know?

CHAPTER
14

*S*huff. *Shuff.*

Jasper's machete rips through the saline forest. Brush and undergrowth, leaves and vine fly upward, coating Seward and me with bits of green.

My legs have no strength, and I lean my head against Seward's chest and listen to my uncle's heartbeat. It races. Too fast.

I don't figure he planned to carry me in his arms.

I glance up at his face, which glistens in the light that seeps from Jasper's pack. *Love.* My father said it was our word, only ours, but at this moment I think him wrong. I feel a warmth for this man, the same one who curses the weight of two extra books, and no other word seems to fit.

Bouncing through the jungle, I discover a second kind of love.

Jasper stops abruptly. Seward and I crash into his back.

"Easy now. We're almost there." Jasper glances at me. "But you'll need to walk, Luca."

"He'd be walking fine, and I'd still have strength in my arms, if you'd have held your news close to your shirt a bit longer." Seward leans forward, and I step down. My vision blurs, but I see why Jasper calls to my legs. We're heading down.

A cupped-out earth, like a miniature Glaugood, lies before us, its walls steep and green, with trees growing straight up from its sides.

"At the bottom of the bowl lies what you seek."

"Which is what, mate?" Seward's hesitance has returned.

Jasper steps toward him. "Many things."

A shout in the distance.

Amongus.

"If they wrested the dials off the claw, they don't need sight to find us." Seward peers down over the edge. "We be dropping breadcrumbs of emotion on the way."

Jasper points into the hole. "Down. Dials or no, they'll have a hard time following us without vision." He steps onto the steep decline and slides, crashing into a tree. "Use these trunks as braces." Jasper releases one trunk and slides down to another, grasping it and righting himself.

More shouts.

"Go, Luca," Seward says, "and give me these cursed things." He grabs the books from my arms. "I'll bring them with me. Now go."

I take a small step forward.

"Not quick enough." A firm hand shoves me onto the steep slope, and I stumble and crash into a slender shoot.

"You got it," Jasper calls.

My shoulder throbs, and I shake my head clear in time to see Seward clutch a tree near me. "Keep going — look!" He glances up, toward the rim of the bowl.

Figures mill about. One with purpose.

He probably closed his eyes in time.

I release my tree and slide downward, moving in short bursts. My slight frame makes each collision tolerable, unlike Seward, who bears the brunt of force on a weightier body. His shoulders absorb the impact, as each hand holds a book.

Numerous trunks later, we reach the bottom. Before me, a stone path, and at its end Jasper stands in front of a rock mound, clearing the pile. He squeezes into the fresh opening, then pokes out his head and holds up a backpack. "This is for you and them scratchings. You can't carry them by hand; not where we're going."

He tosses the pack to Seward's feet. Uncle stuffs it and slings it over my back.

Jasper disappears again, but this time it takes longer for him to return. When he does, he looks pleased. "Okay. I guess we're ready to go."

"Where?" I look around.

"Down." A woman — Wren — steps out of the crevice. She hugs me long and real. "I see you received my note. Consider your reading test passed." Wren grins at Seward. "And you brought the scoundrel."

Seward bows. "At your service."

I raise my hand, and my jaw drops. "Am I the only one who doesn't understand what's going — "

"Curse it!"

A pile of Amongus tumble onto the floor of the bowl.

"Got to hand it to them," Seward says. "They're persistent."

"Come, Luca!" Wren grabs my arm and pulls. I follow her around the back of the pile and onto a grassy path that disappears into a small cave.

"Those stones were the marker, set by Massa for you. This is the entrance. This is the moment he trained you for." She looks at me wide-eyed. "Only you can get us safely below."

"Safely? Do you know who's down there?"

"Do you trust me?" she asks.

I roll my eyes. "Why is everyone asking me that?"

"Mate." Seward rounds my shoulder with his arm as footsteps pound nearer. "We be out of time for trustin'. If you know the way, use it!"

The first Amongus finds his way around the pile, and I take off toward the cave. I duck inside easy enough. Wren slips in behind. Jasper's head appears — only his head — and he howls.

"I'm stuck, stuck in the pass! Ow!"

Jasper crashes into the tunnel, and Seward scrambles off his back. "Don't know what you've been eating, but you better be hopin' that's the pinchiest we meet." Seward hoists Jasper to his feet. The cave darkens as the Amongus converge on the entrance. "Lead, Luca!"

"Okay … okay …" I rub my hands together and swipe the sweat from my brow.

Blank.

My mind blanks.

Lefts and rights float about, but nothing sticks. I glance to each side. Thin tunnels lead off in each direction.

Wren places her hand on my head. "It's here. It's all here. Relax."

In the distance, I hear Seward's voice. "One's inside the cave!"

"Close your eyes and remember." Wren's voice hypnotizes. "You sat with Massa on the dock. Hear his voice."

"Three in the cave!"

Luca, let us begin the sequence. The first section, the most cru-
cial, and the most dangerous should you err. What is the first turn?

"All here!" Seward shouts. "They all be here!"

"Left!" I scream, and stumble over loose rock into the first left offshoot.

"Luca!"

I turn, and Jasper tosses me his orb. I catch it, face forward again, and crash into a rock wall. "Oh, slight jog right."

And as I run, the words shift, gel, fix in my mind. They are a whole. Unforgettable.

"Now a sharp right."

Seward's voice reaches me. I want to ignore it, concentrate on the route. "Left, left ..."

"They're following, Luca. We can't take them there."

"Veer left, lower your head ..." My three mates catch up in the long stretch. My feet flop down, nearly out of my control, so steep is the descent.

"He's correct." Wren slows me down. "How can we lose them?"

"Without losing ourselves?" I pause and recite the route up to the present. It is dangerous to speak in the middle. Wren gives me no choice.

"When do we reach the pass?" Wren grips my shoulder.

"The pass? I don't know. That word is not in the sequence."

"Is there anything like it? A thin pass, with a drop off on the left?"

"Thin pass," I repeat, forcing myself to focus on the sequence and not her questions. "Deep into the series we will come to 'careful, hug the right. Keep hugging the right. Don't look left.'"

She grins. "Get us there."

We fly forward, and my mind wanders. Time seems to vanish in the series of turns I alone know. The temperature is cool and comfortable. It hasn't changed since we dropped. It makes no —

Crack.

I slow to a stop and plod back to the others, already looking to where my foot fell.

Three dials. Three busted dials, the glass sparkling in the light of the orb.

I look up and smile. "Father. So you were at least this far. Easy left, then slow and whoa ..."

We burst out of a shaft, pass beneath an arch of fitted stone, and gaze out at a subterranean dome. The ceiling is barely visible, rising hundreds of feet before us and reflecting yellows and blues. The path veers sharply right, where it thins to a trail wide enough for one that winds tight against a rocky slope. To the left is the open, airy expanse of the dome. I step to its lip and glance down. There is no bottom.

I pick up a stone, stretch my arm straight ahead, and drop it over the edge. We listen. Nothing.

Wren whispers, "This is where it must happen."

CHAPTER 15

W e don't know yet how well they see."

Wren paces, her voice tense. "Your earlier bread-crumb analogy is accurate. They can trace us as long as they have dials. And who knows what manner of markings they may be leaving? The real danger is not that they find the Aquifer, it's that they find their way out again with the means to return."

She draws us back off the ledge and into a huddle.

"This means nobody can continue on to the thin trail. Our scent must stop here. We hide behind those rocks there." She nods toward the piles on either side of the arch. "They will come quickly down, as did we, and when they reach the drop we can only hope they're blind enough to miss the turn onto the ledge."

"And fall," Jasper huffs.

"And fall," Wren repeats.

"And if they don't?" My voice sounds small, small like me. "Fall, that is."

Seward slaps my back. "Then we will, mate. But Wren is

right — we can't lead them closer to the only thing they want more than you."

We hide behind the two outcroppings, Seward and me on one side, Jasper and Wren on the other. Tucked behind Seward, I feel safe, and for minutes we whisper, speaking fondly about the things we know. Lendi, the wharf, Massa.

Then I hear it.

On the ground, not fifteen feet from us, there is a whirring. One of the three broken dials Father confiscated springs back to life.

"It's picking us up!" I grab Seward's arm.

"No, mate. If I be right, this time it picks up those who approach. Pocket your orb." Seward peeks up the passageway. I press my cheek into his back and feel him stiffen. He turns and gestures me to take a peek, out from the safety of our hiding place.

I look and shiver. A row of Amongus move down the tunnel with speed. All carry dials, two carry orbs. If the rest are still blind, they have adapted very well.

I draw back and try to calm my heart. Their footsteps pound as one, echoing louder as they approach the dome. Seward presses backward, his weight pinning me between fear and rock. Footsteps thunder beneath the arch, until all falls silent.

A minute passes; I tap my uncle's shoulder, and he shifts forward, shrugs. He shushes my lips with his finger and slowly steps out from the outcrop. Seward quickly returns.

"All there, mate. Standing at the ledge. I count nine."

I raise up my fingers and mouth, "There were ten."

He squints and steps back out, then hollers.

"Le'go!" Seward's body jerks forward, out of my sight. I hear scuffling, then more silence. I push back deeper into the crevice, my breath audible. Shadows appear, and I cover my mouth. In front of me, two Amongus feel their way into my hiding place, standing where Seward had been.

One yard away, no more than an arm's length.

"There's a strong reading here," one hisses, raising his dial to his ear.

"Readings are everywhere. Likely Seward's imprint." The other gropes forward, and I shrink my small body yet smaller.

"It's an uneven fix. It's these cursed dials. Broken, I'm sure."

Their dials stretch toward me, whirring, stopping, then jerking to life. *School.* I think of my eagle and my uncoded heart. A cool draft floats over me. Both of the Amongus jerk back. Without my body heat, I'm invisible.

"Blast, it moved." They disappear, and I slowly stand and poke my head around the corner. The rest close in on the other side of the arch, where Jasper and Wren hide. All except for two, the two that pin Seward to the ground.

Think, Luca. Think.

"Nobody matters here but Luca." An order given. "Find the boy."

A busted dial from the tunnel floor gives a faint whir.

You are brave. You are brave.

I leap from my hiding place and race back up the tunnel. I hear motion and grunts, but it's too late to turn back. I grab the dial and stare into its mechanism, press it against my heart. It picks up my warmth and whirs violently.

"Got the other two! I'm picking up a third." I hear one shout. "We have all but the prize."

Oh, Father Massa, I was not meant for this.

I race back toward my friends and duck through the arch.

"He's here! Something moves!"

120

Arms reach, and I weave and scamper through the chaos.

Seward fights his head free. "Luca, run. Run! You're all they want."

I reach the cliff's edge, hold up my dial, and yell. "Then they'll have to come get me!"

They drop Wren and Jasper and converge on me as one. I turn and fling my dial into the abyss, then drop to the ground.

One by one, they dash off the ledge, the dome swallowing their cries.

For a moment, all is still. I slowly stand. I've never taken a life, though I've watched many taken. I wonder if it's the same thing. I know I saved my friends, but I can't help feeling ... less.

Jasper and Wren gather around me. "That was brilliant, Luca." Wren hugs me and offers my uncle a satisfied sigh. "Seward, you have taught him well."

I turn in time to see Seward crumple onto his back, where he grasps his jaw and writhes in pain. From behind the outcrop steps an Amongus, his gaze fixed on me. He cracks his knuckles.

"It is good to have my sight back."

Jasper and Wren step between us, but two backhands later they, too, lie groaning on the ground.

"You've done well, Luca," he says. "If you escaped the blaze, the assignment was to bring you to the PM's isle, but I don't suppose assignments matter too much below." He takes a large step closer. With the ledge behind, there's nowhere to run.

"Truth is," he says, "I don't know my way out. We're already in too far. So the job must be buttoned up here." He cups his hands. "Farewell, Deliverer."

I brace myself, and he lunges toward me.

I feel nothing but the breeze he creates.

His body lurches to my left, his eyes large and confused.

He falls, Seward on his back, the two disappearing down into the mist.

"No!" I drop to my knees. "No. No. No!"

Wren crawls toward me. Blood covers her cheek, and she wraps arms around my shoulders. I rock within her embrace, rock and weep. The tears that fought so hard to escape for Massa fall freely.

"He did what he had to do." Her voice is soft and weak.

"But why?" I pull free and push back from the ledge.

"Because there is much more at stake than you realize." Wren blinks and sways, and Jasper kneels at her side.

"You still bleed." Jasper rips his shirt and wraps it about her head. "You must've struck rock as you fell. We'll take care of it as we can, but ..." Jasper glances at me. "She soon won't be much for walking."

I breathe deep. "Okay. Okay. Give me a moment. I need to recite to here!"

Minutes later we string across the mountain pass. I lead the way, while Jasper's steady hands keep Wren aright. The next hours blur into a strange numbness. The route. Always in my mind there is the route, but it becomes automatic, as Father said it would be, and other thoughts do not disrupt.

Why am I going here? Surely Seward knew of a deserted island free from the Amongus's reach. Why do I need to go below?

And Nine. Nine Amongus fell. There were ten, and I didn't see Mape. He may yet be following. I could be leading him to the water source, the one cared for by Rats. I don't want to see Rats. Living the rest of my life miles below the ground with a bunch of devolved humans. There must have been a different way.

Maybe being undone would have been better.

No. You're on the right path.

The thought, the voice first heard in Lendi's cave, is so clear. I peek at Jasper. His face is fixed — he heard nothing. I rub my temple. I must've bumped my head too. The strange voice seems quite at home inside.

I just wish that I did.

A cool blast strikes me, and I stop, turn. Jasper eases Wren to the ground and stretches his arms.

"How many more turns, Luca? Are we close?"

"Two. Just two directions. Sharp left."

Jasper wipes the sweat from his face. "I can do that."

"And a three-mile windy walk."

He bows his head.

"Leave me here, if you must," Wren says. "Send somebody back for me." Her voice drifts light and airy, like the air in the dome, and her eyelids flutter.

"No, ma'am." Jasper grunts and hoists her up. "If I can haul a net 'a shrimp, I can carry a lady. And I'm not certain who you think we're going to meet. Move, Luca."

I dart left and enter a passageway — one like none other.

It's not rough, but smooth and wide and comfortable. I rub my hand over it. "This is manmade."

"Rat made," Wren whispers, and she closes her eyes.

The smooth walk twists, but soon straightens, and widens and widens, and the ceiling lifts and lifts, and minutes later Jasper and I walk side by side, no longer in a tunnel. It's not a chamber, or a cavern; it's too large for those names. No, this place could contain the entire Swan Inlet.

It's a world. The world of the Water Rats.

CHAPTER
16

W ren. Wren!" Jasper's rough voice is unusually tender.
"The lady doesn't answer me, Luca."

We quicken our pace for ten steps.

And then we stop.

Three figures approach. Three men. Upright men.

It dawns on me that I can see. That I can see well, and that
light is everywhere, though I can't find its source.

"So we'll just ask them for directions to the Rats?" I say.

Jasper looks back the way he came. "Well, I've seen nastier-
looking blokes above." We begin a slow walk forward.

They are identical in height, though not in age. The man in
the center has clearly seen many years, while the other two so
resemble him, it would be impossible to think them anything
but sons. All three have my fair skin, my gray eyes. Their thick,
dark hair, far from my matted dreadlocks, gathers in back and
falls long behind them, swishing as they walk.

They're short, short like me. Short and kind and simple,

dressed in rough-spun buttoned tan shirts and loose-fitting pants. With cords around the waist and gloves on their hands, the men don't terrify. Yes, their dress is odd, their hair unusual, but they strike me as ... normal.

They stop in front of us and say nothing, though their gazes make frequent trips to Wren.

Jasper leans over. "Do ya reckon they speak our speak?"

"We do." The old one steps forward and lays a hand on Wren's forehead. His eyes glaze, and he nods to his sons.

"Thank you for carrying Wren. Will you allow us to take her the rest of the way?"

"Listen." Jasper turns away from him. "You might know her name, but I don't know yours, and I've been carrying this lady too far ... I can't have anything happen to her."

"You'll see her again shortly." He touches the back of her head. "But not unless you allow us to help her."

I squeeze Jasper's arm. "We've done all we can. You couldn't have done more."

Jasper bends over and whispers in Wren's ear, "You stay with us, lady." He hands her to the sons, who together grasp her beneath the shoulders and knees. They carry her awkwardly toward a cleft in the rock wall and slip into the shadows.

"Whoa." Jasper lumbers after them. "Where did you take her?"

"No place that you can follow. Not yet." The older man gestures to Jasper. "Come back, friend." He pauses. "And to you, young Luca, welcome to our home. Look at you." He strokes my cheek, and his eyes roam my face. He steps to the side and faces Jasper. "Jasper, you are also most welcome to call this your dwelling."

"You know us all," I say.

He smiles in answer. "You may call me whatever you like, though most say Etria." He gestures over his shoulder. "Many wait for you. May we proceed?"

I want to. I feel so comfortable with this man, though one look at Jasper and I know he doesn't share my peace. Besides, Father never told me I should follow a greeter once I arrived.

"I'm sorry," I say. "I wish I could. I need to find, at least I think I need to find ... Oh, Wren told me to reach the Water Rats and the Aquifer. Could you point out where they could be found?"

"Yes. I'll take you to them." He spins and walks away.

"Not trusting that man," Jasper whispers.

"That's wise," Etria calls back without breaking stride. "I haven't yet given you reason to!"

"Well, the directions end here," I say. "Maybe he's the ... the Rat keeper, or something. Maybe he keeps them all locked up."

"Locked up?" Etria's already out of a normal man's earshot, but he laughs deep and rich.

"It doesn't seem as though we'll have any private conversations." I yank on Jasper's arm. "Come on. For Wren's sake, come on."

~

A half hour passes, or maybe it's an hour. Time blurs below. It's unclear whether danger or safety lies before us, but as Seward said, we're past the point of trusting. Besides, I have no more directions. Ahead, Etria stops and stretches. "I'd forgotten how refreshing a walk can be."

Ahead, the stone beneath my feet comes to a sudden end. My eyes sparkle, and Jasper curses.

I couldn't have said it any better ...

We stare out over a shimmering sea. An ocean. A magnificent lake with gentle swells tinged yellow and red, rivaling the most beautiful of sunsets above.

The painting ... Wren's painting. She must've been standing right here when she painted it.

And through the middle, a path of translucent stones pokes above the waterline — flat, smooth, and stretching clear to the far end.

Etria raises his palms to the sea. "Luca, meet the Aquifer."

"Beautiful." Jasper bends over and dips in his hand.

"By it, all life on earth is sustained," Etria says. "Including yours. You two must be very thirsty by now. Drink."

Jasper and I stare at each other. I'm first to find voice. "Freshwater? This is all drinkable?"

"Of course. We release liquid-state water to a depth of a few meters above the Aquifer for beauty sake. Its source, the layer of hardened rock from which it is extracted, lies below. It stretches thousands of feet deep and spreads out hundreds of miles wide. We mine the fresh water and propel it up to your diverters." He points, and I blink.

Exploding out of the Aquifer on both the right and left, two columns of water rise from the sea. Cylindrical waterspouts hundreds, maybe thousands of feet tall, bend and twist, sucking water toward the rocky ceiling.

"Amazing what can be done, is it not?" He gazes at the top of the columns. "The waterspouts strike rock, where our suction plates draw the water farther on, seeping toward your world through cracks and fissures until it's ten feet from the surface. Your pumps and diverters take it from there." His face is proud. "You stand before the highest point of the world's only attainable aquifer." Etria bends, scoops up a handful of water, and drinks. I need no more urging. I scoop up water with both hands. Jasper drops to his knees and laps like a dog. The taste is cool and wet and perfect.

I've found the water source. My father descends to this same place …

I slowly rise. "Wait. If you mine the water, you're a … you're a Rat."

"As I said, call me what you will, though I do admit that, though necessary, *Rat* is not my favorite name."

"I'm sorry, I'm so sorry, we should …" I yank off my pack and fumble for the light rod still trapped inside. I turn my head, extract the contained energy, and hand him the rod. "I know it isn't as many as my father usually brings, but please, I came down here under different circumstances. Please don't turn off the water. Nobody knows I'm here."

"Oh," Etria says, removing the rod from my hand. "I doubt that."

I slowly turn to face him. The rod is gone. I glance around our feet. The rock on which we stand shimmers like a rainbow prism.

"What did you do with the light?" I ask, bending down and stroking the warmth of the glow.

"All in time. Now come," he says. "My people wait."

I follow him onto the first stone, and then the second. Slowly, we journey across the freshwater sea. So much water. A treasure without cost. What my father once said is true: "Whoever controls the source controls the world."

Lendi could never contain his wrinkle at the sight.

CHAPTER 17

C louds?"

I'm so taken with the sea and the two swirling columns that we're nearly across before I focus on what drifts above.

"Massa tells me that they are not as beautiful as yours." Etria witnesses my wonder. "I believe him. We can try, but no copy rivals the original. Yet you can do marvelous things with mist and airflow and light. Yes, we call them clouds."

"Best fake clouds I ever seen," Jasper pipes up. He's been quiet since Wren was taken, and I long to discover the streams of thought that flow through his mind. I wonder a lot of things about Jasper. Of all my companions, I know him the least, yet here I am, seeing the most astounding things with him.

Jasper strains forward. "That noise. Have we arrived on Holiday?"

I jerk out of my thoughts. It's a playful noise, a rollicking noise, coming from the mass rising before us. Dusk has fallen over the world of the Rats, and though I can't see clearly, the sounds hold nothing to fear.

"These are the Dwellings, the Dwellings on the Rock." Etria points at the mountain of stone. "They're anticipating. Surely by now many can see us approach."

"Many what?"

"Many people, Luca."

The music, for that is what Jasper heard, gets louder and more beautiful. I stare at the mountain, and as I look, it shifts, clarifies. Specks of light dot its slopes like a thousand fireflies in the heat of evening. The mass does not rise gradually, but rather in an intentional symmetry, in plateaus. Both sides of the mountain resemble giant sets of stairs, and the flats are covered with movement. The mountain is alive.

It's not a mountain at all. It's a crystal city.

"Most people's dwellings are toward the base. You, however, are headed to the summit. I think you will find our community quite beautiful," Etria says. "If you walk the shore where city meets sea, you will eventually reach the artisan market. Perhaps in the morning you will find time to explore, but tonight, Luca, there is a gathering ... and you are the guest of honor. No disrespect meant to you, Jasper."

"None taken."

We step off the path. Directly ahead, a broad road continues, winding gently up the mountain. Clearly a main thoroughfare like Swan Boulevard, the street weaves through rock-hewn dwellings of all sizes, its edges lit by thousands of dots of light, and randomly placed patch-prisms of glowing stone. There, similar to the spot I encountered earlier, light refracts like a rainbow, bathing all who stand nearby in shifting color. In that glow, thousands of faces stare down at me. Jasper is here, but I feel naked, a one-person parade.

Surely it's a mistake. Nobody knows why I came, why I came so soon on the heels of Father. I only need a place to hide. For me, for Father Massa, until I can figure out what to do; how to keep us both alive. I bury my face in my hands.

So much for hiding. Wren, I need to talk to you about this.

An ovation begins.

"Well." Etria turns to me and bows. "This welcome is not for me, so I will take my leave of you. Follow the lights. I'll see you shortly."

I gaze around. "I never wanted to be the center of this attention." I turn back to Etria.

Gone.

"Sure," I mutter. "I mean, go ahead and fade into the backdrop. Leave me surrounded by ten thousand extremely excitable Rats, with no clue where I'm going. Might as well."

I wind through the dwellings to the cadence of my name. "Luca! Luca!" I smile and wave and wonder. Do they do this for Father when he comes?

Jasper swaggers, pausing every so often to offer an awkward bow. I'm glad he's here, but he's not my uncle. Seward should be walking in Jasper's place. My face feels hot, and I turn from my posing companion. Little girls run out and throw flowers over my neck. It doesn't help. Seward is the reason I live. His dreadful choice is the reason he does not.

I close my eyes. I don't understand any of this. I just want him back.

"Oh!"

I collide and my eyes pop open.

Beautiful.

I'm off the road. It veered sharply; I didn't, and standing before me is a Her.

I've seen plenty of Hers before. I've gone to school with them. Purchased from them at the wharf. Noticed them and stared at them. More than once, I've gazed and pondered, Is that Her my match? Will we someday be together? But that's as far as I let my mind travel.

Because I'm short and agemate Hers are always tall, and I'm not like Lendi, big and strong with Hers fighting back wrinkling smiles as he struts.

Maybe I'll be the first New Pertian in centuries not to be matched.

I once told Father my concern and he said nothing, but later that night he laughed. A big laugh, clear and free.

"What, Father Massa? What brings you such joy?"

"Your words," he had said. "You would not be the first. Now, perhaps you will be the second New Pertian not to be matched. That is a distinct possibility."

His statement was not comforting.

But now I stand in front of a Her and I can't move ... Can't because my eyes won't stop roaming, pausing in places they should not pause. Inside, I warm, tingling in places I should not tingle.

Help.

No, I take that back. Please, don't help.

"Luca."

She speaks, and I flatten down my shirt, clear my throat. How do I return the greeting? My lips refuse to move and I stare at her skin, light and perfect, and her hair, raven black, cascading down in waves to her shoulders.

"My name is Luca."

"Yeah," she answers with laughter in her voice. "I know."

"I walked off the road."

She glances behind me. "I noticed that too."

Around us, a new sound. A giggling. A laughing. Her mates all look and smile and laugh.

"Do you plan on staying here? Off the road?" she asks, and her voice is music. "With your hand on my hip? Generally, that spot is reserved for my own hand."

I look down. It is there! My fingers, on her. I gently move my pointer and jerk my hand back to my side.

Hah! There! I officially caressed her right there! Oh, Luca, you should be undone!

"I'm so sorry. I'm going to start walking. Because that's what I do. I walk. I mean, right now, I walk ... I don't always walk."

She nods big and slow, and I back onto the road.

"Do you walk? I mean, of course you can walk. You know what? That sounded dumb. Forget that. I'm going to vanish, gone. I mean, walk gone ... er, walk."

I turn and stumble away to a chorus of laughter. My name echoes from all around me, but I tune it out and replay my words to this Her in my mind.

Stupid. Perhaps the most stupid words I've ever spoken. And to her! That Her.

Jasper waits, and I catch up.

He seems confused. "How do you know someone from here?"

"I don't," I say. "Do me a favor. Look over my shoulder. What is she doing now?"

"The one you bowled into? Let's see. She's watching us, like everyone is watching us."

"Watching, or *watching watching*?"

"Wait!" His eyes grow big. "She's left her friends and burst onto the road. Well now, she's racing toward you."

"She is?" I grab his arm.

"No." Jasper pries loose my fingers. "Luca, you need some rest. You've been through a day. Let's get to the end of this parade and find sleep."

Sleep and a pleasant dream.

Father. Seward. Wren. I'm trapped in a nightmare where everyone leaves.

Well, except that Her; and she can stay as long as she wants.

CHAPTER
18

I reach the end of the road and stand before a great stone building, knowing a few things for certain. Nothing I have heard about this place is true. The Rats are beautiful and brilliant — how else could they have created all this? It's also clear the PM and his Amongus do not control this place, not with this much excitement wrinkling up the dwellings.

Actually, I know a third thing, and my heart thumps with the thought of the girl I just met. Tall Topper girls never jumble my thoughts, twist my tongue. They certainly never cause a wrinkle. I fear that a life joined with one of them, though the safe, expected choice, will now be a real letdown.

"Luca, I think we're supposed to go in. At least that's what Etria wants."

I follow Jasper's finger. Ahead, Etria and his sons stand at the doorway, beckoning us on. They hold open the door, and we step inside a grand ballroom filled with light and marble and statues. Only the ground is clear rock.

It's the museum, minus the beautiful painting.

In the center of the floor, yet another circular prism-patch fills the hall with light. We approach it and stare down. Shadows pass deep beneath the floor, and the prism within the hall bends.

I stare at Jasper and shake my head. What is this place we've reached?

Jasper exhales and faces Etria. "Wren. How is she?"

"Have no worries, Jasper. She is beyond fine." Etria rounds my shoulder with his arm. "Now, let me show you to your place."

On the far end of the room is a chair, wooden and simple.

A chair in a hall filled with light. My second mother's dream!

"That's for you, Luca." Etria stretches out his hand.

"Can you find another for Jasper? We've been traveling a long way, first down and then up, and — "

"I will find a comfortable resting place for Jasper, but this chair has waited for you. *We've* waited for you." Etria gestures to one of his sons, who marches toward my only remaining friend.

"No," I say. "I want — no, I need him to stay."

The son removes his right glove and light explodes from his hand. Grabbing Jasper's forearm with the other, he bends down and presses his palm against the prism. Both of them vanish.

"Jasper!" I break free from Etria and race toward the light. "Where is he? Etria! Where are they?"

"They are shadow, passing beneath," he says quietly. "Luca, you have so many concerns. They aren't needed." Etria straightens. "All will be explained. Return to the front."

What choice do I have? I've fallen into a crazy world. "Can I know where you're taking everyone?"

"Yes." Etria's voice firms, and he glances over his shoulder.

His vanished son reappears on the prism and regloves his hand. Jasper is not with him.

"Please," Etria says. "Sit in the chair."

Sit in the chair. Sure, I'll sit. I'll sit before I sink into a hole of light in the floor. Father never told me this, any of this. It was just a down and up proposition.

I walk the length of the hall, listening to the sound of scraping beneath my boots. The mood reminds me of my entrance to the amphitheater, except there is no Birthing tunnel, and no Father to anticipate. I test the chair with my hands, turn, and take a seat. This I can do. I glance up and rub my eyes.

People step quickly out of the prism. With hands upstretched and ablaze with light, they explode from the rainbow on the floor, move to their places, and glove their hands. Ten. Fifty. Hundreds appear, until the entire hall is filled with people — pointing, murmuring people.

"That is a little disconcerting."

Etria appears at my side. "I imagine our normal mode of travel will take getting used to." He clears his throat and addresses the crowd. "I now wish to formally welcome Luca to our home. As we had hoped to honor Massa, we will now most certainly honor his son."

I lean over and draw him close. "Honestly, the fewer people who know I'm here, the better." I point around the room. "I didn't come to be celebrated. I came to hide."

"I know. This may take some explaining, but first, let me place your mind at ease." A nod to a son, and the young man disappears into the prism. A minute later he reemerges, but not alone. Seward and Wren, damp but sound, step out of the floor and release the Rat's shirt.

I jump off the chair and run into my uncle's arms.

"Hey, mate, you mess up me clothes." Seward's voice is strong. "Not bad for a pirate, though if they be thinkin' of giving me a ridiculous hair job, well, this is where I draw lines in the sand."

I squeeze him with all I have, not wanting to let go. Ever. But soon he pries me loose, and I look him over. "You fell ..."

"And what transpired between that act of foolishness and now makes no sense. As I fall, I think, 'I be undone. Nothin' remains but the splat.' And then I come to. I only know the Amongus who shared my tumble be here as well."

"No, that can't be." I shoot Wren a panicked glance.

"It's okay." Etria steps between Seward and me, eager, I think, to regain control of these proceedings. "The other gentleman is ... presently miserable. All things can now be spoken of."

Wren approaches me. "Do you remember this hall?"

"Sure. It's like your museum."

"Go farther back. Do you remember *this* hall?"

I stare around, and my gaze falls on the chair. "I remember the chair, and a man in it."

"Welcome home, Luca," Wren says. "You're finally home."

I stumble backward. "Home? I watched my home burn. Wait..." I shake my finger. "You lied to me about the Rats. Probably everything."

"Allow me to help." Etria raises his hands, pleading for calm. "All, please sit down, and Luca, please sit in the chair."

The hall obeys, and I look to Seward. "Listen to him, mate. If he meant us harm, we'd be undone long ago."

I leave his side and take my place in front of a peaceful crowd. In the corner, I see her. The Her.

I guess it would be rude not to stay a little while.

CHAPTER
19

Etria strides around the hall, thinking, it seems, how to begin.

I'm so tired. So tired of waiting.

"Maybe you could simply tell me why I'm sitting in this chair and why you gave me a parade?"

Etria raises his eyebrows. "Massa told you nothing."

I glance at Seward, tongue the inside of my cheek. "Yes, that seems to be a nasty little habit of Father Massa's."

"Would you allow me to share a bit of history?" Etria whips toward me with a flourish. A female groans from the back of the crowd.

I yawn. "Sorry, go ahead. It's been a long day."

Etria sits down at my feet, his legs crossed. "Have you heard of Rabal?"

"Of course. Rabal and the Nine. The miners who found the Aquifer," I say. "Probably this Aquifer. Nine stayed below, only Rabal surfaced."

"We in this hall, and everyone you see in our world below, are descendants of those ten men."

"Okay, well …" I point at Seward and Wren and pat my chest. "Almost everyone." I smile at my companions. They don't smile back, and I bite my lip. Hard.

Etria continues. "Everyone. But that explanation will come in time. What you have just spoken about Rabal is true. If you were taught anything more, I think those words will not be as accurate."

He snaps his fingers, and his son brings him a large book. "For completeness, I will read the rest." He peeks at my Her, who steps behind a column. "I'm told I get long-winded when I tell the story from memory."

Etria flips through the pages.

"The story of Rabal, and his place in the world. And so it was decided among us that Rabal should surface, for we have need of materials and machines if we are to create an underground home. Rabal will also inform our families of the path to the Aquifer. This we, nine in number, set our hand to on August 14, 2058."

"Who wrote that?" I crane forward to see.

"Robert Blythe, one of the nine." Etria flips forward in the book and continues. "Lane's family has just arrived, bringing with them news. The diverters we constructed are working. It is entirely possible that this aquifer will indeed meet the world's future need for drinkable water. Rabal has provided us with every piece of drilling and pumping equipment needed, as well as airshafts, pressure equalizers, and everyday essentials such as food. Our one need is light. If we are to be self-sufficient, this need must be met, and soon."

"The light rods," I whisper.

Etria flips forward.

"It is now understood that Rabal will continue to live above. It is the only way to secure scarce items for us below. Furthermore, he sends word that rumors of the water source have spread, that there are those on top who would control it for ill gain. Indeed, there are those staking our claims, claiming our identities. They declare their authority over the Aquifer. This group of nine men deceives the world. They must not be allowed to find us. In the evil and panic above, all the secluded beauty of this place would be destroyed."

"The Council." I stare at Seward, who stares back. "The beginning of the Council of Nine!"

The ground heaves and shakes. Walls and statues rattle. And from high above, one small chunk of marble tumbles downward, exploding on the rock behind Etria. Throughout the hall, concern ripples along with the tremor. Faces turn grave, but Etria raises his hands. "We know the life." He turns to me. "The rock bed is a product of the tectonic plates. It exists due to their shifts. Where was I?"

He clears his throat and glances down at the book, taking one more peek at me before continuing. I know the look; I saw it on Walery. He wants to know if I believe his explanation, if I believe him.

It is not true.

The voice is clear, and once again not mine. I glance over my shoulder to find its source, but no one stands behind me. *What's not true?*

The voice is silent. I'm going insane.

"Rabal has therefore—" Etria raises his gaze. "Are you paying attention, Luca? *Rabal has therefore, in his wisdom, felt it necessary to create a barrier between the world above and the world below. That barrier will be the route. Only Rabal knows it.*

The nine of us who remain, along with our wives and children, are in agreement with his decision. Though a barrier is needed to protect the Aquifer, to protect the beautiful, we hold no ill will against the Toppers, many of whom we remember as friends. We covenant never to turn off water to the surface. Those above are our brothers. At the same time, if the news is true, the darkness that settles over the surface cannot be allowed to reach the light we enjoy below."

Etria glances up at me. "Are you following?"

I rub my face. "So the water flows no matter what? What of the exchange? Of my father? Of the light rods?"

"Hear this well. There is no exchange. I'll say this again: there never has been any exchange. True, your father brings us light rods to continue the ruse, but we learned long ago how to exploit the Aquifer's energy and reuse them. They are of no new value." He pauses. "Water flows upward because it should, not because a yearly deal is struck."

"We call you Rats, monsters ..."

"And this we accept. In fact, this misconception is helpful ..." He flips a few pages forward.

"We could not imagine the hate of the Topper's Council. Their desire for power and control is insatiable. Rabal has retreated to an island home with his two sons. His shrewd business dealings have secured the finances available for us to build a life below-ground, but it has created enemies. The Council of Nine has offered Rabal their consultative services, but it is clear that they only seek the route to the source, and the power they could obtain through its possession. They have ordered countless excursions to find us, and many have reached the dome. Rabal has imposed this final safeguard: The directions to the Aquifer will pass solely through his family line, to his sons and their sons. His esteemed

position as peacemaker of the surface world should protect their family from the Nine's wrath.

Yet even this may not be enough. Rabal believes he must sow the seed of untruth about us. Our names must vanish. Our humanity must be forgotten if we are to live. He has declared us unhuman, animal in nature. It is to be taught, accepted. Sadly, we have come to this point; fear alone protects us from those above."

"You started the lie about this place? Your ancestor did that?"

Etria shakes his head. "Yours did."

A heavy silence descends in the hall. "Do you ever wonder how it is that you, Luca, you were chosen to be the Deliverer of the surface world?"

"Every single day," I say quietly.

"Of course." Etria stands. "You were chosen because you know the route, and the only ones who know the route are — "

"Rabal and his descendants."

For eleven years I have stood and pledged allegiance to my ancestor. I stare at Seward, who nods. Of course. His story, Etria's story, they all fit; they all make sense. All except for one thing.

There is no PM.

"Seward, you said there was no peacemaker."

"I wouldn't lead you wrong, lad."

I walk toward Etria. "But you just said Rabal was the first, and his two sons ..."

"That history lies in another book, but it is easily and painfully told. Rabal passed, and his oldest son assumed his position. The new PM. Once again, the Nine placed themselves in his service, all in an attempt to attain the directions that were buried in his mind, now in your mind. He refused their assistance, and was, as is said by the Toppers, undone. By committing this foolish act, the Council unknowingly cemented the barrier between the Toppers and us. They destroyed one of two who knew the route. Wisely, the younger son fled the island, and proclaimed he had knowledge of the Water Rats' demands. He would be the Deliverer. He would come and meet with us. And he has — he and his descendants — for hundreds of years. Through the myth of exchange. Through the myth of a hideous underground race. Through the myth of our need for light. Through the directions the Deliverer alone knows. These myths have protected the Aquifer all this time."

I step around Etria and pace back and forth. I know nothing about who I am, nothing about who my father is. I'm lost.

"So the Council—"

"Took over. Instituted the Amongus. Coded your children. Robbed you of humanity. The legend of a peacemaker lives on to cement their control."

"And this chair ..."

"And this chair" — he smiles broadly — "is where Deliverers come when they pass on the route to their offspring. There have been none so wise as Rabal's descendants. For hundreds of years, they have been our judges. Without crime, we need no enforcement, just the wisdom that rests in here." He points to my head.

"No, no. That can't be how it works."

"Thinkin' it be true, mate," Seward interrupts. "Janus disappeared, as did Linus before him. There was no sign of undoing."

"Two good men. They made two fine judges." Etria pauses. "We had hoped Massa would assume his place, but from Wren I heard the Fates held otherwise." He spins me toward the crowd, his hands on my shoulders. "But now again, ill winds have shifted, and our fortunes are favorable. With one so young, we can rest for many years."

"Blime!" Seward screams, and jumps to his feet. "What a fool I be! How could I not see the possibility?"

"What?" I ask. "What's wrong?"

"The exchange be a sham? This changes everything. Massa has no reason to share the route. He knows water will flow either way. But the Council doesn't — they would never believe that — and their desperation to secure the Aquifer will grow." He looks Etria in the eye. "So follow it through. By now Massa has been shown to the world as undone. New Pert searches for Luca and finds his shanty burned to the ground. There is no Deliverer, and the world wails, believin' that come the next seventh of the seventh, water will cease to flow as the exchange fails. What would you do if ya thought you had less than a year to live? Toppers know nothing of your … kindness. Do ya have an inkling of what this news be doing on the surface? In the best of worlds, people patiently hope the Nine will save them. In the real of it, without Luca and Massa, what carnage may follow!"

Etria nods, as if thinking, and then shakes away the thought. "The years, and I believe the need, for a Deliverer are over. Toppers will find out in time that they no longer need fear us."

If any Toppers remain.

Seward paces back and forth. "Then think on the reverse! What if my brother breaks and does speak the route? He endures more than a little duress. Have you no sympathy for him?"

"He would not do this. He will not speak our destruction." Etria addresses the crowd. "Massa's death is tragic, but it ends forever all presence of the route on the surface. There is no one who knows how to reach us now that Luca is home." His face lightens. "Yes, Luca is home."

Etria spreads his arms. "The coronation of Luca, our new judge, is in one week. Until then, People of the Rock, rejoice!"

"I ... I ... need some time." I run out of the hall to thunderous applause. Once outside, I scan wildly. *I could escape.* I stare down the mountain at the Aquifer shimmering in the distance. *I could cross and ascend and maybe the Amongus have left ...*

A hand pulls me into the shadows.

"What my father does to you is not fair."

It's the Her.

"Your father?"

"Etria."

I pull away. "The Etria?" *Oh, this relationship would never work.* My mind's a blur. Beside me, her warm breath breezes softly on my neck.

"Luca, do you want me to leave?"

"No. *I* want to go home. I want Father and Old Rub, Seward and Wren ...Well, they're down here, but Lendi's not, and he can't give me the silent treatment forever. I need to ... What is that place?"

Deep in my mind, I find a match for the small triangular building before me. "I remember the windows, looking in those windows."

"Lots of people do." She smiles. "That, Luca, is where you and I were born."

CHAPTER
20

I start to shake.

Born here. Why was Mother here? Why did Father take her on a descent? There are plenty of clinics on top.

"That can't be true," I say. "I don't want to be here."

"You'll need to face truth sometime." She glances back toward the great hall. "But you heard much tonight. Too much. Come, I know a place."

She grasps my hand, and we slip off the main road. In the distance, another prism glows.

She slows at its edge and removes her glove. Her palm, it shines. "Hold your breath." She whispers, glances over her shoulder and grabs my arm, reaches down and presses her palm onto the light.

Falling. I'm falling, but only for a moment. A current wild and free catapults me forward. We're in water, and I force open my eyelids. Lights pierce down from above. Thousands of orbs race above our heads, while shadows streak by. Figures. People?

My body chills and then warms, and for an instant I feel myself implode.

And then I am fine.

The Dwellings, the hall, the triangular building have disappeared. Wet spray coats my face and I step backward, pressing against a rocky hollow.

I stand behind a waterfall, the girl at my side. She releases my arm and comes forward, reaches her hand beneath the torrent.

"What was ... How?" I feel my arms. I'm still whole. "Where—"

"First the how." She slips on her glove, and the night falls dark. "Our city is built upon the solid surface layer of the Aquifer, but ten feet down something else exists. We call it the stratus, a fifty-foot deep lake of liquid water, left behind by our miners. When mining operations deepened, the stratus was left unused and free flowing, until by accident a light rod was dropped. Not only did it pass through the hard surface, but for a few moments the light scattered the rock around it, leaving temporary access to the stratus. The rod had been dropped on a crystal node, a uniquely permeable area of rock. We now mark all the nodes we find."

"The prisms," I whisper.

"We now harness light of the same frequency that exists in the rods, capture it as a liquid, and paint it on the palms of our hands. This allows our hands, like the rod, to scatter solid rock and open the Aquifer at the nodes. The matched frequencies give us moments to drop into the stratus, which is what we just did. After the drop, you must know the city. From underneath, the refracted light on each node draws the light on our hands, and us as well, forward; a simple electromagnetic connection. The closer to the surface we travel, the faster we move, until we upturn our palm and allow ourselves to open the node from beneath. Make sense?"

"No." I focus on her hands.

"These gloves shield our eyes. We remove them only for travel and fresh applications."

I lick my lips and stare at my boring palms. "Of course you do."

"As far as the where. This is where I go to think. I bring my problems to the falls, open my hand, and let the water wash them away, wash me clean." She peeks back at me. "Come on, Luca. You've been lied to your whole life. It's time to let the lies go."

"Lies? What if this place is filled with them? What if what I learned above is true?" I pause. "I don't even know your name."

"No, you don't."

The girl is the most infuriating, alluring Her I've ever met.

"Would it be too much trouble for me to know it?"

"No. That would be fine."

"What is it? What is your name?" I groan. "Did I ask properly?"

"Talya. And yes, you did." I run the name over in my mind. It's a good name.

"Now, Luca. Come join me."

I straighten and shuffle forward, my eyes on the slick stone beneath my feet. I reach my arm beneath the spray, feel the weighty power of the water, and draw my hand back to my mouth. Fresh.

"I can't believe this place. Any of it." My legs weaken, and I fall into Talya. She eases me back into the cleft and lowers herself beside me.

"I don't think my father knows of this node. It's so dim that when one passes through the stratus as shadow, it's barely visible, but you don't need to hear more tonight. Let your mind rest. All you heard will be waiting for you another day."

The rush of water washes away Etria's words, and we sit in silence for what feels a forever. My mind holds nothing. Thoughts flit like butterflies, slipping through my head.

Talya hums. A quiet, haunting hum. I search for the words, but they remain hidden.

She finishes, and I don't want to speak, or for her to speak. I want to rest in the song's afterglow.

Minutes pass, maybe longer, and the beauty of the melody blends with the rushing of the falls and the song that seems to sing on.

"Is it all so different?"

"Huh?" I ask.

"Above, is it all so different?"

"There are few smiles. There is no laughter, except on Holiday. Feelings ..." I peek at her. "Songs — all forbidden. We live but we don't *live*. And beneath it all is an anxiety, a strange below-the-surface fear. We're taught to hold that emotion in check."

To speak it, to speak my world plainly, sounds so harsh to my ears; I feel a need to defend it. "It's beautiful too, with the warm sun and the ocean breeze ..." I glance down. "But it's dry — dry and lonely and cruel."

"But you're not those things."

I think of the march of the undone, the hundreds of times I watched worlds end for errors made, not for guilt. For fear of those cursed dials, I did nothing. I was nothing.

I peek at Talya. "Sometimes I am."

"Not when you were little." She smirks and folds her arms. "You, Luca the Golden Child, you were a brat. Our little star. Everyone adored you, cared for you, loved you."

There's that word again.

"Not that they didn't love the rest of us. It's just that you were the first of your kind —"

"What kind? The first confused, anemic kid? You know, on top I'm Other in every way. Why should it be so different down here?"

Talya pauses and touches her fingers to her lips. "Maybe this is best left for my father to tell."

"Please," I say. "I need to know who I am, and I'd rather hear it from you. I need my truth, from the beginning."

"Yes, you do," she whispers. "It just had never happened before ... a love union between a Topper and a Person of the Rock, and then a child ..."

"My father is a Topper."

Talya gently sways.

"Which means my mother was a Rat."

"Of course."

The world spins, and my body collapses into her lap. She strokes my hair as the rushing of water fades into the distance. But her hum, it remains with me, softly, gently ushering me into the darkness.

~

"Luca, Luca. My apologies for my daughter." Etria leans over my cot.

My room is spacious, and light pours through the open window. It's morning. Or the morning after morning.

"Talya is filled with ... enthusiasm. She had no right taking the judge of our city on a pleasure tour through the stratus before he had adequate rest."

I grunt and prop myself up on an elbow. "Where is she?"

"Contained." Etria rolls his eyes. "For her good and my sanity.

Which brings me to another, more pressing issue. We have a guest, and I need a judgment as to how we should proceed."

"I haven't taken the job yet. I ... need some time with Seward."

Etria sighs, and for the first time I sense frustration. "I've not asked you to take a position. I've called you to assume your position; it is who you already are. Your birth, your descent in the line, dictates this for you. Centuries of judges have taken the chair before you arrived, each with joy, I might add. Their blood is in your veins. You are like them in every way — "

"Every way?"

Etria bends and speaks slowly. "You are like your ancestors, including Rabal, in every way."

"Did any of them have a Rat for a mother?"

Etria stiffens and tongues the inside of his cheek. "No, in that tiny point you are correct. You are unique. But should that fact not draw you to this place all the more?"

"Did any of them have a father who was still living? Who was trapped by tormenters? How about those tiny points? Did any of my ancestors have a father in the hands of a wicked council when they happily assumed their position?"

"No."

"Father Massa is your rightful judge."

I lie back down, shut my eyes, and wait. When next I crack an eyelid, Etria hasn't moved.

"You don't take a hint. Fine. One time. What judgment do you need? Can't I make it from this cot?"

"Come."

We exit my dwelling, situated just beneath the great hall, to sunlight — only there is no sun. Instead, sourceless beams of light dance off the rocky ceiling and mirror against the sea, shining in the distance. We march down the mountain and into a dwelling with no door.

My heartbeat skips, and I cast a panicked look at Etria.

"I assure you, Luca, he's quite harmless."

There sits an Amongus, still dressed in New Pertian red and gray.

Guilty. That's a fair judgment for the one who struck Wren and Jasper, who lunged at me, who went over the edge with Seward.

His eyelids are squeezed tight, his hands pressed firmly against his ears. Beautiful music sounds from a box in the corner, and around him stand easels, paintings of the Aquifer in all its glory.

Like those from my cellar.

"How'd he —"

"Eight of them fell together, likely from the dome cliff. We had no warning, and they landed across the sea. They were found dashed on the rock below. We quickly reversed the dome's airflow and were able to catch the next two, setting them down gently. My sons brought them to me and I discovered, with great pleasure, Seward." Etria circles the Amongus. "This one has not been so pleasant. Do you know him?"

A pang of fear strikes inside, and I nod. "I know what he's done. And you leave him here with the door open? He could leave anytime."

"Yes."

"But he doesn't."

"If you want my thoughts on the matter, this man cannot handle the beauty. The appreciation of the lovely is an appetite that must be fed, or it dies. In that sense, this man is already dead."

"Good. That's what he deserves because of his deeds above; he undoes the innocent. He has earned his own undo —"

"Mercy, Luca. Mercy. He knows no other world."

"Neither do I," I snap.

Etria wraps his arm around me. "Not true. You began life with us. It's why you wonder, why the things above seem so strange, why they feel wrong though you don't know why. Wren has told me of your talks." He looks into my eyes. "Your foundation is mercy."

"I was here with my mother ..."

"During your early years. Massa visited as often as he could, but when you turned five it became clear that Massa needed an heir, or he would be provided one by your Developers. Janus, who was our judge at that time, gave Massa, Alaya, and you his blessing to ascend and begin a life together. Given your symbolic importance, and the chance Alaya was taking should her origins be discovered, another was sent to watch over you, to assist Alaya with your transport and care and protection should the need arise."

"Wren."

"Yes. Alaya's sister."

I knew it. Somewhere I knew. The peace I felt with her. She felt like family, even above.

"But Jasper says he found — "

"The Amongus were waiting. Your father expected their move. He emerged first, hoping to draw them away. Alaya was to wait, to slip out later in the darkness. Lastly, Wren was to deliver you to your parents. Obviously, all did not go as planned. Your mother was intercepted — undone, as you say — but for all our sakes, the Fates watched out for you, and Wren delivered you to Massa."

"Who fell deep into depression." I stare at the Amongus. "He hardly spoke to me, hardly knew me."

"I do not know about those matters."

No wonder I was so Other. I reminded him of all he lost.

A tremor rumbles the room, and I stagger. The Amongus braces his hands on the floor.

Etria strokes the ground as Seward strokes the sea, feeling, listening. A shade of worry fills his eyes, but he quickly strengthens his face. "But that is history, and I called you to dictate this man's future."

I look at the Amongus, lean in front of him. His dial rests on the ground. It registers nothing. Overloaded, I'm sure.

"What is your name?" I ask.

"I don't believe he can hear."

"I need him to hear."

Etria snaps his fingers, and his sons walk through the open door. Each takes hold of an arm and pulls. The Amongus, so powerful aboveground, quickly surrenders. He snarls and glances up at me. "Undo me now, but do not leave me in the hands of these beasts."

I stand silent, and he spits on my boot. "Undo. Undo! This is no life."

An urge, strange and untried, overcomes me. I reach out my hand and place it on his head, and as I do the words string together, filter into my mind. I try to change them, to alter the judgment, but I can't. They are a whole, not to be separated.

"This man lives his judgment, his torment." The voice is mine, but the idea, it feels rich and settled. Like Father's when he spoke to the Amongus. "But so that he is not tormented further, he must go outside the camp, to the broad space across the Aquifer. He may always return, for food, for fellowship, to live among us. Or he may choose to risk his way to the surface. The choice will be his."

There is silence.

I shake my head. "I … uh … I don't know what I said there. It just came out."

Etria folds his arms. "You gave a very wise judgment. Sons?"

They glance at each other and pull the Amongus from the room. I see a dimming of light outside the door and hear the half shriek of an Amongus. Clearly, he's just discovered a node.

"You see where you belong," Etria whispers. "You felt it. It is your gift, and your responsibility."

I walk with Etria out onto the street and stare. People move about, pausing and smiling. They take their leave of me with winks and hugs. It is beautiful. More beautiful than the source that quenches our thirst. That is water, surely enough, but the cries and the squeals and the hurts and the joys — this is life.

I peer through a window. A man embraces his wife inside their dwelling. She kisses his neck and he bends, scoops up children into his arms. They climb on him as if he were a recreation tower. I want it. Longing fills me, and I want that.

"If I do this," I say. "If I become this judge —"

"As I said, you already —"

"Nope. Stop. Rule number one: you will not interrupt me."

Etria cocks his head and offers a slight bow. "Agreed."

"Rule two: I don't want the chair. I don't want the hall. Or the applause or anything that sets me apart." I point at the family. "I want that. No more Other."

"I … don't know that the option exists. You are special. We could not regard you otherwise."

"Then don't regard me." I push by him and march down toward the Aquifer. There's a man I need to see, and I know where I'll find him.

CHAPTER
21

I walk toward the shimmering water, my face tight, my fists balled. Strange; all around me is talk and freedom, but my face has become what I hate about those above. I feel bound.

Perhaps there is more Topper in me than I thought.

It takes some time to pass through the Dwellings, skirt the outdoor market, and reach the Aquifer, but soon I stand on its shore, peering out at the underground sea. On my left, a group of children squeals and plays in the sand. But the man I seek wouldn't be found near them.

I turn my back on the children and walk. I pause, kick off my shoes, and feel the sand squish between my toes. It is cool, like the Shallows. It's in my memory.

"Well, Old Rub, this would be a place you'd like to see ..."

There he is.

Seward sits alone on a stony shelf overlooking the water. I pad toward him, climb up beside, and plunk down. He neither nods nor turns, and we sit in the quiet.

The squawk of seagulls interrupts the moment. *How did they reach this place?* The birds round us, begging for handouts, but soon realize we aren't in the mood and fly off. I peek at my uncle. I don't know where my mate is, but he's far from here.

Finally, he speaks. "What's the difference, lad? Tell me, between where we were and where we are?"

I pick up a stone and skip it into the sea. "Are you kidding? Is anything the same? Salt water, freshwater. Amongus, no ... Well, one Amongus. No freedom, total freedom, being wrinkle free."

"Are you free? Am I free?"

"Not completely," I say quietly, and exhale. "Birth still dictates what I will be, and I'm still Other."

Seward glances down. "It be truth that above we are watched, directed, controlled. We have lost our souls. Most Toppers are no longer wild men. It's why piracy isn't about the gain." He gestures toward the water. "But be we any different here? Is anything real? Take the sea; you could walk across it. It's been tamed. Those clouds be the work of skilled hands. The air we breathe, the cool of the day — all controlled, directed. Hearts be free, but the body is trapped in a forever of comfort and safe."

He stares out again. "And to think I spent a life desiring this, Massa's world. I knifed for it."

Suddenly he grabs a rock and hurls it into the Aquifer. After a great splash, the water stirs, then ripples, then stills. "Does the true sea do that? Can I dent it?" Again, he hurls a stone. "Ripples be the same every time." He gazes into my eyes, his on fire. "I'll miss it, Luca. The wildness of life. The danger of feelings and sudden storms and shark attacks. I'll miss life."

I don't know what to say, but inside, desperation grows.

"So, mate" — his voice quiets — "live on, safe and secure."

"And you?"

"Only you know the path to the surface. I have no choice. I'll find honest work. Piracy is no longer an option, or I be judged most severely by my mate."

"Why are you being so hard on me?" I frown. "Coming here wasn't my choice. Who brought me? Huh? What have I done?"

"You've blasted forgotten why we came."

I shake my head. "No, I remember it all. I need to stay alive. You said it yourself."

"But why? Why live, Luca? For the comforts? Then you be in the right place. Or did another concern drive you here?"

Father Massa.

Seward sighs. "You didn't know him. You saw a quiet fool drowning in sorrow. But remember, as you judge this world, your father is torn up in another. And my brother be a great man."

A great man.

The panic inside turns to dread. In the flight, hiding below seemed reasonable, but the backside of all things wasn't known. Seward is right; with the exchange just a sham, Father would tell them nothing of the route, and be treated most severely for his silence. And the surface, so filled with fear, could spiral out of control.

"You're my hero, and a great man," I recite. "And tomorrow, you'll be great again. That's what I told him before every descent, when his mind was rough and the night was bad."

"Your hero? So you lied to him once a year." Seward stands and brushes off his hands. "Well, mate, for certain, you have important preparations for your big moment. I go to find Jasper and Wren. I didn't speak to the former last night, and for Wren

I have many questions." He takes one last look at the glassy sea. "Enjoy the view."

I sit alone on the ledge. Seward hates me or is disappointed in me or pities me — I can't tell which. I only know he suffers, and Father suffers, and none of this was the plan.

I never had a plan.

I toss pebbles into the water, watching the ripples expand and vanish.

Same. Same. Same.

CHAPTER
22

Seward's wrong.

I have nothing important to do. I wander through the Dwellings, the weight of Seward's words heavy on my heart. Though I'm hugged and greeted, welcomed and cheered, there's no denying that I am again alone.

My wanderings take me around the roots of the mountain-like system of homes, and as I walk, small shops appear, not so different than those sprinkled among the residentials topside. Clothiers and bakeries and salons line the streets, and I pause to gaze through a shop window.

A second too long.

"Oh, Luca, we need to fix what was." A woman rushes out and grabs my arm. "Oh, yes, we will rid you of these." She lifts my locks and lets them flop. "I declare, you'll be thanking me soon." She leads me to a chair. "Every time I see Massa, I tell him the same. 'You'll be on the front edge of a whole new style.' But he only laughs. Never makes it to the chair."

No, he never made it to the chair. He should have, though. He should be there now.

"Hold it." I lift my hand. "I have no credits, or whatever you use here."

I am ignored, and an hour later I stand, my hair, golden and smooth, pulled back into one braid and falling down my back.

Won't sit well with Seward.

"Say, I ... I need to speak to someone. Do you know Talya, Etria's daughter?" Women glance at each other, smile and nod. One waves a hand my way and proclaims, "Isn't that an irony? Such strange and wonderful things happen when they turn of age."

She reaches for my hand and leads me to a back room bathed in yellows and oranges.

"A node?" I ask. "Inside?"

"We paid handsomely to build on top of it, but ..." She removes her glove. "It's grand."

No. I'll do this node thing with Talya, but not—

Too late. She slaps down her free hand and my stomach drops. I surge forward, cooling, cooling, and then warming again. I open my eyes in a small room drenched in light. Talya reads in the corner. My escort pats my back and disappears. Before a hello forms on my lips, Talya slaps shut the book.

"You can't be here."

"I ... I don't even know where here is. You can read too? Never mind."

Calm, Luca.

But I can't calm. A loose, woven tunic falls over her upper body, curves around her thighs. Her arms and legs are light and beautiful. My gaze traces her lines, and my fingers stiffen, wanting nothing more than to trace them as well.

"Luca?"

I swallow hard. "I'm sorry, sometimes I stare. See, I was there, and then suddenly I was here. Honestly, I just asked if she knew you and then — "

"This is not a good time or place for explanations," she hisses. "Father would say that I am not the appropriate one to receive your attentions. The city is filled with fine choices. All would show you around."

"But I don't want plenty of people. I sort of want one people — I mean, one person. I want you." I kick the ground. "What I'm saying is, I want you to show me around ... No, I don't."

"You don't." She rises and nears me.

I exhale hard and push my hand through my hair. It's sweaty. "Yes, I do."

"You're a bit hard to follow." Talya stops directly in front of me, a bit too close, or maybe not close enough. Either way, I'm rooted.

I cover my eyes; it's my only hope of forming a complete thought. "I need questions answered, and your father won't help me."

I crack my knuckles and watch Talya's eyes soften. "That's why you came? For answers to questions?"

"I came to you."

"Yes. You did." She smiles, and I warm and wonder how long her mood will control mine.

"If I do this, which I shouldn't, we need to return soon. Before my father does."

I turn and march toward the door.

"If we are going to avoid Father, we best travel as shadow." She yanks my newly done hair, and I take a breath.

Cool. Warm.

Books.

Thousands and thousands of books. They line the walls, floor to ceiling.

"This is a good place," Talya whispers. "As I'm always here." She closes the door into the back area. "It's the study room."

"You can study anything?" I ask. "Whenever you want?"

"It's a library, Luca."

I don't recognize the word, but pretend that I do. I nestle into a chair and massage my scalp. I've never been transported by the hair before. For a long time we sit and look at each other, though our gazes, I think, land in different places. I shift, but don't want to leave this stare.

"You speak very little for somebody with questions," she says.

"Oh, right. I, um … I've never seen this many books."

Talya glances out at the stacks. "The library is great, but it gets tiresome. All the books written from the same perspective. All written belowground. I wish we had some of yours, from above. I would love to know what you know. You've seen both worlds."

"We don't have any books." I exhale. "Not quite true — I found some. I brought two with me."

"Where?" She perks up.

"My bag. Wherever that is. I lost track of it my first night in the hall."

She bites her lip. "It's still there. Nobody is allowed to touch anything of yours without permiss — "

"Talya, of course! She was to be at home. Have you seen her?"

Etria's voice is muffled, but unmistakable through the door. Talya drops to the ground. "These next minutes are not going to go well."

She climbs beneath the table, and I shuffle my chair in front of her. Etria's eyes fix on us through the clear partition, his jaw tightening.

"He's coming. I'm sorry, Talya, I didn't mean to cause trouble—"

"Quiet, Luca. Answer this. What do you think of when you see me?"

"What?"

"Quick. What do you think of?"

The door opens.

"Talya. This is the height of folly," Etria snaps, bends over, reaches out his hand ...

"Hope," I say quietly. "I hope."

Her hand clasps my ankle.

And with her touch, the room lightens and we both disappear.

CHAPTER
23

We pop out of the water rock and find ourselves in the midst of peaceful woods, beside a quiet stream. The journey to the hall for my books had been quick; the trip here required a mighty breath.

"Hope is good." Talya's eyes sparkle as she hands me my backpack. "Very good." She winks. "And I like the hair."

"Won't your father —"

Talya gently places her finger on my lips.

Just keep your mouth shut, Luca.

We turn and wander along the bank.

"Few people come out here, to the treed outskirts. These areas were all planned by past Deliverers, and for the Deliverers. Everyone wants you content. We tried to bring as much of your world into ours as we could."

For a moment, it feels real. The gurgling water, the piped-in breeze, the rustling in the trees — if you didn't know the original, you'd be hard-pressed to find a flaw in the copy. But I do know it, and so does Seward; the wild is missing.

"Are we heading somewhere in particular?" I ask.

"We're walking to Wren's." She slows, glances at her feet. "Walking. Hmm." Talya smiles broadly. "She's an outlier, choosing to live away from the Dwellings. She tends to the trees and the shrubs. During her years above, her home fell into disrepair, and much that's green overgrew, but I think her plans were to return. My mother says she used to take me to this stream before Wren left surfaceward." Talya throws back her hair. "If Wren's here, this is a good place for us. I think my return home will be unpleasant. Father and my two brothers are searching right now, but I don't think they'll look outside the Dwellings."

I nod. "They don't trust me."

"Judges function outside the rules. You define our system. You can do whatever you please, and the people will not question. No, it's me they don't trust. Now that I've turned six thousand."

I freeze. "Years?"

She smacks my shoulder and it deadens. "Days, you idiot. I've reached joining age. I have one hundred days to find a companion, or one is found for me."

Please say you haven't.

I swallow, but the dryness remains. "Have a, have you …"

"Not yet. And until I do, my brothers keep close watch over me."

We walk in silence. The stream bubbles, but I'm suddenly grim. "Do you have any prospects?"

"I have a possibility. At least I hope I do." She glances down. "I've known him for a long time."

I want to ask more, to find out who the bloke is. I could surely find him guilty of something.

"I'll just judge this whole system as unfair. Can't I do that?"

"You can try." She pauses. "But judges come and go. The systems keep life in place."

Systems. Yes, Seward was right. Things here are not so different from above.

"But now, Luca, could I see a book? I'd love to look at one. A really old one."

"Take your pick."

She reaches in and pulls out the red one, Massa's.

"That belongs to my father. He always held it, and when it wasn't held, it was hidden. Even from me."

"Maybe I should take another —"

"No." I push it toward her. "Go ahead. Read it. I'd like to know what's in it, and my reading isn't great."

She nods. "Well, it's handwritten. Page one says, 'To Luca, my son, whom I love.'"

I slow and regain my step. "That's a nice start."

"'I want you to know everything, and as I may not have the opportunity to tell you, it is my hope that someday you will find the truth in this book. First of all, I want to tell you about your mother.'"

I snatch the book back from Talya, close it, and gently place it back in the pack.

Her eyebrows furrow. "Don't you want to know what Massa says?"

"I can't. If there's even a chance I'm going to stay here, I can't. I can't know more about him or hear more about him. If I stay, I need to forget."

Talya leans into my shoulder. "And if you don't stay?"

168

"Your father says that's not an option."

"My father has been in charge too long." She steps in front of me, presses her finger to my chest. "What does this say?"

"It says that there are some desirable things here."

Talya winks. "This is good." She glances over her shoulder. "We're here."

Ahead, a cottage rests on a spread of green grass. It's a welcoming site, surrounded by trees and beside a large garden. Constructed of logs, not stone, the home could have come from the wealthy Telurine neighborhood of New Pert. Smoke churns from the smokestack, and the door stands open. We walk inside. It isn't the quiet moment I'd hoped for.

"What is going on?" I glance at Talya.

"The group now be compete, just as you predicted." Seward pushes back from the large round table and stands. "Though I admit I was not expectin' his daughter."

"Oh, I was." Wren rises from the table where Jasper relaxes, and embraces first me, then Talya. She points to two empty chairs and moves to shut the door. "Luca, I will not delay. Time does not favor us. Now that you've heard what's expected from you here, the moment has come for you to decide your course, and in some ways the course of us all."

The crackling fire should warm the small cottage, but I feel cold. Cold and tired of decisions. Talya runs her hand along the dark stone, and then breathes deep.

Wren notices. "Yes, we are off the Aquifer. Nobody pops in here. Any guests will be coming the old-fashioned way. Please, sit."

I don't feel like sitting.

"Why did you bring me down here, Wren? Weren't there other places Seward could have stashed me? Secluded places.

Maybe the outer Northern Territories?" I ask. "I could have taken care of myself."

"That's me lad!" Seward slaps the table. "Thinkin' like your uncle, you are."

"Haven't you read your father's book?" Wren says quietly. "Why else would I teach you to read? Didn't you see what Massa wanted for you? He wanted you to experience what he never himself received. Freedom."

"You call this freedom?" Seward hisses.

"Easy, man." Jasper lays his paw on Seward's shoulder, but he pulls free.

"Yes. Freedom ... the freedom to choose." Wren walks into her kitchen, returning with two cups. She reaches both out to me. I shake my head.

"Denying both options is the only choice you don't have." Wren hands one mug to Seward and the other to Jasper. "Your father wanted to give you the world. All of it. What if I would have withheld this part from you?" She takes her seat. "You have a rightful place here. Respected. Honored. How could I deny you at least a glimpse at what could be yours?" Wren exhales. "But now I've completed my course. I've watched after you. I've brought you above and back again. The length of stay is left with you."

I rub my forehead. "So all this — the hasty descent, our near undoing? This was to teach me to make a choice?"

"No," she says. "The timing of this trip was accelerated. Massa's disappearance wasn't foreseen. The danger that exposed you to ... Massa knew nothing about the timetable for those matters, and I believe we have Seward to thank for a timely rescue."

I glance at my uncle and give a tight-lipped nod.

Wren picks up the pot of tea and begins to pour. "I left the note and brought you down to save your life. And in so doing, perhaps bought Massa some more time, though I don't imagine it is comfortable time. We left your father behind, but he would not hold that against you. Even Seward, if honest, would agree." Seward lowers his head, and Wren continues. "You have seen your birthright below." She turns toward Talya. "And all that could go with it."

Wren marches over to the fire, stares into the flames. "The world of the Toppers is not what it was. A civilization in tune to Massa's every breath, as well as to yours, needs only days to fall into chaos. New Pert, the Swan, the wharf; the world you knew is changing, likely filled with the panic of a people convinced that in less than one year water will cease to flow. Not even the Amongus will be able to control the anarchy."

"Etria said that when the Council sees you mean them no harm, all will be set to rights," I say. "They will know there is no need for a Deliverer."

Glasses tinkle on the shelf as a tremor works through the house, sloshing Seward's tea onto the table. Wren grabs a nearby towel and wipes it dry. "Those still alive will know. But the decision to resurface goes beyond you or your father. Surface hoarding and violence will intensify. And the tremors. Luca, all this needs to be weighed in your decision." She raises her eyebrows. "Yes, the tremors. The water source exists on a fault line, but these are not the once-a-decade rumblings from beneath. These are not the movements of earth."

She stares into my eyes. "A question for a bright young man: What would you do if what you thought you needed to survive lay thousands of feet down, and you didn't know the narrow path to reach it?"

It hits me. "Blast my way through."

The room is very quiet.

"The Council," I say. "They're trying to dig their way down. Blasting from the surface." I stare at Talya, her eyes wide. "Eventually your sky will fall." I turn away, look at Wren instead. "But if I leave, they're waiting to undo me."

"Perhaps. But now that you have seen their prize, I think you have information they will want — about us, about how best to proceed. Though I shudder to think how they would extract it from you. Remember, the Aquifer is their goal. You and Massa are still the only ones who know both the way down and the way to the surface."

It is silent. Jasper speaks.

"I don't envy your choice, Luca, but I've made mine. After years on that island, speaking to critters to keep myself sane, well, this is a dream. A crumbling dream, but a fine one, none-theless. I won't be going back up."

Seward rolls his eyes. "Then I'll take the other. If by any means I can surface, then surface I will. It's not perfect, and it sounds as though it be less perfect still, but it's real."

"So is this, Seward." Jasper exhales.

"You be bewitched."

"You've never had it so good."

"Fool!" Seward rises.

"Pirate!" Jasper pounds the table.

"Men." Wren sounds weary. "If I was an Amongus, each of you would be in for a good debriefing. Luca, take some time. But your choice must come soon. I suggest you stay far from the Dwellings ... Movement through the Aquifer renders you too easily detained. Your coronation is mere days from now." She gestures behind her. "Take the back room as your own. You'll find a private entrance. Come and go as you please. Walk the stream and think. I find it helps me."

It's too much to place on me. Too much, and I whisper to Talya. "I'm going to be living here then."

"I know. That's good. But please ..." She turns me around and reaches into my pack, removes Father's book once again. "Don't make this decision alone."

Wren smiles. "A very wise young lady."

CHAPTER
24

I spend the evening with my parents.

Mother Alaya's words fill the book's beginning. Each day recorded as a journey of life taken with her one and only child. Life below is chronicled as well — it reads like a joyous time. Woven through the pages is a combination of excitement and fear. The idea of life on the surface terrified her, yet she believed that, perhaps as an ambassador of goodwill, she would melt the Toppers distrust of the Rats.

Mother felt certain she could find a sympathetic soul on top.

Her last words tell it all.

Your father has slipped through. It is my time to leave you, but in the safest of hands and only for a while. It is dark inside the tunnel, and the air, it weighs heavy on my lungs. You seem unaffected, and this makes me smile. Outside, I see a sky, and an orb — the moon by Massa's description —

guarded by an uncountable number of attendants. Lights shining, twinkling, even shooting across the sky.

I go now to be with your father, and to wait for you and plan for a time when this separation is gone. When there is but one world, not two. You embody my hope. You are the one who comes from two. I trust this book and your life to Wren's care.

Come soon, my son. Come soon.

Mother, the one who loves you.

From there, the scratches take a painful turn, as a despairing Massa tries to make sense of his life. Guarding what doesn't need to be guarded. Losing what should never have been lost.

Trying to show me love though he has lost all hope.

It is a love letter, a lifelong love letter filled with words he could not say.

My father was a great man.

I close the book and my eyelids feel heavy. A pounding from outside the cottage quickly changes that.

"I know he is here, Wren! Let us in."

Etria!

"You are the temporary judge until Luca's coronation, but does this give you the right to enter my home?" She raises her voice, and I believe it is meant as a warning to me. "And with your sons as well?"

"Were he alone, no. He could wander as he pleased. But Talya's with him. I sense it. I have seen them together, seen how they stare at one another. It is not proper at this time, and with her in the middle of her six thousand." He pauses. "Long ago, a suitable selection was made."

"By her, correct? It was made by Talya?"

"This is a matter for my household, not for your discussion. I will not see my daughter risk Alaya's fate. Toppers are Toppers."

"Which Luca, as we know, is not."

"But he is half-bred, and that ends this line of talk. He is meant to be our judge, not part of my family. Step aside."

I quietly twist the handle of the back door. It flies open.

Talya winks. "It's about time you came out."

"What? How long have you been out there? You can't —" I peek over my shoulder. "Your father is here too!"

"Talya!" Etria calls. "I hear you. Come to me!"

She nods me out and we dash into the woods, toward the sound of distant water. It's no small stream ahead — waves crash and pound against my eardrums. Downed branches and leaves crackle beneath my feet as we leap logs and dodge trunks. The tree line ends abruptly, and we pop out onto a rocky ledge. I see from the front what I had only known from behind: a majestic waterfall. Beneath the unreal glow of a nonexistent moon, there's a sparkling plateau and another waterfall, and another, and another, disappearing into the muted subterranean sky.

"Seven falls in all. The lowest and largest of the falls is formed by a crystal spike in the Aquifer." Talya stares over her shoulder, at the three figures stepping free from the brambles. "The other six are simply porous rock." She is talking faster now, and I see panic in her eyes. "We can't go any higher. I'm sorry, Luca. If I had gone home, they wouldn't have found you."

Etria's voice rises above the water's fury. "We most certainly would have seen Luca at the coronation, isn't that right?" He folds his hands. "Now, daughter, do not disgrace me further before the future judge. Come. Obey your father."

I take hold of Talya's hand and back toward the churning pool.

"With respect, Luca, that hand is not yours to hold. I know you are not yet familiar with our customs, our systems."

To the top, Luca. Take her to the top.

"Talya, do you trust me?" I shuffle to the water's edge.

"For no understandable reason, yes."

"Remove your glove."

"But once in the stratus, if we even reach it through this stone, we'll only be able to access the small node behind the lower falls."

"Don't aim for the node. We are going through solid rock, to the top."

"But I'll see no prism. What will pull us?" Her breath quickens. "What if my light doesn't separate the rock? We'll be trapped in the stony layer. No one has ever risked something like this."

"Do you trust me?" I speak, but the words are not my own. The certainty is not my own. I am filled with something, something Other, and I stare at her with unblinking eyes.

Talya slowly removes her glove, and a beam of light pulsates around us. "Luca, you are the bravest person I've ever met."

We grasp hands, and she slaps her palm down upon dark stone.

The heat is overwhelming, but we reach it, a stratus without current. Talya strokes my face, gazes about, locates the small node, and we accelerate upward. At the last moment she shifts her hand, veers to the side, and our world falls into heat and darkness.

We are inside solid rock. Slowing, slowing. If we come to rest, there is no light node to pull us on. I will be undone. Talya will be undone, encased forever inside a stone.

Up, up.

Splash.

I break the surface of a different pool.

"Talya? Talya!"

She bobs to the surface, shivering and wide-eyed and beautiful. "Where are we?"

"The pool ..." I sputter and shiver. "Above the top waterfall — at least ... at least ... that was the hope."

Talya's breaths are shallow, and she swims closer. "Luca, if you leave this place, take me with you."

A chill works its way through me. There's nothing I'd rather do.

"But I heard, Talya." I halve the distance between us. "Your father has selected someone for you."

"By the rules he upholds, it's not his right. Not if I select first." We move together, and she places her arm on my shoulder. "But by our rules I must be pursued, and may not pursue."

"Talya!" Etria's voice is faint. "Where have you gone?"

She smiles, and I smile. "Tell me how I pursue."

"Cup your hands."

I've never made that gesture; always it is given to me. But I lift my hands from the water, waiting. Talya looks at them, her eyes sparkling. She fits her own ungloved pair into mine and drinks. I do the same.

"That's it?" I ask. "Don't get me wrong, I like that, but — "

She draws her body against my own, and presses her palm against my chest. Every nerve fires and screams. There is warmth and want, and I wrap her in my arms.

Okay, I like this second part a little better.

"Are we leaving?" she whispers, grazing my ear with her lips.

I don't want to talk about the choice, not now. I want only to stay in this embrace. But the question hangs like a cloud, and I pull back, stare into her eyes. "I can't promise you anything. I can't keep you safe. Think of Alaya — "

She presses her finger against my lips. "Are we leaving?"

I slowly nod. "My whole life, I prepared to come down in order to save the world above." Another tremor, and I glance at the sky. "Now I have to ascend to save the world below. My father needs me. If Wren is right, maybe many more people than him."

"You are a great man," she says.

"I'm just a boy."

"Not anymore."

It strikes me; I have discovered a third kind of love. The affection for my father, the kinship with Seward — neither compares to the emotion I feel right now. To leave Talya would be to leave part of myself.

"Do you need anything from your dwelling?" I ask.

"Yes. Father is certainly shadow, searching the stratus, so I need to get there quickly. We'll meet at the base of the mountain," she says. "At the first stone of the crossing."

"Be safe," I whisper.

"Always."

We hold hands and dive. Aided by gravity, the trip down is much simpler, and we emerge at the base of the falls.

"Courage," whispers Talya, "and speed." Again, she drops away from me into the stratus. Standing alone, I feel her urgency. I dash toward the bubbling stream and pound along its bank to Wren's, my heart on fire.

I race through the back door and grab my pack.

"Stories and prophecies. Prophecies now fulfilled." Wren kneels by the fireplace, eyes closed, arms outstretched. She wasn't speaking to me.

"Wren!"

"Welcome back. We have so little here from the past. The deep past. Leave us the books."

A Wisher? Wren?

"Ask your question, Luca." She turns and rises, before sitting in her rocking chair.

"You were just … Well, it looked like you were — "

"Praying."

"Yeah," I say. "Like the Wishers; they do that. I always wanted to ask why. Why the dials don't work on them."

"Their hearts have been seized by a strange affection, one that seems to render the coding inadequate. I met with them often above." She sighs. "They are one of the few things I miss from the Topper world. Treat them well, Luca. They will do the same for you, and more." She holds up a finger, listening to sounds I can't hear. "You must go. Trouble awaits. But please, leave the books. Carrying them with you could be quite … dangerous."

Inside, I burn. *They are mine, found by me, meant for me!*

"I didn't carry them this far to leave them below!" My voice softens. I don't know where that outburst came from. Wren's done so much for me. "Why do you ask for them?"

Wren turns toward the fire. "Where you're going, they will slow you down. They are too precious to lose. You have no idea what lies in the pages."

Leave them here. It's where I want them.

Again, the voice speaks, this time gentle, urging. Like the

rumbling of the stone, it comes when it pleases. Wild, unpredictable. But not frightening.

Insanity should not be comfortable, but it is.

The rage inside relents. There's no reason to haul them. I've committed pieces of Father's book to memory anyway. The words, like the route, will be safe in my mind, while the books … I remember the library. They will be much safer here.

I undo my pack and hold my sole possessions in my hands. I glance at Wren's kind face. "Okay." I set them on the floor. "Keep them safe."

"Good-bye, Luca, my pride and joy." She stands and peeks at the books. "You, though small, have just become our greatest Deliverer, and our most severe judge." Wren smiles. "I hope we see you again."

"It's a good chance."

She catches me again in her gripping stare. "If you should return to New Pert, do check in on my museum, will you? Perhaps you'll find something that will guide you on your way."

I grin, remembering tea in the rooftop room.

"I'll do it for you."

"No." Her face turns grave. "Do it for you."

CHAPTER
25

I reach the Aquifer, its last reflection kissing the subterranean sky.

Evening People move around me, their words calm and relaxed. They have no idea that their judge-to-be is trying to escape.

Those who recognize me pause to offer congratulations. I receive them, but have no urge to talk. Instead, I scan the crowd for the girl who makes me complete. Strange; I met her so few days ago. I shouldn't feel as I do.

"Luca!" Seward calls from the ledge, a stone's throw down from the crossing. He runs toward me. "What be your business down low among the rabble?" He glances up the mountain. "Shouldn't a judge be preparing for his big day?"

"He should," I say cautiously.

"Mate!" He catches me up in his arms, whirling me around and setting me down. "Think of it. The wild sea, the smells of the wharf..."

I stand motionless, and he steps back. "You be fixin' to leave soon, as it were."

More silence.

"You weren't goin' to leave without me."

"It wasn't a conscious decision, Uncle. I escaped down, now I escape up. All I do is run. Seward, I know you want to leave, but think what happened to my parents. The odds for you don't fall favorable, not after your conduct with the Amongus on the way down."

Seward breathes deeply. "Will you be makin' me beg?"

His eyes are desperate, pleading.

"As much as I'd like to hear that ..."

Seward frowns.

"There's no need." I place my hand on his shoulder. "I wouldn't have made it down safely without you. I don't think I'd make it back up either."

Seward's head falls back and his eyes close. "Thank you, mate." He dances away across the rocks, spinning on the third crossing stone. "There's no good in waiting. Darkness is close. We need be moving on."

I follow him onto the first stone and watch him skip nearly out of sight. Minutes later, he reappears, none too pleased. "What be your hesitance?"

"None," I whisper. "Another goes with us, that's all."

"Jasper? I don't know if I can endure—He seemed set on this place."

I stare up the street, still waiting for the shape, the form that fits against my own.

"Not Jasper? Well, it can't be Wren," Seward says. "She's put in enough time away from home."

It's late. Talya should be here by now. Shadow to her dwelling, shadow to the shore. Unless the unthinkable. Unless Etria and her brothers contain her.

"Who, Luca?"

"Talya," I hiss, with fury and concern and confusion. "Talya," I whisper.

"Oh, Luca. Her presence in our merry band wouldn't bode well for her."

My narrowing eyes dart to Seward. "For her or for you?"

"Easy, mate. Easy. Right you are to question." He puffs out air. "You would've made a grand judge."

Half an hour later, I am still with Seward. Only Seward.

"I need to go after her," I say. "It should take moments. If I don't return — can't return — you need to understand. I will assume my role as judge. Talya is my choice. I won't leave her."

"Please, you can only play the fool so many times before the Fates catch up to you."

"Too late." I glance toward the top of the city. "I've already become one. Good-bye, Seward." I run up the main road. *Talya. To Talya.*

My legs scream as I dash through her open door and blink. I'm face-to-face with Etria.

"Welcome, Luca. To what do I owe this honor? At this hour."

Think, think . . .

"As my coronation draws near, I wish to consult your daughter."

I have no idea what I'm doing.

"She's through that door."

I peek over his shoulder. "I don't believe you."

"Please." He gestures. "See for yourself that you have no reason to question me, though you've given me good cause to doubt you."

184

I turn the latch and pull. Talya looks up, her face tearstained. "No, Luca. Stay out!"

Too late. Strong hands push me forward and slam the door behind me.

I run to the corner, where Talya sits with her head buried between her knees. "Get up. This is our chance!"

She glances at my hand, then at the floor. "Marble. The floors, even the walls of our back room, are marble. There's no escaping this place."

"You can't push through ..." I rub my hands along the walls. "Can't we try?"

Talya removes her gloves and tosses them onto the ground. She raises her hand. Her palm offers no glow. "I've been swiped clean."

I kick at the floor and slump to the ground.

"So what happens now?"

All expression, all life has drained from her. "You will be our judge by week's end. I will shortly be attached to Harani, the son of my father's partner, to secure a deal made years ago. I will watch you and you will watch me for the rest of our lives, and someday you will be attached as well. You shouldn't have come."

I stand and close my eyes. A boldness, and with it a trail of words, pounds in my brain.

"How could I not? This isn't our end. Rise and prepare."

Eyelids flutter open as the unbidden words escape my mouth. "Okay, that's happening more and more. Thoughts and words fly in, and sometimes out. I don't know why I said that or what we'd be preparing for — "

Talya hops to her feet and throws her pack over her shoulder. "I like your words. So how do I prepare?"

"I don't know. The voice didn't say."

She shakes her head. "That would have been a great time to make something up! Let's stand by the door."

We do, and wait. And wait.

A shout and a thump from the other room. The door swings opens. Seward winces, massaging his hand. "Didn't mean to strike your father. But the man left me no choice. Luca, I want to go home."

Talya runs out and bends over Etria. "Nobody strikes anybody here. You hit him? In the head?" She strokes his hair. "He's okay, isn't he?"

"It wouldn't have done much good to whack his thigh. He's fine. Well, as fine as a sleeping man can be. He'll come to with a bit of an ache about the fore." Seward glances out toward the street. "I'd not like to be here when that occurs." He turns to me. "Sorry, mate, it took me awhile to get the hang of the travel." He lifts his pointer finger. "A jolly woman from the salon tried to touch my hair. 'That won't be happenin',' I says, 'but I'd sorely appreciate a dab of light. I should at least give the stratus a try.' Confusing, it is. I popped out ten times before I found you."

Talya stands. "This isn't how I wanted to leave my father. But we need to go." She grabs the back of Seward's shirt and I fist the back of hers. We dash to the node outside Etria's dwelling, Seward presses his finger into the prism, and we plummet down. Suddenly, we stand damp, but warm, on the far side of the Aquifer. It's dark — very dark — but I recognize the wide space and the tunnel to the surface behind me.

"Where we go, light will not be our mate," Seward says, flecking the light off his fingernail. "Tell me you still remember the way, lad."

"I know it."

I remove the orb from my pack and rub, the heat drawing forth a yellowish glow.

"All right. When I get going in the sequence, I can't speak much or I lose my place — "

A projectile barrels into my chest and steals my breath. I tumble back, the orb falling from my hand and rolling over a smooth rise of rock. Before I can scramble away, Seward and Talya crash down beside me.

The captured Amongus.

He sits on Seward, and with his free arms presses Talya and me against the ground. There is no escaping the strength of his hands.

"Listen ..." In the distant light of the orb, his gaze flutters, wild and fearful. "This is the world you ... This is the place you sentenced me to. I can't go up. I can't remain. I need your ..."

His face twitches, and he releases Talya for a moment; only long enough to wipe his forehead. Sweat drips down on Seward.

"You need what, mate? Other than a kerchief," Seward asks.

"Nothing from you." He turns to me. "From you. The directions, the way out. Do you know them?"

I nod.

"Lead me out!" he screams. "Lead me out. Please. Lead ..."

The Amongus starts to cry.

I peek at Seward, who returns the glance.

I have no words. There's no way an Amongus can be trusted, but I've never seen one cry before.

"What a dear man."

Talya? You don't know.

"Of course you can come." She slips from his grasp. "He can come. Can't he, Luca?"

"Oh, mate," Seward whispers. "Don't let pity sway you."

"I did when you asked to come along."

My uncle pauses for a moment. "But the difference is clear. You know who he is. He'll reach the surface with knowledge, not of the route, granted — that he'll not remember — but of this place. He'll have us, and undo us, and then what of Massa? Who will save him?"

I stand up. "If I do this — if we let you come — will you harm us?"

The Amongus moans. "I don't know. I don't know what I'll do."

Talya steps forward and hugs him. The Amongus stiffens, stares down at her. "Luca, that's enough. This truth is enough for me."

I exhale hard. "Okay, then we go. Four started the descent, four will go up."

Seward shakes his head. "A tragic turn, mark my words."

I brush myself off, and Seward retrieves the orb, but Talya, she stands statued, gazing at the Aquifer.

"It's hard to leave home."

Seward steps to her side. "You may want to give it a second thought. There will be no returning as I can see ... What's that? What's happening?" A thousand dots of light illuminating the distant city grow dim.

"They wouldn't ..." Talya squints. "They would! The stratus is so near the surface beneath the sea. They come!"

Surging nearer, a multitude of light beams set the Aquifer on fire. Like underground shooting stars, they neither slow nor surface.

"Father has alerted the city." Talya grabs me and runs. "They'll take you by force. We must get off the Aquifer!"

We sprint away from the shore as the sound of voices echo in the tunnel.

"Luca! Talya!" Etria's voice grows faint. "There is no choice for either of you!"

I scramble forward, wanting only to be the same, loathing the feeling of Other. I was pursued down. Now I am pursued on the ascent.

I am Luca. I am special. And for that, I am cursed.

CHAPTER
26

We ascend in silence, though there is much to say. All energy must go toward the climb.

Shuffling feet and shifting stones seem but a few steps behind us, but each time I pause, my heartbeat alone throbs in my ears.

Seward gently turns my head toward the task before us. "Etria's fallen away long ago; their knowledge of the route be no greater than that of the Toppers. He wouldn't leave his world."

But I'm not so sure. His only daughter is at my side. How far would Father pursue if he thought me in danger? Until he dropped. I'm sure of it.

I take another peek back, think I see a shadow shift behind the last bend, and plod on.

Always, the Amongus walks two steps ahead, glancing over his shoulder at each decision point, and nodding when I gesture the correct direction. He seems to feel an urgency.

But a hundred turns later, even I'm convinced there is

none, and we pause often to rest. Talya, especially, struggles to breathe, though she does not say it. I wonder if I am leading her to an undoing. I wonder if Father harbored the same thought about Mother.

We reach the thin path and wind slowly upward, hugging the mountain that rises this time on our left. The path has crumbled since last I walked it, as if thousands have wound its span, though I know that can't be true. After several slips, we reach the archway and pause. Five dials lie on the ground. They whir and spin.

The Amongus gently gathers them. I swallow hard. Seward stares at me and folds his arms. I hear his unspoken words, feel their truth — you can't change an Amongus.

But for good or ill, the die is cast. The one I fear strokes the dials and glances at each one of us in turn.

And then suddenly, violently, he flings them, one by one, over the edge. He stares out after them. An Amongus without a dial is nothing. He just threw his life away.

"Phale," he speaks without turning. "My name is Phale."

A name. I suppose they all do have one. Mape does, though as the head of the New Pertian regiment, he's a unique case. The others, they have nicknames: Stinker. Barker. Fishlips. I've never heard a name offered.

"Phale," Talya repeats. "I like it." She points over the edge. "What were those?"

Phale stares at me. "Those are *our* judges. I make no decision without consulting them, and their verdicts are final." His face softens. "Pieces of metal and glass. Owned by pieces of metal and glass. What have we become?"

He walks through the archway and up the tunnel.

"Are you still concerned?" I pat Seward on the back.

"More than ever. At least before we knew the enemy. There be safety in that — Whoa! To the ground! Take cover!"

I pull Talya to the floor and shield her body with my own. For a minute the tunnel rumbles, as a thin crack widens and works its way up the right wall. The tube eventually falls quiet, and I remove my hands from my head. I rise slowly. "I think that's it."

Suddenly, the ground heaves, opening beneath my feet. Rocks crumble from the ceiling of the passageway. Seward, Talya, and I leap beneath an outcrop, but in the darkness ahead, Phale disappears in a plume of smoke.

"Phale!" Seward hollers. "Every one, farther away from the cliff!"

We cough and sputter and climb over fallen rock, making our way forward to where Phale lies, a boulder split inches from his head.

He winces and straightens without help. "Don't attend to me." He lifts me to my feet. "We need to move faster. Blast his blasting! Mape's explosions won't stop until he reaches the Aquifer. There's always been talk of it. What else could this be?" He wipes dust from his face. "The directions in your mind — the tunnels and turns — they will become meaningless soon. They'll be obliterated."

"The Age of Deliverers is over," I say.

Phale lifts his hands. "Massa is gone. You should be gone."

I stare at Seward and Talya and start to shake.

"We don't know, mate." My uncle eases me forward. "Phale doesn't know either. Massa's a tough old bird."

"Even tough birds sink," I whisper.

"Please, Luca, we need to move." Talya cocks her head and strokes my hair. "If we fail doing something great, that's okay.

We'll be okay. But to give up here? In between? To save nothing? You weren't made for this end."

I sniff and cough.

And yell. I've never yelled before, and I don't know where it comes from or why now it pushes free, but it's filled with love and anger.

I will not die here.

I dash forward. Two hundred some turns await. There's no time to waste.

It is a hopeless quest. To stop the blasting. To protect the fragile world of the Rats. To calm the frenetic world that waits on the surface.

To free Father, if he lives, from the council's hands.

But I am not alone, and here between worlds, for the first time in my life, I feel free.

CHAPTER 27

I jog around the corner and fall to my knees.

"Hold on!" I touch the tunnel floor. "It's slick, wet."

Seward steps to my side. "How close are we? To the surface, I's askin'."

"We're near." I perform a quick mental check. "Twenty more turns."

"Mape's goons be blasting out the center of the isle, sure enough." Seward peeks up. "It's a good bet it'll get a lot slicker from here." He rubs grimy hands over his dreadlocks. "If seawater already be seepin' through, these tunnels will soon give way, fill ... Everything will fill."

"Is your sea big enough to swamp the Aquifer?" Talya asks.

Seward and I exchange glances, and he climbs higher. "Nothing holds back the sea."

I scramble in front of Seward, turn right, and slow. A smile gentles across my face. We are in the worst of places, but there's no containing my glow.

"What is it?" Talya asks.

"Sunlight. Real sunlight." We move toward the warmth, and the tunnel stops abruptly. I poke my head into the day.

Glaugood. We stand at the bottom of the mini Glaugood I discovered days ago. But the trees we used to reach the base are gone. In their place, trucks heavy with dirt and stone climb a circular road around the perimeter, while empty trucks chug back down the path, ready to be filled. Heavy machines and drilling crews slosh about the bottom, which, like us, is submerged in two feet of water.

"There's no way out of this mess," I whisper.

"Correct." Phale's voice strengthens. "A straight line. Seward first, then the girl, and finally you, Luca, directly in front of me. March, Seward."

Nobody moves.

"Please," I say. "I led you out. I gave you choices, a chance at life. Why do you do this now?"

He rounds my shoulder with his arm and gestures around the bowl. "Show me my choice. 'Oh, hello, Mape. I've decided to join these fine people. Please let me walk away safely.'" He looks off. "You know what I am. What I do. What options do I have?"

"No, Phale." Talya turns, horror on her face. "Nobody owns you anymore." I wonder, for all the emotions Rats feel — for all the fullness they experience — has Talya ever known betrayal before?

Phale takes a deep breath — a thinking breath — and gives his head a quick shake. "March."

"Last march of the undone." Seward steps forward, pauses to speak in my ear. "Once an Amongus ... Maybe next time, a bit of trust in your uncle be warranted."

We slosh out into the cauldron beneath a clear blue sky. For a minute, we stand unnoticed, and in those moments Talya turns toward me. She straightens and clasps her hands. I study her face; it is at peace. I have extracted the most beautiful creature from the depths of the earth, led her to destruction, yet she is at peace. I feel a tear make a clinging descent down my cheek. She shakes her head, smiles, and speaks. "We are doing something great. We aren't done yet."

I want so to believe her.

Slowly, the machines fall silent. Truck engines die. All is quiet.

"Mape!" Phale calls. "I want to see Mape."

From the top lip of the cavernous hole, he appears, one eye bandaged.

"Well, this is a surprise. And a welcome one. Only ... what became of the others?"

"Undone. And if it's blame you're looking to pin, look no farther than this boy." A heavy hand shakes my shoulder.

"He's not a boy," shouts Talya.

Mape shifts, and even from our distance he appears amused. "With that hair, I'm not certain what it is. But the girl ... I don't recall a girl in the net."

"She was a find. A surprise." Phale crosses his arms. "Strange things lurk below. Had you the patience to wait me out before proceeding with these accursed explosions, I could have finished the job without stones falling on my head."

"It seems your time below has liberated your tongue. An unwise condition when speaking to a superior." Mape pauses. "Still, perhaps understandable given your days underground, and forgivable due to your success. As for the drilling, this is not the world you left, Watcher. The PM loses power by the day.

Without Massa or Luca, the mainland has teetered. There are riots. There is looting. We control only a small quadrant on the Swan. We need control of the water and the Rats' domain, and we need it quickly. The Council authorized the haste. And I say it's about time. For too long, freakish monsters have laughed at us. Why should the Rats not pay us tribute? We sustain them with light."

Talya yells, "You do nothing of the — "

I slap my hand over her mouth. "Not the one to speak to right now."

Mape's eyebrows lift. "Luca has learned something in his absence. Let's hope he is as wise when he appears before the Nine. Bring them up."

"No!" Phale grabs my shoulder.

"No?" Mape asks.

"No?" I peek back at Phale's determined face.

"I know how the truth spins, Mape. I know where the credit for this capture will fall. I've spent too much time in the darkness not to receive my accommodation for this assignment." Phale points toward the tunnel. "*I* bring them in, or we return."

"This level of subordination surpasses debriefing!" Mape yells.

"Debriefing be hanged. I've experienced worse!"

Mape looks away, and his jaws clench. Nobody but Father has ever challenged him. At least not that I've seen. Mape turns from the edge of the bowl and then whips back around, his finger pointed at Phale. "I will do this. Once."

"March, Seward. Up the edge," Phale calls.

The four of us wade to the road and start the circular climb. We reach the lip, and a voice pushes up from below.

"Do we keep blasting, Mape?"

Mape stares at me, and I drop my gaze. "There is no need. There is an easy way down ... if you don't destroy it."

"Halt, for now!" Mape orders. "But all machinery remains on the isle in case Luca should forget either the path or his newfound wisdom."

It's done: The shelling. The digging. With my words, all can stop. But the price is more than I can bear. I see it in Talya's eyes. That horror of betrayal has returned.

Welcome to the world of the Toppers.

CHAPTER 28

The world is dark today.

The brilliant sun sparkles against a field of blue, and in the distance thousands of ripples return the favor. But in the space between, where I live, the world feels dark.

The Council. The thought of them fills me with dread.

My father. The thought of him fills me with longing.

And Talya. A strange void grows between us as we walk, something no words can breech. To her, again, I have become Other. She sees good and bad and wrong and right, and her conviction draws me, but she's not stuck in-between. If providing them with the path buys a little more time for Etria and his people, gives me clues to my father's whereabouts, it's a wrong I'll consider.

My world is gray.

We push through the jungle and toward the beach. Phale and Mape speak in hushed tones behind me.

"And what of Jasper?" asks Mape.

"Out of my reach below. The same for the Curator."

Mape grunts. "Maybe for the best. Five is too many for one man to bring up."

"Seward!" Phale yells.

My uncle stops but does not turn.

"Did Jasper tell you where he beached his boat?"

Seward turns his head to the side. He exhales loud and slow. "What if he did?"

"I fancy a boat." Phale folds his arms. "My pay in credits — "

"Is sufficient." Mape sounds upset, and I quicken my steps.

"After my recent days, no. It's not sufficient. Eight Watchers were undone. I faced the fear you would not. I want a boat."

I turn in time to see Mape yank Phale nearer. "If you knew the conditions on the mainland, you would not waste time with thoughts of personal gain."

"If it is as bad as you say, I think a boat is a wise thing to acquire. Seward, lead me to Jasper's shrimper."

My uncle hangs his head and veers left, away from the main lagoon.

One tiring hour later, we reach the craft. Hidden beneath a weave of palm branches, it sways smartly back and forth against a makeshift dock.

"I'll follow you to the PM's isle." Phale gestures toward the four of us. "They will ride in my new reward. Seward, untie it and step in … That's right. Now the girl. And Luca, the prize." Phale follows me into the boat, turns and stares. "Then again, Mape, you could simply come with me."

Mape stares at the boat, spits, and clenches his teeth, and his own dial starts to spin. "I hate this craft. I spent months soaked in it, curled up in it, cursing the day I saw it. Rain, cold … I swore I'd never set foot in it again."

Phale raises a palm and lets it drop to his side. "Fair." He sighs and stares out toward the sea, and whispers into my ear, "It will take him some time to reach the lagoon where the other ships are anchored. You should have a sufficient head start by then." His voice breaks. "Thank you, Luca. Greet my wife and baby girl ... and thank you for the sky."

Phale steps back off the boat and launches his body toward Mape, crashing into his midsection and toppling him backward.

"Hold on, mates!" Seward cranks up the engine, and the shrimper chugs into the depths; from there we witness the strangest of fights. The Amongus exchange body blows, each fierce enough to be the end of me, yet none seem to take effect. I can't watch. Win or lose, this is Phale's last stand, a final battle fought for us.

The motor gathers speed, and Seward sets his course. "The mainland, I suppose."

"Yeah." My mind whirs. *What just happened?* "The museum. Wren says there's something there I need."

"That isn't going to be easy, mate," Seward says. "Then again, when you're involved, nothing's easy. A trouble magnet. That's what you are."

Talya takes clumsy steps toward me, her legs unused to anything but the firm certainty of bedrock. She draws me close, humming softly into my heart.

"Were you really going to give your council the path?"

"The truth?" I peek at her. "I don't know."

She rests her chin on my shoulder. "The truth works for me."

Talya glances back, and her breath catches. She grasps my head and cranks it toward the isle.

Phale stands alone, his arm raised in the air. He's waving. An Amongus is waving.

Talya and I wave back.

It's a strange world we live in, one where my heart now hurts for an Amongus. No, not an Amongus: Phale.

"Luca?" Talya kneels. "Have you been on this boat before?"

I shake my head.

"Then you are a very well-known young man ..."

She straightens and points at the decking, to a scratch that is weathered but clear.

L-U-C-A

"Why is my name on the boat?" I trace the etching with my finger.

"I wonder more about this." She raises a metal band, the sunlight glinting off tarnished gold. "Why was your mother on the boat? It's an anklet from one of our artisans, one mothers are given at birth. It bears your name." Her voice softens. "It belonged to Alaya."

I reach for it, stroke it. I know this craft's history; Jasper told me. I believe all the words surrounding my birth. Talya would not lie to me, but holding proof settles it, pushes the truth deeper. I am a Topper. I am a Rat. I belong everywhere and nowhere, and I alone can save two worlds.

Don't be arrogant, Luca.

I pocket the anklet and acquiesce to the gentle voice in my head. "Well, Father and me," I whisper.

He must still be alive.

Father Massa, I'm coming. If I can figure out how to find you.

CHAPTER
29

I float into a fitful sleep.

Heavy eyelids rise and fall, and I drift away only to jerk awake. Always there is Seward, who whistles a tune I've never heard.

"When did you know?" I ask.

"What, mate?"

"That Phale was on our side."

Seward turns. "I still don't know." His fingers grip and regrip the wheel. "You believe far too easily. Am I on your side?"

I chuckle at the thought. "Well, yeah, you're my uncle."

"But be I on your side? I work for them, you know."

I nestle down into a pile of nets and rope. "I doubt you still have a job."

"Luca, don't trust anyone. Not even me." He reaches for a balled-up windcoat and flattens it over his thigh before drawing it around his Water Rat garment. "We scratch by, trained to fear, to doubt. It's the way of the Topper world, and from what I saw of Etria, it may be the way below as well."

I point down below the deck to where Talya sleeps. "Not Talya. She's, she's —"

"Captured your senses. Captured your heart. You be especially blind when it come to her."

I shake my head. "You don't know her like I do. But I don't expect a pirate to understand those feelings."

"Because castoffs and scoundrels never love."

"I didn't say that —"

"And we live only for ourselves."

"Seward, I never meant —"

"And we never settle down, and never feel alone, and never long for the time when we return from sea and can rush into a woman's embrace." His eyes glaze and the mood about us grows heavy.

I pause. "I'm just saying I like her. That's all."

Seward licks his lips. "Okay, mate. But what do you know of her? What do you know of her that *she* hasn't told you?"

She reads?

Seward raises his palm. "I rest my case before the judge. Oh, don't feel bad. Talya's easy on the eyes. Better to be betrayed by a looker —"

"Betrayed? What are you talking about? She's totally dependent on me up here. She's never been to the surface. She needs me."

"Okay, lad, okay. Just speakin' pirate to pirate. I've never known anyone to be who they say they are."

"Even Massa?"

Seward breathes deeply. "My brother came close."

"You mean comes close. He comes close, right?"

Seward winces. "Yeah, lad, to be sure, that's my meanin'. You'll find Massa."

I'll find him? You mean we.

Uncle's face lightens. "Ah, there it be. The lights of Freemanl Wharf! A sight for sore ... eyes ..."

"What's wrong?" I push myself to my feet and join him at the fore.

Seward cuts his engine and turns off the floodlight. "Just days away, lad, and our world," he rasps, "it burns."

Fires dot the shoreline, licking the night sky. Blazes spring up, die down, and then reappear with new intensity. Small explosions, followed by shouts and cries, riddle the wharf.

"There will be no landing here." Seward's face turns grim, and he turns the wheel. The shrimper creaks and its prow turns out to sea. "I think we will not be able to tell friend from foe."

"They're just people. Lost and misinformed." I yank the wheel back around, and the confused boat swings back. "This is our home. New Pert. I need to tell them all is well. That the water won't stop after all."

"Is all really well? The riotin' is no longer the main concern. How long, now that you've escaped, until Mape begins blastin' again? I tell you they've already begun. How much deeper can they dig until the weight of the ocean crushes in, flooding every last tunnel? Flooding every Rat below and destroying the Aquifer?" Seward turns. "I tell you, the end is nearer now than we think." He presses his finger against my chest. "Your escape marked the beginning of it."

I think hard. "Unless we can stop the blasting."

"And, young mate, how would you propose to do that?"

"I don't know, but Father might."

Seward rubs his face and lowers his gaze. "You and the girl

have your path. I was never a world saver. That's Massa. Me, I'm the back-stabber." He nods at the chaos in front of us. "If this is my world, so be it. I will take my chances on the sea." He gives me a quick glance, and the next word comes soft and weighty. "Alone."

"You're going to leave us," I say.

He gazes at the coast. "Aye. At the first safe docking point. The rest of the journey is yours."

Mine. My insides wilt. Thus far, there has always been Seward. Through every danger, every decision. At the same time his words don't surprise me. He's the unpredictable one. Father, the steady; Seward, the wild.

"Okay." I try hard to sound brave, but my voice cracks. "Find us someplace solitary."

"Thank you, mate." Seward stares off, then spins the wheel and shouts.

Another craft rams into the shrimper, and Talya leaps up from below. "What did we hit?"

She joins us at the edge of the boat, and we peer into the darkness. I tap Seward's shoulder. "Risk some light, Uncle."

He flips the toggle and his floods illumine the sight.

Talya steps to my side, gasps, and covers her mouth. "Why?"

It's a barge, though no captain stands at the helm. Motionless bodies litter the deck, forming a gruesome cargo. Yet the undone still speak, their dials whirring and spinning.

Twenty, maybe thirty undone Amongus on their final voyage out to sea.

Seward heaves a grappling hook over its railing and draws the barge close. "Arrows and knives, all. The mainland is lost, Luca." He exhales hard. "I always dreamt of throwing off their cursed authority, but never in my worst nightmares did the deed end like this."

From the crimson deck, a groan. Soft and pained.

"Someone's still alive." Talya climbs onto the rail and leaps onto the vessel.

Seward glances at me. "Full marks for pluck and compassion. It will get her undone, but, full marks."

I shove him and follow Talya. Together, we move from corpse to corpse. "Who's alive here?" I say. "Please, I need more sounds."

Another groan. Talya and I haul a carcass to the side, and there beneath lies an Amongus, blood oozing from his stomach wound and his eyelids fluttering.

"What's happened?" Talya kneels and strokes his matted hair. "What's done this to you?"

His hand shoots out and clasps her ankle. "Who are you?"

I jump to her side, and the Amongus stares with wide eyes. "Luca, you're alive? All have been told that you perished — " Coughs rack his body. "It's a hunt, and we are prey. The world has turned."

"Are there more of you left alive?"

He lifts his eyebrows. "Downtown quadrant. On the Swan. A small group still holds. All our families are there." His muscles shiver and twitch. "It's the same everywhere. New Pert. The Outer Territories. Queland, Vittoria. Sydney has fallen." He pauses. "But the worst is New Pert. Rioters beam their actions to Sowt Afrika, Sowt Amerika. It's over. Leave here, Luca. Though I know of no place to flee."

Talya turns to me. "We need to help them."

"Excuse me, lass," Seward calls from the boat. "But consider well the ones for whom you accumulate favors. You be speakin' about helping those whose job it is to undo. You be speakin' of the enemy."

"Phale wasn't an enemy." She takes the Amongus's hand. "What's your name?"

His gaze wanders and then focuses. "My name? My name ... It's Connyr."

"And do you have family, Connyr?"

He nods. "Aye. A wife and two daughters. Barricaded in the quadrant."

"Luca will get them out." Talya rests her hand on his heart. "You have my word."

I cough hard, and Seward throws up his hands. "Ah, yes, we will waltz in and lead out a triumphant procession of the accursed — "

"Shut up, Seward," I say. Talya looks at me with pride. I can see it — every ounce of her believes I will rescue Connyr's family.

Such confidence from a girl is most disconcerting.

I push my hand through my hair. "How do we get to them?"

"Through the Swan River. Streets are overrun. But you will not reach the inlet. You can't."

Talya cups Connyr's cheek in her hands. "Rest now. Luca will deliver your family."

Who is this young lady I brought up from inside the earth? Seward is right: I know nothing of her, except she is the bravest girl I know. That, and when I am with her I feel brave as well.

"We'll get them out," I whisper, hoping Seward doesn't hear.

"I don't blame the people," Connyr rasps. "Not after the things I've done ..."

Connyr is no more.

I stand. "Uncle, we have to go toward the museum. Wren

208

told me it was important to visit it again, and with the fear the building creates inside people, it would also be the Amongus's last holdout. While I'm there, I need to greet Phale's wife if she lives, and bring Connyr's family to safety. I need a boat to do all these things, and I need a crazy pirate to captain it. Basically, I need you. After you help me, I'll ask you for no more favors. You may disappear from my life if you want."

"There will be no after," he says dryly. "We'll all perish in the attempt."

I climb back into his boat and help Talya over the rail. "What would you do if you could see your brother again?"

My uncle raises his hand. "I'm not fallin' for this manipulation."

"What would you tell him?" I ask.

Seward glances warily at me. "I'd say, 'Not a day passes without me bein' proud. Not a day passes without me feelin' regret.' And I'd tell him he raised a son who puts me to shame … Blast it, Luca. Find one of the scum about my size. If we're going to do this, I'll need to look the part."

I pull the red uniform off the nearest man and locate an intact dial. "Here you go. I bet you always wanted one of these."

Moments later, Seward, every bit the Amongus, churns the boat toward the mouth of the Swan. My mind focuses. For the first time I have my own hopes, my own dreams. And I think I love Talya.

What a time for my world to end.

But the thought of Father still buoys me. I haven't seen him for months, but every moment I feel it more strongly — he's still the center of everything. What will I say when I see his face?

Not a day passes without me being proud. Not a day passes without me feeling regret. And I love you.

CHAPTER
30

S eward idles the engine at the mouth to the Swan.

"Can you keep this lumbering jug of a boat in the center of the river?" Seward pulls me toward him. "If the shoreline be held by looters, then perhaps an Amongus like me running the shoot is a dangerous proposition."

Seward sits low in the hull, and I move to take the wheel. "Anything I need to know?"

"Go fast, mate. Go fast. And do not stop. When you reach the inlet, I'll take over, and you two become my children. If the Fates favor, we'll be allowed into the safe zone Connyr spoke of. If it remains." He winces. "But we'll never get in with your hair ... Talya, search below deck for some hats or hoods."

We race toward the river, gaining speed and volume. Its mouth is not hard to find. Bonfires fueled by the keels of ships rage on either side, and kids stand, arrows in hand, waving us nearer.

Friend or foe? Friend or foe?

Seward covers himself in a blanket. "Just don't stop."

I reach the mouth and wave. From the left bank, a cautious wave back. I fly through the channel and peek over my shoulder at the boy who returned my gesture.

Lendi!

I slow and turn the wheel. Seward's hand reaches up and yanks the boat straight. "What's controlled you, lad? This is no time for delay."

Shuff.

An arrow pierces the bulkhead and I duck, throttle to full. *Shuff.* Another lodges in the seat behind me.

"Stay below, Talya!"

I drop to my knees and we churn forward. From the shore, I hear voices. "He shot the gap! To the boats!" A firing of distant engines, and soon I'm pursued.

"Going below, mate. You best not be seen with an Amongus right now." Seward crawls toward the steps and tumbles into the hold. A moment later, he pokes up his head. "Just don't stop."

I grab Seward's hooded windcoat and throw it over my shoulders.

Words. I need the words to speak.

My pursuer's speedboats make short work of my head start, and they quickly pull alongside both on the left and right.

"Ease, mate," a boy shouts. "It's only the water we want."

"Then why shoot at me?"

"Because it's a quicker way to the goal than to spend all this time gabbin'."

I do not slow. I stare straight ahead and feel their gazes.

"A different look about this one, eh, Jerome? A sympathizer for sure."

My mind whirs. "Been shrimping for a month off the eastern

coast. What's happened here? Aren't you concerned about an undoing?"

Jerome sneers. "By whom? The Amongus are the ones undone in New Pert." A cheer goes up. "We live for today. And tomorrow. Not many tomorrows left, you know. Here, at the end of all things, the Amongus and soon the PM will feel what we have felt all our lives … the only feeling granted us. Fear!"

Shouts of support rise from his mates; I glance into the boat and quickly face forward.

Do I reveal who I am? Would that give them hope?

"Is it like this everywhere?" I ask.

"To be sure, and worse. Rallies are held each evening at the amphitheater. The sectors have fallen. The Council is silent, the Amongus isolated and controlled, except for the fortunate few airlifted from downtown by those accursed kopters." Jerome pauses. "But enough. You seem a likable bloke. Give up your water casks and we'll let you on your way, though I don't recommend the way you're heading."

"I have none."

He scoffs. "That was not the correct answer. Lendi, ready your bow!"

My thoughts spin. *I need help. I need it now!*

"Tell me," I blurt. "Has Glaugood fallen?"

"There is nothing to be gained in that refuge for the weak."

I wipe my brow. "But have you checked the caves? There may be a stash. An ancient hoard. Especially in a lower cave, untouched by the sea. What's found might be enough to send your best mate into a year-long wrinkle."

A cry from the rear of the boat. Lendi presses forward. "P — p-perhaps we let this one by. Just this one. He's one man, and the water he would possess after a month away means hardly a swallow for each of us."

I would embrace my friend if I could, no matter what the outcome might be. Lendi reaches out his hand and strokes the shrimper's hull, then turns toward his companions, his voice strengthening. "So much blood already tonight."

A calm surrounds us. "Lendi, I don't know what's filled you," says Jerome, "but you've filled my barrel many times over this evening. Stay your hand."

Lendi clears his throat. He will not look at me, but I feel his shame.

"How far do you intend to keep this course?" Lendi speaks, his voice tender.

My voice breaks. "Until I find a welcome."

"If … if you carry on to the inlet, know that the north side — the downtown — remains in Amongus hands. There, I don't think you'll receive this kindness. Maybe … maybe you could turn aside now. There are places to rest, safe places I could show you …"

"You speak as though you've stumbled on your kin. The fool's choices are his own. Death soon or death now. His choice to make. To shore!" Jerome shoves Lendi toward the aft of the boat, and the flotilla peels away from the shrimper. I risk one last look at my mate. He stands statued, his face buried in his hands. They lower toward me, cup and raise. I return the gesture.

"Thank you, mate," I whisper. "Thank you."

Seward crawls up on deck, with Talya close behind.

"Quick thinkin', lad."

Talya whacks Seward hard on the shoulder. "I knew he could lead us. When will you stop doubting him?"

"I just …" He massages his arm. "It seemed a might tough scrape, is all."

But their compliments don't take hold. Lendi. Blood? My childhood friend. It's only been days since I've seen him. Since he was compliant, obedient. My best friend is corrupted by freedom, like the entire surface world. He has become a victim of himself.

I need to reach that museum.

We motor on, and though shouts echo from each shore, no boats venture out to meet us and the water is strangely quiet. Ships have always been hard to come by in New Pert, but those with means spent their evenings on the Swan. Wrinkles were harder to detect, which made the waterway ideal for unauthorized trading and unregistered meetings. But tonight we own the river.

The Swan widens and the current slows. I breathe deep. *The inlet.* Seward rises and takes the wheel. I stand by Talya and stare to the south where fires rage, but to the north all is still.

"We go north, children. Luca, your name is Radney." Seward folds his arms. "Do you like that name?"

"It's a strong name."

Seward looks away, and when he turns back he is not the same. "It was the name of my son."

My mouth hangs, waiting. Waiting for an explanation, for a story.

You had a son?

"Close your yammer." His face twitches. "You'll get no satisfaction from me on the issue." Moments pass, and his voice falls, his tone mocks. "Lass, you speak so well of Phale. You jump so quickly to Connyr's aid." He swallows. "But no father should have to pull his own son up from the depths."

My eyes widen. I want to know what happened, but he says no more.

His silence speaks; that's all for now.

CHAPTER
31

Searchlights from the north crisscross the water, stealing my sight. I shield my eyes as my vision becomes one big sunspot, and wait. Another boat has joined ours.

"Who's with you?" The voice from the other craft is gruff, nervous.

"Just my two children. I've been gone a week between sleeper assignments. I was to report to New Pert before a stint in Sydney." Seward rips the arrow's shaft from the seat. "Why was I fired upon?"

"The world is backward. The arrow came from the rebellion. You are fortunate — I've not seen a boat survive the river route for some time." I squint into the light, and he continues. "Yet it is fortunate that you did not first report to Sydney. That city has fallen." He looks us over once more. "Follow me."

Our escort doesn't wait for our answer, but powers quickly toward the downtown district. We follow, easing up to the remains of the Great Swan Pier. As children Lendi and I splashed around its support beams. As teens we secretly discussed our desired matches, though jumpy Lendi never did feel comfortable with the issue.

I tie up the boat and, together with Talya, Seward, and our escort, run onto shore.

Wire, coiled and barbed, stretches far in either direction. Three rows of clumsily built fencing rise, each one higher than the one fronting it. Behind those twisted lines stands a ten-foot, hole-riddled cinder block wall.

"We hemmed ourselves in. About a three-mile diameter of the city is all we control. You cannot remain outside." He whistles. From above the wall, three heads appear, vanish, and then reappear hoisting a wooden ramp. They toss a rope secured to one end of the span over the fences and our escort pulls it taut. Slowly backing up, he and Seward draw the length of the ramp down onto the beach.

"Hurry. Hurry!" our escort urges, though I see no danger where we stand. With the ramp in place, he scampers up and over the wall; Seward follows, and then Talya.

I take one last look around the inlet. Distant shouts fill the night.

"What have we become?"

Nothing that can't be restored. The voice pounds in my head.

"Well" — I shake my head — "you can speak, but you sure can't hear. New Pert falls apart."

I step from sand to wood, and the world explodes in heat and light. The earth drops away; am I falling or flying? It feels like a journey through the stratus, except that pain rips my body. And then suddenly it doesn't, and I feel nothing. Moments pass, silent moments when the ring in my ears eclipses all other sounds. I'm lost in a vacuum, and the world spins, though I'm quite certain I'm on my stomach. I force open my eyes and roll, peering through dust and flames.

The ramp is no more.

"Lu — Radney!" Faintly, my name finds me. "Are you there, boy?"

I can't see Seward, and my head feels light. Angry voices approach. When I call on my legs to move, they don't respond. *Talya! Was she over the wall?* I claw forward, feel strong hands on my back, and remember no more.

～

My eyelids open lazily. I lie on my back, this much I know. I wriggle my fingers, my toes. I still own them.

It is dark, the world shrouded in shadow. The scent of burning wood surrounds me and smoke wafts over me. Wherever this place is, it burns.

Then the smoke clears and my vision sharpens. Twenty feet away I see a crackling fire, its light dancing on the ceiling. Shadows huddle around it, shoulder to shoulder, offering their fingers for warmth. I count twenty bodies, speaking in soft tones punctuated by occasional laughter.

A chill racks me, and I draw a sharp breath. A shadow breaks from their ring, rises and approaches, kneeling down beside me. "Luca. How are you?"

"Cold."

"To be sure. Belzar? More heat for our guest." Another shape leaves the fire ring, and soon arrives with blankets; I feel the weight of the wool, nestle beneath its warmth. Before I can offer a thank you, the giver's shadow resumes its place by the fire.

"Don't try to talk." The man's accent is thick, like none I've heard before. "The explosive landed near, though likely it was intended for the wall and not for you. Terrance removed metal fragments from your leg but they were not deep. You should mend well."

Metal? I lift my covers. Dried blood darkens the loose-fitting browns I received from the rats.

"Are you ... are you part of the rebellion?"

"You aren't going to rest, are you? Very well." His strong arms pull me and my covers to a sit, gently lean me back against iron bars. "Your question. Are we part of the rebellion ... Hmm. I suppose too far from the mark. Please, call me Akov."

"And I'm in a cell with you." I shift against the iron. "I've heard rumors of these secret pens. Holding areas before an undoing."

"Your eyes took quite a flash." Another shadow hoists a lantern. "Look around once more."

In the light's lazy glow, I catch sight of the exit — a circular door, thick and immense, fit into a wall of steel.

A bank vault! Gold bars are stacked in one corner, silver bars line the far wall. "You stole all this," I say. "You broke in here and stole it."

"So quick to judge to the bad. Think, Luca. If we were thieves, we sure didn't get far." Akov gestures toward the others. "Make room. Let's bring Luca around our fire."

The smoke hangs above us and burns my throat, but I'm warm, which is enough. None of the people gathered look frightening or cruel. Twelve men, a few women, and two girls, one about my age.

"Are you going to let me go?" I ask.

"Oh, Luca. You aren't being detained. Terrance mended you. He says you'll be stiff, but you can leave anytime." A girl speaks, and when she does I gasp. Emile. It's Emile, a Fifteen.

I lean forward, feel the pain in my thigh, and cough in the smoke. "Please just tell me where I am. I need to reach ..."

Do I tell them I want to reach the Amongus?

"You wanted to get inside the barricade. You wanted to follow your comrades," Akov whispers. "But you paused, and that pause saved your life. We saw."

"Luck," I say.

"There is no such thing." Emile reaches over and sweeps matted hair off my face. Her touch feels good. Should it feel good?

"You were protected," she continues. "As we all are."

"By ..."

"By the Voice."

How do you know what I hear ... Wishers!

Weeks ago, I would have considered myself fortunate to be in their company. I used to have so many questions. Now thoughts of Seward and Talya consume my mind. "Can you get me into the compound?"

"When you can walk," says Akov.

I throw off my blankets and grimace myself to vertical. I hobble around the room. "I'm good."

Akov rubs his face. "You'll be one more day with us, and then, yes, we will see what we can do." He pauses. "It is a pleasure to speak to you. Most of us have traveled far to reach New Pert. We were born in Siberska and lived on the rim of Lake Baikal. But it, too, dried. We journeyed far to reach this place, and have picked up a few stragglers these last days." He glances at Emile.

"We've been waiting for you, Luca. We were forewarned of your return, and your distress." Emile gazes into me.

"Who told you? Wait ... let me guess. This Voice spoke to

you." I tongue my cheek. "And since we're all listening to the crazy voice in our heads, did it happen to say anything else I should be aware of? Maybe a clue about my father's location, or something useful like, say, how to get over that wall without blowing up?"

"More was said." Akov grows somber. "Luca, you must stay alive. Much depends on it."

Above us I hear a slamming of metal.

"We're compromised." Akov leaps to his feet, bends over, and hoists me over his shoulder. "Emile, Suzanya, with me. The rest of you, my blessed comrades, don't fear — pray."

"We'll see you soon, Akov." The man who blanketed me now smothers the fire. With perfect precision, the entire group slips silently out of the vault and into the elevator.

"Where are you going?" I call. The door slowly closes. Akov waits, listens. The sound of clanking vanishes.

"They go to find a way out for you," Akov whispers, and another minute passes.

"Maybe it was nothing."

Akov exhales. "It's never nothing. Now it's our turn. We'll take a different path."

We enter the stairwell, climb one flight, and stop. "Luca, pain or no, you will need to run." As Akov sets me down, I feel his heartbeat quicken. Before I can ask him what lies before us, he peeks through the glass of the stairwell door and bows his head. I steal a look, and my jaw drops.

The Wishers stand, hands clasped, a wall blocking the elevator door. Across from them, men. Shouting men. Men with guns. *Where did those men get guns?*

"The Amongus boy! Where have you sheltered him?" They

point their weapons at my protectors. As one, the Wishers drop to their knees, lifting their palms to the sky.

A shot rings out, and a woman slumps to the ground. Then another. I can't bear to watch, but I can't turn away. I've never seen this much hate, or this much sacrifice.

They hardly know me.

Akov gazes into my eyes and whispers, "Luca, they do this for you." Tears stream down his cheeks as he lifts his head toward a room filled with undones. "They're now home; *their* role in the prophecy is now fulfilled. But you still have a part to play. *You* must complete your task."

But I don't know this prophecy. I don't know my task.

"Onto the elevator! They must be below." A young man, far too young to undo another, punches the elevator button, and soon the life-takers disappear.

"Now." Akov pushes out into what is now a chamber of death. I limp over toward the first body, but Akov's hand jerks me back. "These bodies no longer need our attention. We go."

Together with the girls, we push out into the night, winding through the shadows.

My leg is on fire when minutes later we reach the cinder block wall—all that remains of the Amongus's defenses.

Call your name.

The Voice wasn't Akov's, and I obey at once.

"Radney! Radney!"

A rope flings over the top and lands at my feet. I barely have time to react before Akov ties a loop in the bottom and sticks my foot into it. He then gives a quick tug and it pulls taut, hoisting me in jerks skyward.

A single shot rings out and draws my eyes downward.

Suzanya has vanished and Emile is undone, with Akov

alone kneeling at her side. He looks up, cups his hands, and disappears into the darkness.

"Oh, my boy!" Seward reaches up and lifts me down to safety. "We thought … Well, I thought …"

He gently lowers me to the ground, where Talya draws me near.

I soak in her touch.

"I never left the wall," she whispers, "I knew you'd come."

"You don't know the cost." I pull free and let myself mourn for those in the bank, and my tears turn to rage. I no longer know who to hate.

Yet some truths are certain. Wren was right: the Wishers gave everything for me.

~

Outside, in the vault, I'd found a tiny pocket of peace.

Within the blockade, all is mayhem.

Men, women, and children rush about, though where they are going is not clear. There's a fire here as well, a blazing bonfire stoked by a pile of Amongus uniforms — and a man with charred skin feeds the flames. Tents by the hundreds fill the spaces between downtown buildings. Broken glass and an occasional body accent the chaotic scene.

I finish my retelling of Akov and Emile and what I saw in the vault. Seward's face is tight, unreadable. Talya can't stop hugging me.

We are sitting in silence when the Amongus escort walks smartly over to us. "Still alive. The Fates are with you. As I told your father, there was a fight around the pier, and we pushed them back long enough to build the wall. You should have stayed nearer. Nothing is safe outside."

A woman screams in the distance.

The escort rubs his tired face and continues. "Inside, you may fare little better."

Kopter blades cut the night air, and within the walls scurrying gains purpose. Everyone presses toward the marble stairs, the only lit-up area I see. Rotors thump overhead, and the kopter slows and lands on top of the museum.

"The Council airlifts us food and water, removing us twelve at a time. Twelve," the escort whispers. "So few. Kopters land on the hour, but there are too many who are hungry, thirsty. Landings on the minute would still not be enough."

"Where does it take you ... us?" Seward asks.

"To the PM's island. By Council decree, the PM has withdrawn all Watchers from the mainland. The promise is that our families will be cared for on the isle, and we will be safe."

I whisper to Seward as privately as I can. "Perhaps what we needed was not so much in the museum, but *on* the museum." I point at the kopter. "Would this take us to Father?"

Seward perks up and straightens. "Aye, Radney, that it might." He pats my back and turns to our escort. "I thank you for safe passage. However this ends for us, we are in your debt."

The Amongus frowns at Seward's hand and then nods. "Very well."

The three of us walk quickly toward the marble stairs. Ten Amongus, still dressed in pressed uniforms, guard the entrance. There will be no sneaking by them. Not in this crowd.

"Even if we can get into the museum now, there is little chance they can airlift us this soon!" I shout above the noise. "And I have some commitments to keep!"

Seward rolls his eyes. "To a pair of undones, who will be none the wiser!"

Talya grabs my arm, and my uncle's ear. "We'll meet you here in three hours. You find a way to get us on the kopter."

I look at Talya and then Seward, who scratches his cheek. Finally he straightens his uniform. "No problem, mates. I'll see to that tiny issue right away."

We wander the streets asking Amongus if anyone knows Phale. It is not a wise thing to do, not when every person here should know my face. No, it is not the wise thing, but with Talya at my side it feels right.

"Wife of Phale?" we shout.

"Who's calling me?"

A hand reaches out from the shadows. "Has Phale been called to the kopter? Take me to him. Take me away from here!"

She shakes my arm until it aches. I wrench my limb free of her grasp.

"You're ... You're really his wife?" Talya steps nearer to the woman. "We bring news."

"News? There's not time for news. Take me to him!"

It's not her.

The Voice confirms my thoughts. "What about your son? Where is he?"

"He died in the riots. My precious son, my precious ... Where are you going?"

"Son, huh?" I catch Talya's gaze, and we hurry away from her, but a widows' chorus has begun:

"Phale!"

"Tell me of my husband!"

"Have you found him?"

"Can I board the kopter?"

Desperate women leap at us from the shadows, and we duck behind a tent to wait until the frenzy passes and the only noise

224

we hear is the usual cries. "I think we can resume our search," I say.

After hours of failure, Talya trips over success. Literally. She stumbles over a woman sitting cross-legged in front of her ripped tent.

"I'm sorry," Talya says. "Wife of Phale? Do you know where I might find her?"

The woman's eyes grow and fill with tears. She clenches her teeth, as if willing her face to calm. "My man's name is Phale. What word?"

Talya looks closely into her eyes, hugs her, and lets tears fall. Inside her embrace, the woman softens, dropping her head onto Talya's shoulder. If everyone would allow Talya to hug them, they would feel much better.

Of course, I wouldn't.

"We bring news of him," I interrupt. "We last saw him two days ago, alive and well. He asked us to greet you and your baby daughter."

The woman crumbles backward onto the pavement, rocked by heavy sobs. She claws at her face, and then her tent. Talya kneels and moves closer, but receives a kick in the face for her effort.

I jump to Talya's side and help her to her feet. "Did I say it wrong?"

"No," Talya whispers. "I think you just delivered a message. And I don't think it was a greeting."

Foolish me. Any baby daughter would still be with the Developers!

We back away from the picture of grief. I'm unsure I want to find Connyr's family, though I am rather certain I know where they'll be found. I wander the perimeter of the wall until

I reach the main gate. Amongus, still dressed the part, discuss news from the world outside.

"Any patrols would leave through here. Their families would wait for them …" I glance around and see a group of thirty huddled near a fire. "There."

I wander over to the group. "Connyr? Do any of you know a—"

A woman stands. "Connyr is my man."

Do I tell them they're widows?

I clear my throat. "Connyr's wife and children have been granted room on the next kopter."

She casts me a sideways glance. "Without our men to speak for us, we can't get on. We—"

"This special honor is due the family of a man who displayed great heroism, and great compassion," I say, and with my words women wail. They know. Their men will not come home.

Talya lays her hand on the woman's head. "There is room on the next kopter for the three of you. Do you wish to come?"

"I wish many things," she hisses.

"Go, Meline. Go." Another woman pulls two girls to their feet. "Here, take your daughters and go. Nothing remains for us here."

Meline squints at me. "There is room for us? The PM has never rewarded his Watchers for kindnesses. How is this true?"

I tell the truth. "I don't know."

Meline thinks and stares at her children. "Come, young ones. We are leaving."

"Without Father?" her youngest cries as she latches on to her mother's leg.

Meline fixes her eyes on me.

"Yes," she says. "Your father has provided the way."

Talya leans over. "How are we going to do this?"

I don't have a clue. I harbor no plan. But I am nearer to my father than I have been for some time, and the nearness emboldens me.

Father. I'm coming.

CHAPTER
32

We weave our way through the crowd to the museum.
Hope vanishes on the way.

There is no way to reach the marble steps, much less climb
them to become one of twelve passengers. Not given my size,
and not given the ten — Wait. I count again: eleven Amongus
guard the door. There is a new Watcher. One who looks con-
spicuously like my uncle.

"Leave it to a pirate," I say, and tuck escaping hair back
beneath my hood. "Follow me."

We press into the mob. I jump and wave and shout wildly.
Seward slaps the Amongus on his left, who catches my uncle's
wrist and lowers it forcefully to his side. The Watcher strides
down into the crowd, shoving, throwing bodies out of the way.

He stands before me, looks me up and down. "There is a
familiar feel to you. We have met."

Barker! I drop my gaze. The undoer who violated my home.

"I don't think so." I point at the stairs. "You may know my
father."

"Your father ..." He raises his eyebrow. "Let's hope your
father is as honest as he is crafty. Go, Radney. And daughter
Talya. Go. And the three guests. Go!" He yanks us all onto the

stairs. Seward turns smartly, and we all pile through the oaken door and into the museum.

How I've missed this place.

The statues are broken, but the ceiling is still beautiful, and when the large doors thud behind me all is quiet. For a moment, sanity is back. Home is back. I'll climb up and have tea with Wren and talk about history and the weather, everything and nothing.

"Room for six more!"

A voice from the roof. The door behind us opens and more Amongus pile in.

"We can't separate!" Seward says, and dashes upward. I grab one young girl while Meline grabs the other, and together we pound up the steps with Talya close behind. We are all focused on a singular goal until we reach the tearoom.

"Talya!" I turn. "Take her. I'll be right there."

I step into the room, my sanctuary. Stars twinkle through the skylight and I dash to Wren's rocking chair. She's gone. Of course she is, but she feels here somehow. A half-filled cup of tea rests on the stand, along with an open book covered with scratches — Wren's writing:

The Voice spoke again tonight in fragments I do not understand. Pieces I heard:
The Prophecy

"Okay," I whisper. "About time. What are you all willing to die for?"

Words must be shared . . .
Hope must be shared . . .
The End . . .
The end can come . . .

It all depends on Luca ...

*Here in the quiet, I can't bring anything together. May-
be tomorrow, Luca can.*

"Sorry, Wren. He can't. Words. Hope. Endings." I scratch
my head. "If this was supposed to guide me, we're in trouble.
Bits of a prophecy aren't enough."

Lower on the page, a tiny scribble.

*There's a pounding on the museum door below. It's time
to leave.*

"Luca!" Seward hollers. "Time to leave!"

I fly out the room and burst through the door onto the roof,
where the thump of rotors blows me back a step.

Seward helps me up and runs toward the kopter, throwing
me in and landing beside with a thud.

"That's twelve!" the pilot shouts while skids lift from the
museum. "No more!"

We ease into the sky as another family explodes onto the
roof.

They are left behind, at least for another hour. Yet they are
lucky; they made it through the museum. I stare down at them.
An Amongus with his wife and child, locked in embrace, their
faces desperate.

*We could change places. We could wait one more hour. Then
I could read more about that prophecy.*

I think of Lendi. I stare down at the Amongus.

I no longer know who is friend.

Seward gazes at his feet. Missing is the triumphant wink,
the I-have-accomplished-the-impossible. There is only shame.
I don't want to know what he did to get us aboard.

The thump of kopter blades is hypnotic, and I fade in and out of sleep.

"Veer left, Haifer," the lead Amongus yells to the pilot, which yanks me back to consciousness. "Detour to another isle." He stares back at Seward. "Needing your guidance."

Seward slowly rises from his place and plunks down beside the pilot.

He gave it away. He's giving Father's dropping point, the first step to reaching the Rats, to this Watcher. I feel a sting inside that quickly subsides. It's less than ideal to give away the location, but many Amongus are already there, probably drilling again. Little harm can come in a few more knowing. At least this is what I tell myself.

"There." Seward points toward a speck of light that grows and sharpens. The pilot curses.

"What is this? There's Teria, and Gershon!" He circles the island, slows over the excavation, and quickly flies off. "I dropped them off at the PM's isle. We were told that's where we'd stay." His voice softens. "I've dropped off hundreds ..."

"They'll all end up here. The Nine have lied to us," Seward says. "You've seen our fate with your own eyes. Your next assignment is a prison camp. Sloshing in the muck toward the world of the Rats."

Haifer glances back. "I have just enough fuel to deliver you to the Council's isle, but then my flights are done. I'll radio the others. All flights end now. I won't enslave us again."

Seward leans back and pushes his hand through his dreads. He did it, and more. He got us off the mainland. He secured us transport to the PM's isle, the most likely location of Father. He's driven a wedge between the Nine and the Amongus.

But when I close my eyes I see the family on the museum

231

roof. They will be waiting, expecting kopters that will never arrive. The barricade will not hold up long. Without airlifts of food, the Amongus are trapped.

Phale. Connyr. Haifer.

Amongus. Decent men.

Seward glances toward me and raises his palms. In that one look it's clear; he knows that he's severed the last supply line into New Pert and doomed thousands of women and children in the process.

He's just assumed the role of judge.

It's a lot of moral weight to fall on a pirate.

CHAPTER
33

The kopter thumps down into a clearing surrounded by dense forest. The sun hints its arrival, and I rouse Talya, who drifted off long ago. The pilot shuts down the engine and the rotors slowly still.

"Everyone off," Haifer says. "I will give you your instructions."

Soon we stand circled beside the transport. It feels so peaceful, so different than the Amongus's last stand along the Swan. A distant inland cry interrupts the moment, and Meline draws her children close.

"Until now my orders were to direct all men to follow that path down to the beach in order to meet with the council," Haifer says. "I was told they will welcome you with a brief Ceremony of Gratefulness. There you'll receive well-deserved accommodations."

"Ceremony of Gratefulness." Seward barks a quick laugh. "I bet the beach be littered with boats."

"It is." Haifer's face tenses. "Women and children were to

follow the other path." He points the opposite direction, toward a cut in the forest. "It leads to the PM's mansion. The PM will comfort you with pleasant living arrangements. Your men will join you shortly."

I shake my head. "It didn't dawn on you that it would be unlikely that a PM, if he existed, would have thousands of spare dwellings waiting on a secluded, tropical island?"

"It did not." Haifer draws a deep breath. "I do not claim to have given this assignment any thought. We were perishing on the mainland, and hope was offered." He straightens and draws a deep breath. "But now, after seeing this treachery with my own eyes, I myself will go speak with the Council." He glances around. "I must verify the origins of this deception. Where the rest of you go is your business — you need not fear reprisal from me."

Haifer walks briskly toward the beach, pauses, and turns to Seward. "I know you are not a Watcher. I know this. But, I reasoned, allowing you on the kopter seemed a good way to bring you to the Nine should your story prove false." He faces me, cups his hands, and bows. "Be safe."

The others in the circle fix their gazes on me, blink, and rub their eyes. They glance at each other and bow, cupping their hands and moving toward their paths. All, including Connyr's family, take the path to the mansion.

But there is no mansion ...

Moments later only Seward, Talya, and I remain.

Seward climbs aboard the kopter and pounds the instruments. "Oh, that I could fly one of these. But I left the sky to the birds."

"Father," I say. "Where would they keep him?"

Uncle jumps out of the flyer and points toward the dense trail. "There."

"But that's taken by the women, the children."

Seward walks toward it. "They take it to their own undoing. Mark my words. Nobody reaches the fictional home of the fictional PM."

"They'll all perish?" Talya gasps. "How do you know?"

"I don't know anything." He smirks. "But, lass, on the sea you be floating, shifting without a worry, then a breeze, strange and warm, strikes your neck. And the thought comes: Get off the water. A storm comes. It be intuition — the water be clear as glass — but the sense has never failed me yet." He waves us onward. "I feel it now. There be sadness along that path."

"And, uh ... do you feel *how* all these thousands are undone?" I peek through the dense trees. "Beasties? Amongus in waiting?"

Seward plunks onto the ground. "That's yours to figure out, mate. I got us here."

An hour passes, and we haven't left the kopter. I had hoped to see the pilot return. Hoped his return would give direction to our steps.

I don't know which way to go.

Trust your uncle.

The Voice. It alone has guided me. I exhale and stand. "We follow the women's path."

Seward leaps to his feet. "'Tis a miracle. The young mate speaks! Onward."

Talya stretches and pads to my side. "Luca, I believe in you."

At least one of us does.

She takes my hand and the three of us vanish into the trees.

～

235

Rabal lived here. My ancestor. Maybe this is my true home.

One step in and morning's light is swallowed by dense growth. We quickly come to a fork in the way. "Luca?" Seward calls.

I glance back and forth. All is thick and green. "No idea. How about left?"

"Left it be."

Seconds later, another choice. And then another. It becomes easier to simply recite the sequence already buried in my head.

The walk is steep and painful, as the trees encroach onto the path. Leaves, broad and cutting, slice through our arms, and the sounds of unknown beasties surround us. Light from the sun barely penetrates down to the forest floor. Still, the path is well worn, though filled with forks. Hundreds of choices later, we come to a stone arch. It's the first manmade object we've seen.

Seward pushes to the fore.

"Seward! Stop!"

He freezes. "What is it? Snakie? Beastie?"

"Here." I hand him a stick. "Take small steps. Don't take your eyes off the ground."

He taps the path before him and takes one more step. "It's only water, mate! In front of us, through the arch, it's a pool." He clears his throat. "Aye, how a drink of fresh water would soothe."

He hands me the stick, and I fire out my hand and grip his shoulder. "No, keep it. Tap first."

Seward leans forward and dips his staff into the water. "I feel no bottom. It just falls away, falls ... away ... I owe you a life. Mine. It's no pool, it's the swirl of a stream that tumbles down some distance. There's no seeing the bottom. We stand above a waterfall breaking, from the sound, on rocks that we don't need to dwell on — "

"Seward," I say, stroking the arch, "if Rabal once lived here, what better way to rehearse the route to the Rats, to teach his sons —"

"Than to cut a path to the beach in the same sequence! This would be the point where Phale and me tumbled." He takes a step back. "We've reached the dome. Blime, the Council has had the directions to the Aquifer right here, beneath their noses. No doubt they've hiked this many times, memorized every turn." Seward pushes me back away from the pool. "Lead the way, mate, just not through the arch. No need spending time there."

I bite my lip, step to the front, and glance down. The distance is cloaked in darkness, but from the depths I hear the crash of water. I close my eyes and imagine dark silhouettes riding the waves.

How many must have fallen!

A smell overpowers me, one I met on Connyr's barge. It's sweet but turns foul in the nose. It thickens, and in this place there's no escape.

Death is here.

"I reckon this a convenient burial for families who make it up this far." Seward stares down at my side. "Like the blind Amongus who pursued us through the arch, and off the ledge, they never see it coming."

"But why end their lives?" Talya covers her nose, her sense of smell surely more developed from years belowground.

Seward shakes his head. "The Amongus leave the island, no doubt convinced they're on their final assignment before 'settling in' with their families. But when they see the dig on Massa's isle, they'd know it be more than an assignment. It's the reason they were rescued, once again, for bondage. Feelin' deceived, they would demand to return to this isle and their families."

"Unless there are no families to return to," I say. "But why would they continue to work for a council that has undone all they hold precious?"

"Because they don't know freedom." Seward guides me along a thin ribbon of earth rimming the pit. "We need to be movin'. The price paid to reach this point was high." Seward gestures down. "The price paid by the fallen higher still. We honor them by finding Massa."

I take Talya's hand and we press forward, dense jungle on the right, rocky pit to the left. Foliage reaches from the jungle and roots stretch spindly fingers onto the path. It's an old path—I feel it. On any other day I would walk it quietly, listening to the heaviness. But this is a sad day, a red day. Too many people, including children much younger than myself, likely were undone.

Do I hear a moan? Yes, but faint amidst the crash of waves. I pause and listen.

Silence.

I clench my teeth and dip back into the forest, leaving the maybe behind. My feet grow heavy. What if swimming in all that death there is a small life?

I can't bear to think of who it could be.

~

Hours later, we still hike. There is only our breath, the crunch of leaves, and the route. And then I'm out of words. "This is it. The directions end here."

"To be certain they do." Seward walks cautiously forward.

"It ends with water." I rub my face. "Rabal had a flair for the symbolic."

We wander the shoreline of a small lake, each of us scouring its banks. We don't speak. We pretend it is a typical lake and that we expect to discover nothing unusual. But we all know who we look for, who we do not find.

Nightfall instead finds us, sitting on a downed tree and staring: Seward at the ground, Talya at the sky, and me at the water.

Father. Where are you? I need to hear from you.

It's getting harder to remember his voice.

I wish I still had my father's book, but I sigh, thankful for the passages fixed in my practiced mind.

Talya places her head on my shoulder. "What are you thinking?"

"People keep saying that the surface has shifted, and that the world has changed." I run my fingers through her hair. "Nothing has. Fear and anger, they've always been. Suppressed, but simmering. The Amongus have always been pawns of the Council, slaves to a nonexistent peacemaker. And even now that they know of the deceit, it changes nothing. They continue to work for the same men who destroy their loves.

"We're told Wishers are evil, but they gave their lives for me. We're told our leader will care for us, but we end up undone. We're lied to all our lives. We teach lies to the children, and they pass them on to theirs, and after years of the drumbeat, lies sound like the truth. That's when the flip happens, and what's real and good sounds like insanity."

We traded the truth for a lie.

My heart is heavy. "I want to know something for certain. Anything." Talya lifts her head, and I continue. "Do you know anything beyond a doubt?"

"Yes. But I also believe in this." She presses her finger against my chest. "Sounds like your father did as well."

We sit in silence.

"I think he did. I think he trusted me. It said so in his book, but those passages are lost to me now."

Talya nestles closer. "What do you remember? Recite for me. I want to know him too."

I close my eyes and see the pages, recall the words that speak of a time so far away.

My mind flips forward to the last chapter.

Odds and Ends. Mostly Ends.

You need to know, son, what the world doesn't. You need to know how deep the deception goes, and the reason it must continue.

Here is the piece: The PM is no more. All is the Council. And the Council seeks to destroy from their home on the isle.

"Even Father wrote of deception," I say.

"Go on," Talya says quietly.

Which isle, you may ask? May you never see the PM's isle. May you never walk the walk you know so well and descend to where much debriefing cruelty is accomplished. This is the only piece I will withhold from you, my son.

"The walk I know so well … we just did that." I straighten. "And descend. Descend to where the cruelty is accomplished."

Descend, Luca.

I slowly rise and walk toward the lake.

"Luca?" Seward says. "Mate. What do you see, lad?"

"Descend!" Behind me, Talya exclaims, "All good things come from below."

She hurries to my side.

240

"What manner of foolishness moves this company? What is your purpose? Is it not Massa?" Seward shouts.

"Massa," I whisper.

"For Massa." Talya nods.

I step into the water. Blackish swirls surround my ankles and I can't see my feet, but the footing is firm, firm and rock. Talya joins me, and we slowly descend down a submerged stairwell. Water reaches my waist, my chest, and I fish for the next step. There are no more.

"There's no sense to this," I say to Talya. "How do we drop farther? We're not fish."

"No. But we have to try. Let's find out what secrets this lake is willing to share." She winks at me and dives, her body swallowed by the splash. I wait. Twenty seconds. Forty pass, and all ripples vanish. She does not break surface.

"Don't follow her, mate. Don't —"

I dive and power forward. A strange undertow pulls me deeper and deeper — there will be no surfacing. I swallow and feel a subtle shift in direction. The unnatural current pulls me on, even as my lungs suck the last bit of oxygen from my breath. Up; I'm pulled upward, and my head escapes the water's grasp.

I gulp and sputter, and then frown. There are no trees. All is rock, rock and Talya dripping and glowing in the light of a submerged rod. I climb up out of the pool and cough. Talya comes to my side. "I think we're below the lake," she says, and we continue down a thin rocky corridor.

It veers right, and when we peek around the corner Talya's fingers grip my arm.

We have come to the end, and the end is a chamber about the side of our old shanty, roughly hewn into stone. The ceilings are low, and five chairs scatter throughout the room.

In the far corner sits Walery. He does not blink or move; he is here but not here. I don't know what's happened to him, what they've done to him. But my gaze bounces from Walery to a crumpled body in the near corner. One which is gaunt. Staring.

Father.

I run to him and fall to my knees. He breathes. He lives. I lift his head onto my lap and the tears fall. Talya weeps at my side and gently cups Father's cheek in her hands.

"Father Massa. Oh, Father Massa, I've come for you. I'm here." My words fight out in spurts, landing small and muffled on his ears. Five minutes pass, and still he does not speak. He stares at something beyond. Something through.

"I've come so far," I whisper. "I need you back. I need your counsel. We all need your help. Those above. Those below."

Still nothing.

This is worse than not finding him. Before the dive, my father lived on as last I saw him. Strong, vibrant—a man who could trample Amongus beneath his feet, remove their dials, and sail into the sea.

He was my hero.

I don't know the remains of this man.

I glance at Walery, and his gaze shifts to me. His eyes hold no emotion. They simply fix on the spectacle.

"I don't think Massa knows it's you," says Talya. "Tell him something only you would know."

I'm suddenly angry, furious at my father for being so weak. So many lives ended so that we could find him. I ball my fists and then force them open. "Okay, I'll try."

I speak of Old Rub and the shanty. Of his brother, my new best mate. I tell him of the last time I saw him. What he said, the strength that surged through him. When I finish, I lay my head on his chest and listen to his heartbeat. Steady, but oh so slow, the space in between each beat so very long.

Father, where are you? I look around. *Where are we?*

Talya is no longer at my side. She kneels in front of Walery. "This boy has been through a lot."

"That boy is the reason my house burned. That boy is one of them."

One of them. One of them like Connyr? One of them like Phale?

Talya nods. "So he's one of us. Just a boy."

"He works for Mape — at least he did. He failed. And what did he fail at? My undoing! He wanted me dead. He gave me away. He slept in my shanty. He ... he probably got information from Father." I calm and rub my father's head. "But that part was my fault. I saved him. I brought him into our residence. I couldn't watch him become undone."

I breathe deep and look down at Father. *My words don't work; they don't reach. My words ... my words!*

I close my eyes, see the first pages of Father's book, and recite.

They are the words of Alaya. His wife. My mother.

He blinks.

I continue, my first years underground now ringing out underground again. I know I'm missing passages, but I don't stop, not until I reach my parents' trek to the surface. Alaya's last moments.

"Stop," Father whispers. His eyes roll back and then steady, focus on my face. "Stop, Luca. I see you."

I hug him and Talya hugs him, and slowly his arms lift and round my shoulders. He hugs me back, and the weight of wet clothing vanishes as I soak in his embrace. We ease him to a sitting position.

This is all I've hoped for. This moment, a miracle.

Father squints at Walery, and then frowns before gazing back to me. "The Council found you? It's all I hoped would not happen."

Inside, I feel a squeezing. Where is the joy in seeing me? Where is the laughter, the relieved smile? My father feels pain. I've brought him more anguish.

I failed.

"No, Father Massa, we were not found. We came on our own. Talya and I came for you."

"Oh, Luca. What possessed you? There is no release from this place." He slumps. "The only thought that kept me strong was that you might be kept safe. The current does not reverse."

I slump too. What was I thinking? What can a broken-down man do in a world gone mad?

"I love you, Father Massa," I say quietly, "and so I hoped ..."

Father buries his face in his hands, and when he removes them his face is light. "Forgive me, son. I am very glad to see you."

He looks around the cavern as if for the first time, and notices Talya. My father gives me a small smile before addressing her. "You are not a Topper."

"Greetings, Judge. I'm Talya."

The smile is now gone, and Father Massa's face returns to sadness. "Judge? Here marks the end of the judges' reign. Luca, there is so much you need to know about me, about what it means to be a Deliverer, about my brother."

"Seward. I know. It know it all, I've seen it all. The chaos. The Aquifer." I exhale hard. "And the news, I believe, will be traveling in the other direction. The Council's control has vanished since you've been gone."

I peek at Walery. He hasn't flinched.

Speak no more here.

The Voice again reverberates in my head. If Father is right

and we will never leave, spoken secrets are safe. But I will trust the command, though I don't know exactly what it foresees.

I point over my shoulder. "I will say no more now. Not until we are alone."

"It would be hard to become more alone," Father says.

Talya's eyes sparkle. "Don't give up, Judge Massa. As long as Luca's here, there's hope."

Father shakes his head. "So much like Alaya. You were fortunate not to be spotted as soon as you ascended."

I pat my father's back. "As a matter of fact, she — "

A tremendous splash awakens the deadness of the tunnel. Father tries to stand, but tumbles to the ground.

"This may be food, possibly water." He points. "It has been awhile."

"Or it may be a brother." Seward pokes his head into the chamber. "Many years have faded since we had a face-to-face. Can't say I'm much impressed with how the Deliverer's been treated of late."

Father rubs his eyes, and Seward eases nearer. "Hello, brother."

"Seward." Father cries, and again the sight unnerves me. I came expecting wisdom, solutions, but the man before me is frail and surprised. Definitely not ... helpful.

"You are all insane. Why break into a prison?"

"It's not like we knew what it was like down here," I say.

Seward rounds my shoulder. "My mate speaks the truth. And give us a little credit, brother. Reaching you was no small feat." He grins the sly grin I've come to love. "Are we ready to leave? As I understand the situation, there's a fair amount of work to do. While you were sharing pleasantries, I've learned of some new developments. Leave it to Seward. That's what I always say, leave it to — "

"Seward!" Father and I say in unison.

"So now I will be enduring ridicule from the both of ya?" My uncle disappears back down the tunnel. "Can the younger brother stand?" he calls back. "And here I thought you were roughing it."

Father grimaces and rises to his feet. The three of us follow Seward and reach the far wall, where the end of a rope wedges in a cleft of rock. I follow its length until it disappears down into the swirling pool from which we emerged.

My uncle turns toward us. "So, yes, Seward found a rope. The where of it is a story you will need to know, but I'll tell it when you have the time to appreciate my full ingenuity. And yes, Seward tied it to a tree and dove in, because he thought, Luca is a strong swimmer. No less than a current most perilous could keep him below." He peeks at Talya. "Though I might add that his affections may have the same effect."

After a wink at me, Seward turns grim. "So now a line does exist through that current, but the fact alone doesn't make for an easy sail. Between the pulling and the kicking, it will take a mighty breath."

"Father's not up to that," I say. "He can't — "

"If Seward can swim it, so can Massa." Father straightens.

Seward rolls his eyes. "Did I mention his pride, Luca? Talya, you will go first. I will hold the rope taut on this end. Then Luca. Then I will come. Brother, you will need to hold the rope taut for me. Have your arms the strength?"

"They will."

"Leave me last," I say.

"No. It must be this way. A loose rope provides no aid for the man on the last leg. So before I surface, I will tie the rope

246

around Massa's waist. When we feel the tug from above, all three of us will pull Brother out. It is the only way."

"Well, I guess it's time to enter the stratus." Talya reaches for the slack end of the rope and hands it to Seward. "Do not let go."

Seward bows and braces against an outcrop. Talya takes a deep breath, runs her fingers along the fibers, and dives.

I count. One minute passes.

"Has she tugged?"

"No, but I feel her on the line." Seward frowns. "She still moves."

Another minute passes, and Seward relaxes. "She's out. Luca, swim hard. Don't lose the lead."

I peek at Father, whose eyes again hold tears. "Don't worry, Father. I'll see you soon."

And I dive. At first I swim, the rope scraping my back, but soon the current overpowers and I reach, grasp the line, and fight hand-over-hand toward the surface. One minute, ten minutes — it feels the same. Lungs tighten, burn. I will not make it. Here, after all I have accomplished, I will be undone.

I give one more stroke and rise above the waterline. Life and air and Talya welcome me, and I sputter up the steps. Those beautiful eyes hold relief, and she breathes deep. "What took you so long?"

I shake my head and give the rope a firm tug. Not one minute later, Seward's head pokes out of the darkness. "Stubborn fool held on. Up, you two." Seward clamors up the steps. "Two tugs is the signal from this end. Two tugs on that end and we pull."

I grasp the rope behind Talya and Seward.

Two tugs.

Two tugs.

"Pull!" Seward shouts.

CHAPTER 34

We reel in my father, my thoughts drifting to the man I still don't know.

I'm not certain what's been done to him or how long he's been in the chamber. I only know that in the space since our last meeting, we've changed. My father has always protected me, shielded me. Though he was weak, I depended on him.

Now he depends on me, and I pull all the more.

"He's close." Seward grunts. "A few more ... pulls."

Father breaks from the water, Walery clinging to his back. The boy crawls over Father and stumbles on the subterranean steps before he finds his footing. I look into his eyes — wild, confused — and for a moment he does not move. Then he breaks for the woods.

"Luca! Keep pulling."

I focus on Seward, and together we extract Father from the water like a dead fish. Seward splashes in and hoists him over his shoulder, then carries him onto shore, where my uncle lays him on his side and whacks his back. A few sputters, a gasp, and Father vomits into the grass. Coughs shake his body, and finally he stills, groans, and rolls onto his stomach.

"You couldn't have thought of a different way out?" he pants. "I was not expecting to provide transport for a barnacle."

"No, Brother. I think this is what you deserved."

Talya peeks at me. She can't read them either. They may hate each other, they may love each other. There is no telling from the words.

An hour later we sit around a small fire started by Seward. He breaks out bread and fresh water. "Brother, bringing you to speed is a hopeless task, but Luca, hear this. I have much to tell you about the situation with the Amongus, but first I must tell you of my source. As you know already, I scrounged for a rope. I didn't need to go far, as this lake be roped off. Well, *was* roped off. I wondered who would trouble to ring a lake with cord, and so I walked its perimeter. When I reached the trail on which we arrived, there rested a food pack and a cask of water — I can only imagine meant for you, Brother. I reached down for it, and a woman jumped free of the forest, landing with a scream and quickly grabbin' the provisions.

"But Seward is not long startled, and I quickly overtook her. The Lady of the Lake, she calls herself, and there be a small shelter on the far side cementing her claim. Her friends, they found themselves taken by the pool. Her children as well. The wife of an Amongus, she managed, with luck guiding her feet, to reach this spot. She knows there's nothing for her here, but she watches and listens to those who toss food parcels into the current. Here on this secluded isle, this woman may know more than us all."

Seward gnaws on a hunk of bread, crumbs flying from his mouth as he speaks.

"According to Amongus who travel this path, the Council, too, is in chaos. They be terrified of losing control on the mainland, which, as we saw for ourselves, they already have. All Amongus have been summoned here for immediate departure to Massa's isle. First to drill, then to fight. The war on the Rats has begun."

"War?" Talya asks. "What do you mean, war? What type of war?"

"She did not speak of that, only that the Rats must be annihilated. The water source must be placed under the Nine's control. Only then can they pacify a world gone mad."

I lower my bread and stare into the fire. War. We learned of them in school; wars filled with blood and death. It was hard to believe that in such a short time, the peaceful land of the Toppers could call for such a thing, but I remember Lendi, and the Wishers, and the undone floating in the boat.

"Annihilation." Talya rises and wanders away from the group. She isn't far before she whips around. "They need warning. My family needs warning. There are places they can go. Places none of you know …" She jogs to me. "Luca, my place is with you. But this can't happen." She reaches her hand around the back of my neck. "A loss of the Aquifer? With forewarning, my people might endure. But if the goal is their — our — extermination …" She looks into my eyes, her voice metered and calm. "Take me down. I don't know the way, so you need to take me down. If we reach them before seawater takes them, there is safety for all."

I want Seward to burst in. He always does. Or Father. It is, after all, his advice I came to seek. But the night remains silent — mine alone to fill with words, words that will likely dictate the manner of my undoing.

Tens of thousands of Amongus swarming an isle? How would we get through?

"Of course I'll do it."

She wraps her arms around me, and I stroke her hair. Again, Talya makes lunacy worth the price.

"No, Talya. Luca can't do what you ask." Father's voice strengthens. "He is not the only one who knows the way. Hear me out." He stands. "If what you say is true — if the Amongus are beginning to turn, to question, to doubt, even to hate the Council — if that is their state, they need to see me alive." He stretches his leg and winces. "They have been told I am no more, and that the fresh water supply will soon vanish. They have been lied to and have no hope of survival, save drilling. My life shows them that hope still breathes, that there is another way." He closes his eyes, opens them, and I see Father returning. "Yes, I will go to the dropping point and reveal the Council for the destroyers they are, and perhaps, with fortune, turn the hearts of the Amongus, if they possess them."

I glance at Seward. "But — "

"The mainland needs you, son," Father continues. "You have seen its pain. Spread the word that we are at peace with those below. If New Pert, the beating heart of all surface dwellers, is in chaos, they already know the Council that they trusted is the enemy. Now they must be convinced that those we've hated, the Amongus, could be friends. And if the Amongus can be our allies, then the Rats can be as well." He stares into me with his piercing gaze. "The Fates have determined that I visit the drop once more, and you must convince the world to choose mercy."

"There's just the three of us, Father. How can three do this?"

"Ah, mate. That be the rub." Seward massages his stubble. "Not three. Two."

I stare at Seward, and he continues. "There are many things I could tell you about Massa. But when his mind is fixed, it usually finds a stable place to land. I ... I will see my end at my brother's side. Our destinies be linked. That is" — Seward winces at my father — "if you'll have me."

Father's face softens. "Janus's sons together again. He would be pleased."

"But I'm not pleased!" I jump in front of Father. "I just found you. After all my searching, I found you. I can't lose you again, which I will if you go there. You haven't seen the explosions. There is no way down."

Father strokes my cheek. "Luca, stop. You are not the boy I last saw standing with Lendi." He glances at Talya. "You are a young man. A strong man. If the end of our world tarries, you will make your children proud." He pauses. "Let me make you proud. Remember your own words ... you always told me I would be great again." He grins. "I cannot move as freely as you on the mainland. If either of us is seen, or if we are made leaders by the people, the Council will not hesitate to declare war on Toppers as well as Rats." He pats my shoulder. "No, I must stop the explosions, dismantle the Amongus army, and warn those below. Your job is harder." He pauses. "Convince Toppers suddenly assaulted by their own freedom that riots aren't needed. That the deal has been struck. That they need not war with each other or those below. To that end, Talya, you may be a leader or a martyr. It doesn't really matter which."

I peek at Talya. Father's right. She is proof that we are at peace with the People of the Rock. We must return to the mainland.

Talya draws in a deep breath. She will follow me anywhere, a terrifying and empowering notion.

"And what about those in the middle? The Council of Nine?" Seward asks. "Can we do some undoing of those troublemakers on the way?"

"It wouldn't help. In the minds of the people, the Nine only advise the PM. The focus must be Toppers, Rats, and Amongus. If we can create an alliance, the Council has nothing." Father speaks as though this new alliance has already been formed. The tone settles me.

"We need to get moving," I say. "The only way off this isle lies anchored in the Council's bay, and as the kopter pilot already voiced his feelings, I'd like to be gone by sunrise."

Seward raises his foot to stomp the fire, and pauses. "Lady! Lady of the Lake! I leave you the fire, and half the food."

I see nobody.

"Is she here?" I ask.

"She is." He eases Father to the front. "Now we must go."

We set off through the forest, retracing our steps, with Father in the lead. It relaxes me to follow for a change. Except for turn 114. Father lefts when he should right.

I grab his shirt and pull him in the correct direction.

He frowns at me, and then tousles my hair.

It is good to be a young man.

CHAPTER
35

W hat exactly are we doing again?"
Talya whispers from her position on the beach,
tucked behind a majestic palm. I whisper from the next palm
over.

"We're trying to keep the Toppers from undoing themselves. Father is trying to keep the Amongus from undoing
those below. Easy."

I puff out air and turn back toward the bay. The sun lightens
the east, and the wind off the swells blows cool. It's a beautiful
morning.

Well, it would be.

Arranged on the shore are nine thatched huts, each identical in size and shape. Each has a dock that stretches its finger
out into the bay and a single saline palm stretching mighty
leaves over its roof.

It's hard to believe the evils of the world flow from nine
peaceful huts on an island paradise.

There's no sign of council worry or discontent. No sign of panic.

"Is anybody there?" I mouth the words to Father.

He nods, and points toward a fleet of small boats anchored on the other side of the huts. "Seward and I will take one. You and Talya take another."

"But I don't know how to get to the mainland, or pilot a boat, or — "

Seward slips behind me, and his face hardens. "We both know you are more than you think, young mate. Make southeast. You'll eventually strike a very large piece of land." His tone dries. "That be Australya. As for the how ... I'll key the engine, your job be only to start, full throttle — and again, don't look back."

"Don't look back," I repeat.

"We will see each other again. Pirate's honor." Seward quickly looks away and Father takes his place.

"I love you, son. I am so proud of you. Protect her." He winks toward Talya, who softly hums. "Always, protect her. Well, that and save the world."

I bite my lip. "Don't look back. Protect her. Save the world. Got it."

Father and Seward exchange glances, nod toward me, and pad along the tree line toward the boats. I take Talya's hand and follow.

Their long legs make short work of the distance, and soon Father and Uncle climb into the nearest craft. Seward frantically hops to and fro while Father hauls up the anchor. Seward jumps out and then into another boat, where he repeats his dance.

"Must be ours," I whisper.

"Not likely."

Talya screams. Hands slap over my eyes and mouth, and I'm hoisted from the ground. There is no use fighting.

A distant engine roars to life, and the grip loosens over my arms. I yank my hand free, reach up and tug at the fingers shielding my eyes, and catch a glimpse of two figures, standing in a boat, skipping out of the bay.

Father is free.

The thought brings comforts, but only for a moment. Two figures haul Talya toward the nearest hut.

The hand again blocks my gaze, and I'm carried forward and dropped onto the sand with a thud. I wince and sputter and stare up at five men dressed in white tunics. Though tall and imposing, they peer down at me with kind faces, wondering faces.

"So, you are Luca. Is this correct?"

I say nothing.

"Who were the men?"

They don't know it was Father.

"Amongus, wandering Amongus," I say. "Your jungle is filled with them."

The youngest man glances at the oldest, who continues to speak.

"They wander the jungle ... And their number?"

I think. "How could one know? Fifty? A hundred? Mostly women and children. Little bands here and there. And one great pit of death."

"Reffarian." Another straightens and clenches his teeth. "This cannot go on. The pilot. He warned of — "

"Yes, Kito." Reffarian's gaze never leaves me. "I am well aware of what was spoken, and what tragically has taken place. Luca, how did you come to the PM's isle? Why did you come?"

His voice is hypnotic, and I fight to stay clearheaded. "There aren't many safe places on the mainland. I was holed up on the Swan. There was a kopter, and a seat. I was shoved aboard and ended up here. I've been wandering for a while."

Reffarian kneels before me, as do all the others. "But you didn't wander alone."

"No."

"Who is the girl?"

"Talya."

"Talya," Reffarian repeats. He looks down at the sand, and then up at me. "Do you know why the world is falling apart?"

"Because we thirst."

"No. Water is not the problem. The Rats are. The Rats are the problem. You are old enough to have had your tour. Did you not see the Rats in the museum?"

"I saw the Rat in the museum."

"Was it not frightening?"

"It was not frightening."

"And …" He blinks and squints. "What did you say?"

"I told you the Rat in the museum caused no fear."

"And why not?" asks Reffarian.

Keep them speaking.

"Have you seen her? The museum rat?" I ask.

"A long time ago."

"Then you have not seen her. But what you saw, the creature on display, were you terrified of it? When you were taken from your special room below, when you visited the museum, were you scared of the fact that you are not in control of your life? That a creature like that could turn off your water?" I push up onto my elbows, suddenly unafraid. Suddenly, I am truly Father Massa's son. "Did that frighten you, Reffarian?"

The others peek at their leader, who leans back against the door. "It haunted my dreams."

"I see." My gaze wanders the faces of the Council. "But here in paradise, those dreams can't reach you, and they should not upset you. I will face your nightmares. Now that Father Massa is sadly undone, I must descend next year. How could I do my job filled with fear?"

Reffarian draws in the sand. "Yet I'm told that you have already descended. That you have ascended. That you escaped Mape's hands. And now you are here."

I squint. That smooth voice is probing, reaching. I feel it.

"I told you, I flew here because of the chaos, through no fault of my own. This morning I came across two Amongus near the beach. They said they were leaving, that they were going to find their families. It was my intention to leave you, and the PM, undisturbed. I would appreciate the gift of a boat so that I may not trouble you further. Surely you have important business to complete."

There is a long pause. "Would you consider a trade?"

I look at all these men. They are baffled; I sense it. If I had five dials, all would spin. They have lost control of a world, and now they cannot direct a conversation, especially a conversation with a boy who feels remarkably like a man.

I ponder my reply. I suppose they can debrief me — Father survived the process. I only know I can tell them nothing about the Rats, and I need to find and protect Talya. Father said so.

"I would consider a trade."

"A boat, for the route," Reffarian says. "Surely you understand the precarious position the world finds itself in. One young boy knows the path of exchange. The system of Deliverers was never wise. Fraught with danger, leaving each generation

258

hanging by a thread. Together, we can remedy this, now that your father is gone. Should you ever forget the way, the route would be safe in our hands, a vault of security for the world."

A vault. The thoughts rush in. I see the faces around the fire. I see their bowed heads and clasped hands. I hear each shot, watch them fall.

But you, you must complete your task.

Akov's words.

Protect her. Save the world.

Father's words. Yeah, I'll need a boat.

"I will share the route with you. For a boat, and my companion."

Reffarian glances to his left, and a man rises. He returns quickly with three more men and Talya. She hints a smile and sits stoic at my side.

"Eight?" I ask. "We've been taught you were nine."

"As we are. Discussions can follow, but first let's unburden your mind. Share the route, and then you two are free to stay or leave as you please." He turns toward another council member. "Where's that dolt Fundin?"

Moments later a boy is escorted into the hut. Just a young boy. Maybe twelve, thirteen. His skin is pale, his eyes gray. He opens a book and nervously fidgets with the pages. It's the boy chosen over Walery. I'm certain of it.

"Reffarian, there is no need to obtain the path, not with plans in place ... Luca can't read." Fundin whispers loud enough so that all can hear. "He can't know if he possessed what you seek."

Reffarian lays his hand on Fundin's chest and gestures toward me. "You may begin."

I give Talya's hand a squeeze.

"Left, left ..."

I stand and walk around the hut as I recite, my mind on automatic. I help Talya to her feet. "Right, sharp right ..."

I pause, mouth directions. "Let's see, let's see. Straight away, a long one." I step over Reffarian and open the door. "Left, sharp right. Very sharp right."

Together with Talya, I crisscross the beach, walking the path in the sand. Nine men follow me like obedient chicks, Fundin and his scratching tool leading the way.

"And finally a right."

I help Talya into the boat, and climb in after. "There, you have it. That's the way."

I stare at Reffarian, who stares at Fundin. Fundin's lips move quickly, and minutes later he shuts the book. "It's the same. Exactly. The same route that Massa gave."

Reffarian folds his arms. "We've sent men on that path. They don't return. I do not believe you've been forthright with the truth."

"You expect your men to return from the journey? You saw the gnawing, gnashing creatures that await." I can't help but peek at Talya. Absolutely beautiful. "Surely your parties met destruction."

I glance at the rope threading the metal loop on the prow. Coils fall lifeless onto the deck, where they surround the anchor. Father pulled it up.

"Here it is, something you must know," Reffarian says, and I move to the driver's seat. "You will be surprised to know that there is no PM. That when it comes to the world's citizens, we" — he spreads his arms — "the Council, alone is responsible."

"Yep, I know," I say.

"You know?"

Murmurs ripple on the beach, and Reffarian continues. "Toppers are like sheep without a shepherd, so we must lead with strength. Unfortunately, with Massa undone and you disappearing as you did, they no longer experience the security to which they are accustomed."

"That makes sense. That makes ..." I drop into the captain's seat, and Talya jumps to my side. "I'm sorry, just a little weak from wandering through the jungle." I reach behind my back and feel for the key. Talya straightens and steps between Reffarian and me.

"You and Massa have provided us with inaccurate information, so we have no choice but to forcibly take the Aquifer from the Rats. This plan is underway as we speak."

"Hmm," I say. "Good luck there. I mean, that's a big job."

Reffarian glances around. "Luca, you do not comprehend the gravity of my words, or their implication. The Deliverers are no longer needed. *You* are no longer needed."

"Thank you," I whisper, and bow. "I consider myself dismissed."

I crank the key, and the engine roars to life. The boat spins wildly. Three members of the Council splash into the water and throw themselves at our craft as I turn and grab the wheel, gain control, and power deeper. Two men quickly slip off the hull, and when Talya lugs the anchor toward the prow, and drops it on very unfortunate fingers, we are, at last, free of the Council.

I hear no shouts, but I don't look back.

"They're letting us go, Luca," Talya says. "You were brilliant, but that was too easy."

"I know. If we go to the Isle of Descent and try to warn Etria, they could follow us down. They will think we're going there." I shake my head. "I hope Father and Seward find fortune. But as for us ..." I exit the bay and turn toward New Pert and the world from which we just fled. "We stay our course. We have a different assignment. Nobody of right mind would trail us to the mainland."

Talya nestles down and again starts to hum. That strange melody from long ago.

Why does it calm me this way?

~

The ocean turns restless. So do I.

We make our way southeast, or as near to it as the sun reveals. Talya lies beneath a tarp, her skin glossy red. With her beauty hidden, my thoughts float to my father and Seward and their impossible task.

They'll never break through thousands of Amongus.

At least I should be able to land.

I scan the horizon. We are alone, and I understand Seward's passion for the sea. It accepts your crazy thoughts, reminds you how small you are. But at the same time it surrounds you, protects you. It's everything a good mate should be.

We are alone.

No, we're not.

Bobbing in the distance, I see a white speck. A boat or a trick of the eyes ... I can't tell. I squint, and it's gone, but it festers in my mind. It would be just like the Council to track us.

"I think we're being followed."

Talya breathes deeply. "We probably are."

I bite my lip. Perhaps she has sunstroke. Perhaps she did not hear.

"It looked like a boat, maybe," I say.

She closes her eyes. "I trust you'll take care of it."

Her inappropriately low amount of concern puts my fears to rest. Yes, it must have been a boat. Yes, we are likely being followed. But during the last week, when has this not been true?

I chuckle. Three months ago, I shared my soul with Old Rub, dreading the task that would be mine. Now, I captain a boat on the open sea, sought by the most powerful men in the world, transporting the most beautiful Her I have ever known.

And yet . . .

I miss home. I miss ignorance. I've seen a beauty I can't fathom in the Aquifer, and met a girl who moves my heart. I've rediscovered my father and drawn close to a true friend in Seward. But still I long for the walk up the spiral to my class. I ache for the time when the dials were my biggest fear.

I'm ashamed that I miss my captivity.

The day passes slowly. The white dot makes several appearances, but always it dances in the distance.

Talya sleeps the hours away. Night comes, and she takes the wheel while I close my eyes.

Until the storm.

Pummeling rain, the rarest and most violent of gifts, falls in sheets, and waves swirl, lick, and then slap the boat.

"Capture it!" I throw open the lids of both water casks and lift my cupped hands. Water, for free.

Talya loses her balance and crashes hard against the hull. I stumble to her side, and sweep back her hair.

She laughs, and I stare unblinking into her joy — an unencumbered, unbridled joy that surges through her veins even as we float toward our undoing. There is no fear, only a trust I do not know, one that buoys her through scorching sun and sudden rain.

I want her, but more than that, I want her unconquerable soul.

We ride the crests until the bottoms fall away and we plummet into the sinks. Up and down. Darkness takes us, and southeast disappears. For all I know we are retracing the way we came.

And then, as stealthily as it appeared, the storm vanishes, moving on to bless another sea. Stars appear and our motor makes headway.

"That never happens. Ten full minutes of rain, it never happens ... I no longer know if we're close." I look for clues in the sky. "I don't know how far back the winds set us."

"I think not too far." Talya points at the water, her face blank, her mirth absent. Floating toward us, a flotilla of wood. Decking, drift, mast ...

And more bodies.

The characteristic dreadlocks of New Pert float aimlessly in the water. Men and women — mostly men — swell by. They aren't Amongus. They are us: Doctors, teachers, neighbors. New Pertians are destroying each other.

"I want to put ashore in Glaugood," I say. "It's a deep mine. Nothing's there. Nobody is there. We should be able to set out unnoticed."

Talya looks up from the water. "Set out to where?"

I wait a moment too long to answer, and she turns. My shoulders slump. Talya's great man has no idea what he's doing.

Daylight and the shoreline arrive together. I hold our distance, beyond the reef, and turn south. I don't know exactly where we are but I know we're close to home, and I don't want to risk another arrow-pierced welcome. My gaze traces the shoreline. I puff out air. Fortune is our companion. To the left rises the city of New Pert.

Further on, the arch remnant of Glaugood. I quiet the engine and slowly patter toward the mine and the sea opening I first discovered with Seward.

"This mine is submerged, but it's filled with caves. Empty, except for one," I say. "It's the perfect place to hide a boat and decide what to do ... Oh."

It is far from empty. Faces peer out from every cave. Families, many I'd seen in my previous life. The mine is *filled*. We float into the pit's heart, and I spin a slow circle. Pertians stare down in silence. I duck into a windcoat and pull the hood over my head.

"Who are they?" Talya asks.

I shake my head and kill the engine. "Hallo! What brings you all to this place?"

From a cave toward the top, a raspy voice calls, "You don't know? The city is taken. Savages roam."

"But can this be safe?" I ask.

"Safe no longer exists, but we have nothing they want. They demand all our water, our food."

"So if you hunger and thirst, why retreat to this desolate place?"

The voice falls silent.

"They're waiting for their end, Luca." Talya plops down. "These caves ... can't you smell it? They are homes and tombs. These people are refugees. They have no place to go."

What is happening? A short time ago, I sat in school, staring at the dial in my eagle. I was content, sort of. Content and fooled.

"The Amongus," I ask the voice. "They were barricaded near the Swan."

"Their walls fell." A young woman, gaunt and tired, appears at the front of her cave, a limp child in her arms. "The last I heard, only the museum is in their hands."

I think of the family on top of the marble building, waiting for the next transport to safety. Are they still waiting?

"The savages you spoke of..." Talya says. "Do they meet?"

"They have formed the 'true' council. In the amphitheater," a woman answers. "From there, my eldest son and his friends spew anarchy. In the months that remain, they will no longer be controlled. They mock their dials and broadcast their anger across the world. They demand to speak with the PM."

I can no longer hold it in. "People, you have more than months! Rats will never turn off your flow."

There is no response.

"They are resigned. They can't believe you. I think—I fear—part of them doesn't want to," whispers Talya.

I tighten my jaw. "The amphitheater. We need to get there. But not through the inlet. I can't be sure Lendi will be there to help us this time. But before we go..."

I draw our boat near the cave with the woman and child. "Have you any use for wood? Warmth for your son, perhaps?"

She glances around. "Always, wood is needed."

I unlash the caskets from the hull, and carefully reach them to the woman. I glance around. "Enjoy the fire."

She lays down her child, and grasps the small barrel. She cocks her head, peers inside it and her eyes grow large, a tear tracing down her cheek. Talya hands her the second casket, and I fire up the engine and motor back into open water.

It's time to return home.

CHAPTER
36

We arrive at the Shallows and float quietly toward the Graveyard.

"This was my home. Where I lived with Father." I point at the heap of charred wood. "This was safety. It was a nice shanty, one of the nicest on the shore."

I steer toward the stones. "Rub! Old Rub! Are you here?"

She quickly surfaces and paddles toward the boat. I reach over and stroke her shell. "I'm sorry it all came to this. Stay in the water. Stay low."

"What is this creature?" Talya gazes in wonder, and slowly stretches out her hand.

"A guinea turtle. But Old Rub is more friend than turtle. She alone listened when Father was so far away." I pat her shell, and she dives, taking a piece of me with her. It's a good thing — I know that being far from me at this moment is a good thing — but floating in the Graveyard with Rub is the first normal I feel in a long time.

"There." I wipe my eyes. "The dock where Father sat. I'm surprised it didn't burn. Walery did quite a job."

"I'm sorry. I had no choice in the matter."

Talya screams and I stumble over an empty water cask, ending up on my backside on the deck.

I scramble to my feet, and Walery slowly rolls out from beneath a balled-up sail. He is not the controlled boy I first met, or the dazed one I saw with Father beneath the lake. He is merely a boy, full of fear and sadness and desperation.

"You've been there the entire trip." I shake my head. "How'd you know I'd take this boat?"

He groans and pulls himself up, his body soaked and shivering; the inch of water that sloshes around the deck has taken its toll. "I followed you down from the lake, and watched the man you call Seward prepare this boat. I watched Massa pull up anchor."

"You were on the beach when we were taken," Talya says.

I frown. "You could have taken the boat when we were in their huts, but you waited for us?"

"You freed Massa. I figured if you could find him, you could think your way off the isle." He glances at the house and sighs. "What you spoke of me was true. It's my fault the house was burned. It's my fault you were pursued below. I ate all the food, drank all the water meant for Massa during his deprivation. I'm responsible for more than you know."

"But you waited." Talya walks over and helps Walery to his feet, and then gentles him down on a seat. "And that makes up for it all."

It is Walery's turn to frown. "No. I haven't made up for anything. Not yet. But perhaps I can. I heard you need to reach the amphitheater."

I shrug and raise my hands. "That's the plan. We'll go at night."

"Certainly. That's up to you. But at this point, I think I could be of service, and from what I've heard, what I've seen, traveling New Pert by night is no safer than beneath the sun." He stares at me intently. "I believe you can reach your goal, if you travel ... differently. Remember, I was taught some things you perhaps were not."

Don't trust him.

The Voice inside strikes clear, and I glance at Talya. Whoever owns these strange words is becoming more insistent. Still, they have never led me astray.

"Luca's not too proud to accept help." Talya cocks her head. "Speak on, Walery."

"Uh, hold up. I, I mean we, won't need his help. Not this time."

"Luca, we need everyone's help."

Walery points to what's left of the shanty. "It's the least I can do."

Talya's face shines, and it's not the sunburn. She's convinced, settled. She knows nothing about the route to the amphitheater. She has never walked these streets before. But she believes Walery, trusts him completely.

Worse than that, she believes him over me. A new feeling creeps in. It is not rage or desire. It isn't fear or pride. It's a twisted joining of them all.

Wren once told me a story where a king died bearing all those feelings. She called this wicked combination jealousy.

Jealousy.

"Talya, do you trust me?" I whisper, while Walery yawns and stretches. "If you do, we can't listen to him."

Her hands fly to her hips. "You can't do everything alone."

"I haven't done anything alone! I've always had Father or Seward, and now I have you. I have a feeling about this. I heard."

"You heard."

"Yes. And I trust the Voice."

"I heard no voice," she snaps.

"Do you ever hear it?"

Talya's foot begins an angry tap. "Are you suggesting that I don't know what to do?"

"No! I'm admitting that I never know ... That is, I rarely know without help, but this time I do know without help. Unless you call the Voice help, which it is ... Oh, Talya."

I have no more words. I can't convince her. I tie the boat to the dock and leap out, reach back to help her. She looks at my hand, turns away, and assists Walery onto the dock.

"Thank you, Talya," he says. "Allow me to help you."

I watch Walery holding my Talya's hand and wish he were still beneath a lake.

"Okay, Walery," I say, lifting my hands in a flourish. "What's your grand idea?"

"We follow the diverters."

"The diverters?"

"How to explain this for simple minds ... Water rises from the Aquifer to massive pump lines that use pressure and suction to draw moisture the final feet to the surface. This mechanism is all the work of the Rats."

Simple minds? This simple mind has seen it in action!

"But once it reaches the last ten feet, it must be distributed throughout our inhabited world. That is the job of the diverters — huge networks of flexible piping that run below ground like octopus tentacles. The diverters split into thin fingers that carry water to individual gathering stations, but before they separate, those large diverters transport water throughout each major city."

"That was a very clear explanation," Talya says.

"Thank you."

I can't believe this!

Walery continues. "Care and maintenance of the diverters is Topper work, highly specialized and secretive. The average citizen is not told how to access the network."

I fold my arms. "And let me guess; you know the way to the diverters."

"Well," he says, "it's not as glamorous as your memorized route, but yes, all those taught below were shown the way."

Talya gazes at me triumphantly. I know that look from Lendi: I told you so.

"And these diverters lead from here to this amphitheater?" she asks.

Walery massages the back of his neck. "Not exactly. Entering the network involves a hike, but once we're safely there, you can follow the main line all the way to downtown. You'll be walking right under the mob's feet until you exit the network beneath the hospital. The final stretch into the amphitheater will prove rough, but I think your odds of success are much greater than if you traversed the entire route on the surface."

Don't trust him. Stay on top. Leave Talya if you must. She's in no danger.

But Walery's plan sounds perfect, saving us miles of walking through chaos-filled streets. And the hospital? It's only a few blocks from our destination.

I have to admit the idea is brilliant, and for the first time I push back against the Voice. No advice telling me to leave Talya has any quarter in this head.

"Walery," I say, "I misjudged you. Lead on."

"Okay." He stretches and exhales. "We'll be quite visible until we get out of town. That means we have to hug the shore. Speak to nobody. Glance at nobody."

"How do you know to avoid these things?" I ask.

He pauses. "I was here days ago, before I ... joined your father. We'll be fine. I'm a child, you're a boy. We're not expected to have anything of value. We should be able to slip through to the diverter entrance."

I am a young man, a Sixteen! I wait for Talya to correct him, to insist I'm more than a mere boy. She doesn't.

I don't know how to make things right with her. She's still angry; it's all over her face. And I'm doing what she wants.

Now I have more questions for Father, questions about girls and the third type of love.

Walery leads to our gate and pushes through. Talya, close behind him, pays no heed to me. I could paddle out to Old Rub for all she cares. I sigh and dash after them, peeking first to my left, then my right. Outside my home, it's still — too still for words of chaos to be true.

"Move quickly," Walery hisses. "Follow me."

The houses along Shore Way are burned or deserted; at least I think they are. Once, I catch a pair of eyes peering out from behind Gullier's wall, but it can't be him — our neighbor was always kind to me and he'd at least say hello. I hope he still would.

It's so quiet. The normal bustle of people visiting the shore and heading to the wharf has been muted. As have the birds.

None fly, none sing. Instead, there is only the crunch of broken glass and broken stones beneath our feet.

The entire sector has fled.

They're probably all hiding in Glaugood.

Walery jogs away from downtown, always checking behind him. But there is nobody following besides us, and after half an hour of hugging the shore, I tire of worrying.

That's when Talya pops back into my mind. She's beautiful when she moves; beautiful when she's irritated. I try to think of words that can repair us.

"It looks like this is going to work out," I call. "You know, I miss talking to you. How long until you like me again?"

"I like you now." She glances over her shoulder. "That doesn't mean I enjoy your company."

That makes no sense. Absolutely no —

Engines approach.

Walery veers left and ducks behind a half-standing brick wall. Talya follows. I just slip in behind them before motors rev, and unrestrained voices fill the air.

I peek out from behind the barricade. Twenty, maybe thirty riders hop off their cycles. One screams down the streets.

"Time to give tribute to the New Council!" He laughs. "Bring out your water! Your rations! We have no desire to harm you."

Slowly, people emerge onto the street. From within destroyed homes, beneath ripped tents, they appear carrying cups and flasks and pitchers of water, and lay them at the riders' feet.

"Small gifts do not please." The screamer reaches down, raises a cup to his lips and drains it. He flings it to the ground, where it bounces at the feet of a young boy. "Next week I want your entire quota!"

"But my mother, my sister — "

"Oh, were they thirsty?" he mimics, his face turning dark. "Perhaps a smaller family would not feel the need to withhold."

The boy runs back into his home, while a second rider pours the other containers into a jug and slings it over his back.

"This is most displeasing. Should your sector not fill three jugs? We will return!"

They roar off into the distance.

I look at Talya, who returns the glance. We've been watched the entire time. People are everywhere. Terrified people.

"How far to the diverter entry point?" I ask.

Walery wipes his brow. "Less than a mile."

We run out from behind the wall, eager to escape the city. Fewer people mean fewer roving bands demanding tribute.

We sprint along the curb, and the number of shanties lessens. Those we do see are in better shape, some completely intact. New walls surround many of these dwellings — no doubt hasty attempts at protection.

"Here!" Walery points. We pass Klubarth's mansion, the largest residence on the mainland, and duck into Pert Clinic 23. I've been here before, when I was young and broke my wrist. Walery races past overturned chairs to the elevator and slams the up button.

"This better still be operational," he says.

"You hit the wrong button." I reach out to correct his error, but Walery catches my wrist. "Watch."

The door opens and we step on.

Walery shields the button panel, and when he steps away, six numbers are lit.

"Six numbers pressed in the correct sequence makes up ..."

We slowly drop into the earth.

"Go down." Walery grins and folds his arms.

The doors open and we step out.

I can't believe it. A network of tubes, five feet in diameter, crisscrosses the ceiling. The tentacles stretch in every direction. The rush of water is deafening.

"This is one of the main stations," Wallery shouts. "Fresh water collects here, changes directions, and flows out again within the most extravagant series of tunnels ever devised."

I peek at Talya, who has perfected the eye roll since surfacing. Clearly she thinks the tunnels of the Rats far superior.

I rub my forehead and remember the face of the young boy who brought the rider his meager ration. He stood one mile from this water exchange. I glance up. So much water. So free. Never in danger of running dry, until now, and that only because the Nine are destroying what they're desperate to obtain.

"This one." Walery points at the largest tube, painted bright yellow. "This is your road to the downtown hospital. Once you're there, get on the elevator. The doors will open on the hospital's top floor. From there, I wish you well."

"Thank you." Talya hugs Walery. "How can we thank you?"

Walery bites his lip. "You can't."

She steps back and jabs me with her elbow.

"Oh, yeah. Thanks, Walery."

He bows and turns back toward the elevator.

"Where will you go?"

"I need to … comfort the remainder of my family. They are sheep without a shepherd." His young features harden. "We both have our journeys."

The door closes on Walery, and Talya and I are alone beneath the pipes. She reaches out her hand, I take it, and we walk toward the hospital. It appears she now enjoys my company.

CHAPTER 37

There is no way to be heard, not with a torrent rushing feet above our mouths, and we wander silently through the cut keeping our eyes fixed on the pipe overhead. Orbs illumine the length of the walk, and I wonder who maintains them. I didn't know so many orbs existed in all the earth.

The pipe, the only yellow tube in a snake's nest of red, twists and loops, finally extracting itself from the others and alone leading us through a narrow tunnel. The rush of water is less pronounced, and I'd talk to Talya, if I knew what to say. But she is far from me, preparing, as I often saw Father prepare for the descent. She knows something — I can feel it — and I don't wish her to share the thoughts that occupy her mind.

My thoughts are likely more trivial. I know how far it is from my home to downtown: twenty minutes, tops. Hours later, we still wander.

"I need to rest." Talya releases my hand and sits. Only then do I hear her labored breath.

I ease down beside her.

"What were you doing the day before I appeared below? What were you thinking about?"

She gently scrapes the toe of her boot against the floor. "How to get out of my planned union." She glances at me. "But an escape to the surface of the world wasn't on my mind."

"Suppose not."

She leans her head on my shoulder. "But you were ... on my mind."

I don't understand and say nothing, which seems a very good thing to do with Talya.

"Massa didn't arrive on time. There was talk, there were stories, of you. And I wondered if you remembered me. Faint memories, good memories. I wondered if I'd see you again, and if you would know me, and then, there you were, your hand on my waist."

"Sorry."

"And I knew," she says.

"You knew what?"

"That we who began together would end together. I knew."

Did hours pass? Did I sit up a little straighter at her words? Her certainty strengthens me.

I love you. That's what I want to say.

"Are you ready?" That's what I say.

Together we rise and push on until the pipe disappears upward, and the shaft ends abruptly in front of an elevator door.

"There is no down arrow. I can't mess up the direction," I say, and reach for the button.

Talya hesitates, grabs my forearm, and I see her eyes glaze.

"I'm a long way from home. There's so much pain here. So much."

"I didn't know the half of it, or I wouldn't have —"

Her eyes close and she grabs my shoulders, kisses me full and deep. I stare cross-eyed at her face, her lips gracing mine. I've never analyzed a kiss before, certainly never a real one. Am I supposed to shut my eyes? If so, I don't want to. I want to stand and watch and try to remember my name.

She gently pulls away. "Luca."

That's it!

"This is where we need to be." She faces the elevator and breathes deeply. "Let's do this."

I reach forward and press the up button. The doors slide open —

"Hello, Luca."

Reffarian and three members of the Council stand fixed and somber. They look weary, and I don't think their presence here was part of their plan.

Reffarian's voice is no longer confident, and across his forehead traces a trickle of dried blood. The mainland has not been good to him either.

Mape steps from the rear to shield the Council. I can't imagine he considers us a physical threat.

"Such a trusting soul, Luca," Reffarian growls as Mape grabs our arms and pulls us inside. "Walery has finally proven useful. His time with Massa seems to have helped him see the error of his ways. Speaking of your father ..." He yanks me away from Mape and stares at me with those hypnotic eyes. "Where is Massa? He was in the first boat that left the isle, was he not? You can imagine how important it is that your father remains undone."

I glance at Mape, who frowns. He's thinking, even confused. I see it.

You just found out you were lied to, didn't you? You just found out my father is alive.

Suddenly, I'm not afraid. Talya reaches over and squeezes my hand.

"I shouldn't have doubted," she whispers. "I'm so sorry."

"Me too." I turn to Reffarian. "I don't keep track of Father. Have you lost him?"

Mape backhands me across the face, and I fall to the floor. I stand slowly. "So violent. So pathetic." I turn to Reffarian. "His staged undoing has ended up to be your own. Yet, it is not too late. I would think that if the people saw Massa, it would comfort them. If they saw him, they would have no reason to riot. They would know that all was well, that the Deliverer would continue to make the exchange on their behalf. That I would one day take his place. You would have your precious control again."

"Not of the Rats!" Reffarian hisses. "I would not control the Rats. For too long they have controlled us. That will end. One way or another, their existence will end. I assure you that if Massa went to warn them, he will not succeed. The Isle of Descent is a fortress. Telling me his location is the surest way to save him."

I think. *No. Another lie.*

"If it is a fortress, you have nothing to worry about from him or me. You will conquer the Rats and control the water." I glance around. "Are we going to stay in this elevator forever?"

Reffarian pounds the wall. "I will ask once more! Where is Massa?"

"He abandoned me. I don't care."

The Council looks at each other.

Mape's jaw tightens. "Do you want me to deal with these two?"

"Why do you listen to them, Mape?" I ask. "They have misled you in every way." I pause. "Tell me, where is your family?"

Reffarian slaps his hand over my mouth. "Yes! Undo them! Do it now!"

Talya drops into the corner, momentarily out of Mape's reach. "You were told they would be safe. You were told they would be flown to the PM's isle. You were told — "

"Silence!" Another lunges toward Talya, misses, and crashes to the floor.

Mape pauses. "My family ... they are safe on the isle."

I glance at Talya and kick Reffarian with all I have. My boot thunks his shin, and his hand flies off my mouth. "Safe? They are lying at the bottom of a pit. I saw it. The site of undoing for thousands of Amongus's wives and children. Your men were sent to the beach, your families to their doom. Listen to me!"

With that, all three council members dive toward me. I crumple to the floor, tensing for blows that never arrive.

I peek up. Mape sits on Reffarian, his hands driving the other men's chests into the floor. I've been on the bottom of that move, and can almost feel the Council's pain.

Mape's eyes are wild. "Talk, Wise Ones. Does Luca speak the truth?"

"Of course not!" Reffarian bellows. "Off me. Now!"

Mape peeks over his shoulder at Talya, and then to me. "Massa never lied to me. Never. I nearly stole his life on two occasions, but he was truthful. Luca, where is my family?"

I recount the story of the kopter ride. Of the pilot's instructions and the search to save Father. Finally, I tell him of the pit and the smell.

Mape shakes his head. "It cannot be."

"That's because it isn't!" Reffarian shrieks.

"Do you know Connyr's family?" Talya rises from the corner. "Meline and her two children came with us to the isle. And the pilot, Haifer, do you know of him?"

His face twitches. "Connyr is a mate."

"Connyr is undone," I say. "I — well, Seward — secured his family a spot on the last kopter out of New Pert. The last one. Do you really believe there are thousands of dwellings on the PM's isle, prepared as reward for your families? Do your superiors generally lead with gratitude? What are you thinking?"

Mape looks down at the struggling tunics, but speaks to me. "Why are you here?"

"Because we can't let New Pert destroy itself." I think what to share, what to hold. I wink at Talya. "Maybe if they see me, they will know that a Deliverer lives. Maybe the sight will stay this insanity."

"You would risk entering the amphitheater?" Muscles in Mape's face relax. "Though for you it will mean the end of all things."

I swallow hard and nod. "If we can reach it, we'll tell the people that all is well, and that Watchers are no longer the enemy. We'll tell them ..." I stare at Reffarian, reach forward and grab his locks. I tilt his head until his gaze lands on Talya. "We'll tell them that the Rats are beautiful and never have been our foe."

Talya grins and waves at Reffarian.

I continue. "And we'll tell them that this Council has pit us against each other for far too long."

Mape nods. "You will be undone as soon as you enter. The scene in the amphitheater is beyond words. The people there

281

... Reason finds no quarter within those walls." He speaks quietly. "They undo and destroy and call it freedom, and broadcast their deeds. I have watched it from afar."

"What else can I do?" I ask.

Mape stares at me, a look of admiration in his eyes. There is no hate. No anger. My enemy is no more.

"Open the elevator door, Luca."

I reach up and fumble for the button; doors slide open, and Mape flings Reffarian and his fellow Council members into the tunnel. Their bodies thud and roll — such is the power of an Amongus.

Mape breathes deeply. "Now we go up."

"We?" Talya asks.

Mape presses the button for floor eight, and the elevator jerks and rises. "If my wife is no more, if my children are no more, then this is the end Sonja would have wished for me. She is — she was — good of heart."

His face tightens. "You will reach the amphitheater. I will see to that. I cannot promise you a return."

"Thank you." Talya hugs Mape, who stares at her, his arms pinned at his side.

He glances at me. "She is not from around here."

"No." I pat his back. "You met once before, when we came up from the tunnel with Phale. Mape, meet a Rat."

His eyes widen, and then he looks away. "You are the second I've seen.

"I found the first lost at sea." Mape sighs. "It was my first assignment. I couldn't believe her to be a Rat. She was ... lovely. I thought her adrift from the north. Amerika, maybe Amerika."

Elevator doors slide open, and we exit to an empty room.

"But the order said it was Massa's wife. They said their union was unnatural, and she needed to be undone. After seeing her, I could barely believe it." Mape freezes in the doorway. "After the deed, she haunted my sleep. I heard Alaya. She weighed heavy on me for years, until the haunting grew unbearable. I thought if I hauled her up and saw the creature she'd become, her face would disappear from my dreams. All those months with Jasper . . . I finally saw the remains and convinced myself that my memory of her beauty was mistaken. But that was two years ago, and still the dreams remain. I now see why." Mape's voice cracks. "I'm sorry, Luca."

Did an Amongus just offer a confession?

Mape steps inside the elevator, rares back, and punches through the button pad. A shower of sparks covers him, and he emerges brushing his sleeves. "We won't be followed from below."

Mape destroyed my mother; now he's my protector. I stare at him and shake my head. I should feel something. Rage? Perhaps loss? I have felt these emotions my entire life. But now when the dials mean nothing and wrinkles can flow freely, I'm numb.

Talya is not. She leans over to me. "Are you sure we can trust him?"

"There's no way you could be sure," Mape answers, stretching out the fingers in his fist. "But you have my word. As surely as I have breath, you will reach the amphitheater."

"Good enough for me," I say.

We work our way through deserted halls. Rooms stand stripped and gutted. Beds, blankets — all have been removed.

"They used the bedside tables for firewood," Mape says. "The sick? I will not speak of their end. Now nothing remains, nobody remains. The doors are sealed from the outside."

Though the building stands empty, I walk gingerly down

the stairwell, careful to silence each footfall. Mape shows no caution and leaps down steps in twos. I marvel at his driven nature, every ounce fixed on good. How different the shape of our lives if we'd known, from the beginning, the depth of the Council's treachery.

Mape bursts into the lobby and marches to the entrance. Talya and I join him and together stare out through the broken glass of the hospital's revolving door.

We, uh, just might need another plan …

On the street, it looks like Water Day on Freemanl. People screaming, running. But it's not the same. This is no celebration; this scene is horror unrestrained, filled with jostling and fighting, pursuit and surrender. Small groups of men hoist unfortunate others on their backs. Some of the captured go quietly, others with shrieks. The victims' offences are not clear.

I turn to Mape, who still sports his Amongus uniform, then glance at Talya, with her fair skin and telltale hair, and think of myself, the newly named Deliverer whom everyone has been taught to recognize. It's hard to imagine a trio more unable to blend in.

"Search the floor," I say. "Employee cubicles, especially lockers. We need something different to wear. Something must be left."

Ten minutes later, Talya returns looking adorable in her powder-blue scrubs. In her hands lie two more sets. She drops them on the floor and steps back. "I can hardly stomach the smell …"

"Where'd you find them?" I gag and pick up a shirt and loose-fitting pants.

She bows her head. "Their owners no longer need them."

~

"Three blocks," Mape whispers. "Down this street. How fast do you run?"

I wince. "I don't think we'll make it. Too bad those diverter tunnels didn't go all the way... Wait. The tunnel. The Birthing Tunnel. I don't know if people are inside, but it winds into the amphitheater from the Swan, and there was little activity near the inlet the last time around. Its entrance would be three blocks in the other direction, but once we reach it the way in might be clear."

"There is no good way into that pit, and only painful ways out," says Mape. "But we will use the tunnel."

Mape cups his hands and stiffly bows. I accept the gesture, then turn to Talya and do the same — only she places her hands in mine. Mape frowns.

"Customs are different below." I force a smile. "Listen, Mape, should you make it through the streets, give no thought to me — just stop the drilling. Do whatever you must to make them stop. I've felt the tremors from below. You're drilling will not reach the Aquifer, it will destroy it, and with it vanishes the only hope of two worlds."

Mape's jaw sets, and he nods. "I will consider it my last assignment. Now" — he stiffens — "to the amphitheater."

CHAPTER 38

The next thirty minutes vanish in a whir of shouts and the whiz of stones. As the head Amongus in New Pert, Mape is too well known, and rocks strike our shoulders, ricochet about our feet.

Talya urges me forward, and though I should focus on our flight, I take frequent glances back to where Mape pulls up the rear. His footsteps land heavy and uneven as he dodges left and right, plucking well-aimed chunks of concrete out of the air.

"No good," he says, and my feet lose contact with earth. I'm caught up in the crook of Mape's arm, while Talya is hoisted in the other. Between us, an Amongus covered with blood.

How many blows he must have absorbed! Yet he churns ahead and doubles our speed. We weave through back roads I've never traveled, snaking ever nearer the Swan Inlet.

Rocks no longer fall, and the shouts disappear. Something has happened. The mob no longer pursues. But Mape, he gasps for breath in uneven bursts.

"Duck in there!"

A familiar voice. I know it. I obey it.

Lendi overtakes us, and my mate shoves us into an alley. I want to shout, to embrace my friend, but agony distorts his face and I hold my joy in check.

Mape gently lays Talya and me to the ground and crumples against the wall. Only then do I see the extent of his wounds.

Blood oozes from his face and torso. Crimson shreds are all that remain of his powder-blue scrubs. And an arrow plunges deep into his right thigh.

An arrow?

Talya already attends to the pierce. "What is the shape of the tip? If I pull, will I leave it behind?"

"You must try." Mape braces himself, grabbing a series of pipes, and gives a tight-lipped nod.

Talya yanks, and both shaft and tip pull free, igniting a fresh weep of blood from the wound. She wipes the tip on her scrub. "It's out. This barb was not meant to kill."

"Yes, it was," Lendi says.

I gaze at my mate, a bow across his back, a quiver strung at his side. His hands red with death.

"Lendi, what have you done?" I reach out and take his hands. He shakes and stares down at his palms.

"I'm not worthy of that name anymore. I don't know who I am." He faces Mape. "My four mates and I chased you. It was me who loosed that arrow. I ... I didn't know you were helping Luca. I still don't understand. How are you together?"

I wave off the question. The story is simply too much to tell and time is too short. "We learned of arrows in school," I say, "but they were supposed to have disappeared centuries ago. Where do these weapons come from?"

Mape breathes deep. "Oh, Luca. Hidden behind the walls of their homes, families hide tools of rage beyond what you can imagine. This riot did not begin with Massa or you. It has been festering, waiting for an opportunity. Beneath the noses of our dials, freedom has been biding its time." He closes his eyes. "But now that it's been loosed, we find it has no master." He winces and clutches at his leg. "People were not meant to be controlled. Their fear now fuels their anger." Mape looks from the sky to Lendi. "Who could blame them?"

I peek out at the street. Distant men and distant shouts, but nothing near. "We're only a block from the tunnel's entrance. I can hear the crowd. Stay here, Mape. You've done your job. I need you to begin that last assignment."

I turn to Lendi. "I don't care what your hands have done. Protect this man, as he has protected me. Please, there's no time to explain—"

"No." Mape looks at his wound. "I need saltwater. I need to kill the infection or I will not reach the isle to complete the task. We run."

He bursts free of the alley, and we follow. For a wounded man, he runs with strength and abandon, and soon pulls away, staggering onto the sand and throwing himself face-first into the Swan. Gentle swells of water wash red around him.

I splash in, muscle him onto his back. "We can't leave you! Help me, Lendi!"

"You must." Mape's voice is soft, gentle, and he smiles. *Mape smiles.* "Thank you for the gift."

"An arrow in the leg." I wince at the wound. "Not a very thoughtful gift."

"No, Luca. Today ... today, I feel. Never lose that in yourself."

"Come out, Mape." Talya glances around. "Please let me tend to your injuries."

"Good-bye, Luca."

Mape begins a slow swim toward the deep center of the inlet. His stroke is metered, controlled, at peace. Boats patrolling the Swan fire up engines, surge nearer.

They'll know him. This is his end.

"Come, Luca! Lendi!" Talya calls. "He said we would reach the amphitheater. Don't make his sacrifice in vain. Into the tunnel."

"Uh, mate." A darkness shades Lendi's face. "You don't want to go in there..."

"You're right, but it is my choice, with or without your aid." I place my hand on his shoulder. "Though I'd much rather have you at my side."

Lendi draws a deep breath. "Yes," he whispers. "Yes. I can't undo all I've done, but I swear, mate, both you and the girl will reach the amphitheater alive. I'll cover your flight from the beach. Now go!"

I splash toward the tunnel's mouth, pause to watch three boats converge on Mape, and run. I cannot witness the rest.

Inside the cool of the tunnel, I stumble into Talya's arms and together we cry. Every good person we meet ends up undone.

"Talya, have I loved you well? Have I loved anybody well?"

She straightens, and then grasps my shoulders and straightens me. "You are a great man, and you are about to be great again."

A great man...

The words, mine for Father, hers for me, give strength to my feet. My legs firm, my heart quickens, and my face sets. "We really shouldn't have made it this far."

"No."

And then I hear it. From deep within the tunnel, a chant that sinks my stomach.

"Burn. Burn. Burn!"

Lendi races nearer. "The rest of my band is close behind. There is no returning now. Onward. Deeper into the — "

He staggers, slumps to his knees, where I catch him in my arms and feel the shaft protruding from his back.

"No!"

"Luca, I'm so sorry for everything."

I rock him gently. "No, I lied to you about the books, I lied ..."

"Yeah, you did do that." His voice is faint, and he rests his head on my shoulder.

"You're my mate. You'll always be my mate." Tears fall down my cheeks, burn hot and fierce on my face.

"Promise me," Lendi whispers. "When it's over ..." He cups one palm, coughs hard, and falls limp. "Wash this blood from my hands."

"I promise. I promise."

He inhales short and sharp, and then Lendi breathes no more.

An arrow flies over our heads, piercing the tunnel wall. A quick glance at Talya, and she hauls me to my feet even as Lendi slumps onto the ground. We dash toward the amphitheater, the chant strengthening and my body weakening in equal measure. Lendi is gone, and rage fills me. I want to undo something, someone. Such venom! I've never felt it before. What will I do when I emerge in front of an angry mob fifty thousand strong? What words of peace can I speak?

Don't worry what you'll say.

I can no longer endure the Voice.

"Who are you?" I scream, spinning and clasping my head.

Talya gently lays her hand on my shoulder, and I pull free. "No! Did you not just see what happened? How many must lose their lives for me? Lendi is gone!" I cover my ears and yell. "Identify or leave me now!"

I listen, and my thoughts fall quiet.

On my right is the place where it all began, where I was first told Father was undone. I stare ahead into the light. "Sanity is slipping. Words find home in my thoughts, guiding me, directing me, and I don't know who speaks. I can't bear it!" I stare wild-eyed at Talya.

"No, you can't. This is all too much for one," she whispers, and strokes my hair. "That's why you have me."

I thunk my head against the tunnel. "And if I am losing my mind ..."

"It's okay, because you won't lose me." She kisses me gently on the cheek.

She can say that, but she doesn't know. In a world gone mad, one arrow and she, too, will be lost. I take her hand, lift it to my lips, and release my first initiated kiss. I even close my eyes. My body warms, and my heartbeat races. I feel whole. Hopeless, but whole.

Together, we will meet the end.

"Your purpose awaits," Talya whispers.

We march hand in hand into the light of the amphitheater, and my breath catches in my throat.

My chair is occupied by a man I can't forget; his face is etched into my memory. He watched as we took his family's place on the last kopter to leave the museum.

It's the Amongus.

In front of him, nine men pace the sacred stage, lifting their hands, whipping the crowd into a frenzy.

"Burn! Burn! Burn!"

And in front of them, a boy, just a small boy, drowning in my father's Deliverer garments.

Walery.

A cameraman notices us first, and soon our faces fill the big screen. The crowd reacts — their chant falls uneven and then quiets. The "council," sensing the lull, dances all the more, but to no avail. Finally, they turn. To a man, they stumble backward, and soon the amphitheater comes alive with murmurs and whistles and uncertain chatter.

"Luca."

My name rings from every corner of the theater.

"Let me hear your righteous anger!" Walery screams into the confusion, but my presence has turned the tide, and finally he too spins. His arms flop lifeless at his side.

I don't know what to say, to do. And then it's clear.

I stride forward and place my hand on the Amongus's head. I keep walking toward Walery, and as I reach him I rip my father's robe off his frame and wrap it around my shoulders. My arms rise across my chest. I offer the sign of peace, the one that once brought cries of joy.

From the left, the chant begins. "Burn. Burn."

Soon the amphitheater soars with hate. I know what has happened: The man in the chair has been judged. Perhaps I have too.

"Good citizens!" Walery raises his hands and quiets the crowd. "Your wish is my command. For too long, this Watcher and his kind have controlled us. But today is a new day!"

He points to his left at a raging fire, the fuel for which I do not wish to have explained. Thousands of dials glow red at the base of the blaze, and around it cameras move, fighting for position, broadcasting the carnage to receptor stations throughout the world. Nine pairs of hands grab the Amongus and slowly drag him toward his undoing.

"Innocent!" I yell. "I declare this man innocent! It has always been mine to condemn, mine and Massa's alone. For the first time a Deliverer will be allowed that right. How can you turn so quickly? How can you become as violent as those who have held you prisoner all these years?"

"Innocent?" Walery appeals to the crowd. "Think of the numbers undone merely for feeling, for speaking. Think of your fathers, your daughters! How can any sane boy declare one of them innocent?"

"Were they not under orders?" I yell. "They questioned what they were told no more than you questioned their authority over you. But their cruelty has ended. They understand! The Amongus are friends."

"Friends." Walery circles me. "How many in this theater have known one debriefed or undone?"

The crowd explodes.

"We have all been deceived," Walery says. "I have seen the PM's isle. There never was a PM. There is no leader. The Council's dictated our every feeling, controlled our every thought. So today, and tomorrow, and every day until the water ceases to flow, we will throw off the old form and embrace the new. We will be leaderless no more! The New Council, behind me. The new PM, yours truly. No longer will we live in fear — "

I jump in front of Walery. "Is living in rage a better condition?"

"I'm with you, Luca!"

A lone voice from the crowd reaches the stage, and it throws Walery into a fury.

"Find that man! We will not go back! We move *forward*!"

I run toward my chair and jump upon it.

"Walery does not know the true battle. He has helped the Council destroy you. He has spent time on their isle. He works for them, not you, and he would set himself up as your leader. But only the Aquifer matters, and as we speak the Council has directed all Amongus to take it by force, to take the Rats by force."

"Death to the mutants!" A new chant takes hold.

Talya runs to my side and cries out, "Then death to me! We are the People of the Rock. I am a Rat, I am your long-lost sister! And I bring peace from your long-lost brothers. Humans, like you. Would you destroy me?"

In the confused pause, I scan the amphitheater, my eyes falling on the fountain. It does not flow.

"The fountain." I point to the marble image of the Deliverer. "Do you need a reminder of our peace? See that those below mean you no harm. Remind yourself of your kinship. Start the fountain! Watch the water flow. Though we destroy them, though we rage, water is proof of their goodwill toward us all."

"None is to be wasted." A member of the New Council steps forward. "Only months remain until the exchange fails. We must skim and store rations from every allotment."

I grab his shoulders. "But the water will always flow, unless the source is destroyed. And if you do not believe me, believe in the path that Massa knows, that I know. Throw aside this lunacy." I jump off the chair and run toward the fountain. I lean down to its marble base and flip the switch. "This water" — I rise and spread my arms — "is a permanent gift to you!"

One trickle drips over marble fingers. And then, nothing. There is no water.

No water.

Panic seizes me. In an instant, my life span shortens from years to weeks. Something is terribly wrong.

Seward, Father, what's happened? Is the Aquifer destroyed? Have the Rats been overrun? This fountain should be the first to receive water!

Which means nothing flows to the surface.

"It's gone. It's all gone!" Echoes bounce through the stadium and the crowd stands and storms the stage. "Curse Luca! Burn the Rat!"

Walery tries to calm them, but he's lost control. Without water, his slippery words fall harmless in the chaotic din.

Men rush toward Talya, lift her high, and carry her to the pyre. I press after. *Protect her.* The words pound in my head, but as thousands converge, my height and strength betray me. She is out of my reach. She is doomed.

I'm lifted high and tossed from grip to grip. Punches strike my head and my back as I'm buoyed by the mob's hate, hoisted toward the blaze.

It is my end, but I feel no fear, only sadness — sadness for Talya.

I can't watch the one I love meet this end. Alaya and Talya. Taken by water and fire. They were too good for the surface world.

Speak, Luca. Finish your task. Fulfill your piece of the prophecy. The world watches your undoing.

The Voice, ever my companion, fills my being, the words fitting with Akov's plea. I know nothing about this elusive prophecy, the one scribbled on Wren's museum stand, the one for which Wishers gladly perish. But I now go their way, the way to death. There is nothing to lose. I open my mouth, and the pronouncement comes, firm and bold and complete.

"For as long as I draw breath, I am a judge, I am a Deliverer, and I must speak."

Cameras focus on me as I near the blaze.

"My words, my words now go out to the world. And the words I give you are peace. Peace with those below you and peace with those you once thought your enemy. Peace with the Voice above, the one who spoke you into life, and peace with yourselves.

"And I will not be silent. That Voice pounds in my head, saying, 'What I have done for you will be known below and remembered above, and freedom will be offered to you all.'"

I close my mouth. There is no more. I try to remember what I said, but I can't.

The roar of the crowd intensifies, and, suddenly, it eases. Those around the fire are stricken with a severe quiet, one that spreads throughout the amphitheater.

Cameramen scuttle away to film whatever power has gripped the masses. Hands release me and I thud to the ground, pained but not broken. In the space vacated by hate, a voice rises, faint but clear.

Talya.

How often I've heard her hum the tune, but now the words explode from the depths of my mind. It's a song from the edges of my memory, one filled with words I once heard in the darkness.

One I learned first from my mother. One I sang as a Rat.

One that now stills a mob.

"Amazing Grace, how sweet the sound …"

Her voice strengthens, and the last catcalls fade away. The crowd stands, leans in, entranced by each phrase.

"That saved a wretch like me. I once was lost, but now I'm found. Was blind but now I see."

Walery slinks out of view as every gaze fixes on Talya, and throughout the theater, people — mostly the old — mouth the words. I am not alone; the lines live in others' memories. Surely the Birthers did not sing to them as Mother did to me. Who taught them this mystery?

There is only Talya and the song and the strange weight that blankets us, wombs us — a presence more powerful than hate, than fear.

What is this feeling, this trance that draws us together?

We are not alone, and Toppers scattered about the stage fall to their knees. Are they Wishers? I don't know, and my eyelids grow heavy. I feel a gentle rocking and hear my mother's whisper. When I open my eyes, I, too, have fallen.

How can a song, a simple melody lay claim to the moment? How can it warm and strengthen and reach into our pasts where nothing else can?

And what has Talya ushered into the amphitheater?

"My people! I plea for my people! We are human and have so much more than water to offer." Talya lifts her hands toward the skies.

Talya is a Wisher? Seward was right — how little I know of her.

I have never known a scene like this. It is full, complete, and though her song has ended, nobody moves.

No, we are not alone.

I stare at the crowd, minutes ago so ready to kill, but now subdued and drawn toward an irresistible idea for which they have no words. I felt its tug before, first warming to the strange thought while speaking to Wren, and then rediscovering the passion recorded by Mother's hand.

Above, below; we are not so different.

All around me, people weep. I think they weep in shame, and weep for the years our world has lost. They weep because weeping alone makes sense, and because for the first time they feel the freedom.

Freedom. They're captivated by Alaya's wish, united by Talya's voice. And it hits me: Our future - the hope of above, the hope of below - can't be quenched by the Council's deception or the Toppers' rage. The wailing that surrounds me contains a joy. Hope has survived, despite all controls and punishments; sleeping just beneath the surface, a dormant peace waiting for its time. Waiting for Talya to remind Toppers and Rats of our shared past. Our hope rests in the common peace of this song, and the revelation behind the song, and the Presence I couldn't escape if I wanted to.

And then it rains.

Drops fall gentle and soaking. I've never felt a rain like this, one that drenches the skin but also seems to penetrate further with warmth and peace and a joy indescribable. I marvel at the rain, and then the sight. Throughout the amphitheater cupped hands raise to collect the rare gift.

Hello, Luca. The Age of the Deliverer will soon begin.

The Voice in my head resonates deeper, if that is possible.

"But isn't that me?" I whisper.

Come see.

CHAPTER 39

I scramble to my feet, weave through the crowd, and grasp Talya's raised hands. Her eyes flutter open and I pull her to her feet.

"Come! Come quickly!" We run through the rain and into the tunnel.

"Luca! Where are we going?"

"I don't know. I only know we're supposed to run." We fly into the Birthing Tunnel, and my joy turns to mourning.

Lendi's body.

I can't leave him; I don't know why, but I can't.

I yank out the arrow and toss it far from us. Together with Talya, I muscle over my mate, and we drag him out of the tunnel. Behind us, the sound of rain on water, and as we emerge and face the inlet I blink like a fool, because I cannot speak.

"What's happening?" Talya gently releases Lendi's hand.

The Swan is filled with boats. Hundreds, maybe thousands of boats, stuffed with Amongus, many whom I recognize from

Massa's isle. They rip the PM's mark from their pockets and toss their dials into the water.

But there are more. There's Fundin, the youngest council member, the nervous one, now smiling. And beside him, in the nearest boat, Father and Seward.

For a moment, I cannot move. I can only take in the sight of those before me. I gently set down Lendi and place my hand on his heart ... and watch the rain slowly wash away the crimson from his hands.

I am released!

I shout and splash and swim to my Father. "I don't understand." Seward hauls me up, and I hug them both.

"Oh, Talya!" I turn and pull her in, and suddenly panic returns. "The water. It's off. There is no more coming up from — "

"No, mate. They dug too deep, and the sea always reclaims its own. The isle is no more — the cone above the waterline collapsed in on itself." Seward peeks at Talya. "Nothing below remains."

Talya takes a deep breath. "And what of ... those below?"

Father lifts both hands. "Perhaps they found safety. With all the digging, my guess is they had ample warning. But the Aquifer is no more. Surely it flooded and is swamped with salt."

"So we failed." I stare into the sky at the rain beating down.

"I'm not so sure." Fundin lifts his head and pulls from his tunic a sheet, old and crumpled. Rain soaks the torn page, and he reads. "And Hope will be shared throughout the world. And then the end can come." Fundin's eyes sparkle, and how clear it is now; they are the eyes of a Rat. "I followed you when you left the isle, but lost you in the storm. I wish I would've reached you sooner."

I frown, and he repeats, "Hope? Shared throughout the world? You know, like what was accomplished in that amphitheater? You two were on all the screens."

My face blanks. "What happened in there is lost in a fog..."

"I'll speak it again. Hope must be shared throughout the world, and then the end can come!"

"Why do you keep saying that?" I ask.

"This, Luca, is what the Council truly feared." Fundin lifts the page, shaking it above his head. "This prophecy. These words, ripped from Rabal's ancient book. This is the reason why all books were destroyed. This is why the barrier between the worlds was created. It was never for the Aquifer's protection, as the Rats and even the Deliverers believed. Rabal and his Council conspired to retain power, something difficult to accomplish if the world perishes.

"In this, Massa too played into their hands. Deliverers cemented the barrier. In order for the Council to retain power, to keep down whatever this Hope was, it became clear that Rabal's book must never reach the People of the Rock. See?" Fundin thrusts the page before my eyes. "It says *all* people, which includes those below. For hundreds of years they were cut off, and so the end was delayed."

"Without a water source, the end won't delay much longer." I exhale long and slow.

"Hear me to the point," Fundin continues. "Suddenly a terrifying message arrives from Walery. The Council learns that you, Luca, possess scratchings from long ago, and in their paranoia they order your shanty burned. Those books must be destroyed. Ancient words from above must not reach the Rats."

He grins. "But you did reach them, did you not?"

301

"Luca." Father stares at the shore, at the crowd gathering along the Swan. "While below, of what did you speak?"

I stare at Talya and shake my head. "Etria only wanted my judgments."

"Did you make any?" Father asks.

"Only Phale's, but it was nothing."

A smirk crosses Seward's face. "But did you leave anything with them, lad?"

"No ... Yes! Well, better put, Wren demanded I do. My two books. Father's and one other."

"And can you describe this *other* book?" Fundin's eyes widen.

"It had no title, and I never read it. But it was old. Lendi ..." I pause and glance at my mate on the beach, and my heart aches. "We found it in Glaugood."

Fundin leans forward. "Can you ... describe it?"

I rack my brain.

"It was protected by an undone, and I figured it belonged with me. There was a pair of cupped hands on the cover."

Fundin eases down in Father's boat. He whispers, "Well now, I suppose that could be the one."

A light, bright and piercing, explodes up from the sea, strikes the clouds, and spreads like a rolling wave across the sky. The radiance intensifies, consumes, and in ships and on land men cower and fall. But not all. Some stare unflinching into the brilliant dawn. Father. Seward. Talya. Fundin. And from a boat not far from the beach, Phale and Mape raise their hands to the light.

~

What happens now? Now that hope has reached the Rats and words of peace have touched the surface? Will water fall from above, in quantities enough to satisfy our thirst? And what of our rage, will we release it to the sky and go in search of the Rats, our underground brothers and sisters?

I know nothing for sure, nothing except that the future no longer depends on me. I am no longer Other. I am Luca, son of Massa, one of thousands gripped by Talya's song.

I am small, and small is good.

And along with every other creature that moves, I have a choice.

Talya reaches for my hand and squeezes, while the world collects its breath.